RECONCILIATION
& INDIGENOUS
JUSTICE

RECONCILIATION & INDIGENOUS JUSTICE

A Search for Ways Forward

David Milward

Fernwood Publishing
Halifax & Winnipeg

Development editing: Fiona Jeffries
Copyediting: Jenn Harris
Cover design: Ann Doyan
Printed and bound in Canada

Published by Fernwood Publishing
32 Oceanvista Lane, Black Point, Nova Scotia, B0J 1B0
and 748 Broadway Avenue, Winnipeg, Manitoba, R3G 0X3
www.fernwoodpublishing.ca

Fernwood Publishing Company Limited gratefully acknowledges the financial support of the Government of Canada, the Canada Council for the Arts, the Manitoba Department of Culture, Heritage and Tourism under the Manitoba Publishers Marketing Assistance Program and the Province of Manitoba, through the Book Publishing Tax Credit, for our publishing program. We are pleased to work in partnership with the Province of Nova Scotia to develop and promote our creative industries for the benefit of all Nova Scotians.

Library and Archives Canada Cataloguing in Publication

Title: Reconciliation & Indigenous justice : a search for ways forward / by David Milward.
Other titles: Reconciliation and Indigenous justice
Names: Milward, David Leo, 1974- author.
Description: Includes bibliographical references and index.
Identifiers: Canadiana (print) 20210360984 | Canadiana (ebook) 20210363401 | ISBN 9781773635194 (softcover) | ISBN 9781773635408 (EPUB) | ISBN 9781773635415 (PDF)
Subjects: CSH: Indigenous prisoners—Canada. | CSH: Indigenous prisoners—Canada—Social conditions. | CSH: Indigenous prisoners—Canada—Psychology. | CSH: Indigenous peoples—Canada—Residential schools. | LCSH: Indigenous peoples—Canada—Social conditions. | LCSH: Indigenous peoples—Canada—Psychology. | LCSH: Discrimination in criminal justice administration—Canada.
Classification: LCC HV9507 .M55 2022 | DDC 365/.608997071—dc23

CONTENTS

I wish to dedicate this book to my kookum, Angela Michael.
It is with sadness and yet hope that she recently returned to the Creator
after having been a residential school survivor
and the most kind-hearted grandmother anyone could ask for.

ACKNOWLEDGEMENTS

I wish to thank Kent Roach and Murray Sinclair for their invaluable advice and assistance in helping this book begin its development. I would also like to thank Fiona Jeffries for her invaluable assistance in bringing the book to its present form. I would also like to thank the peer reviewers for their helpful insights and perspectives.

1

THE LEGACY OF RESIDENTIAL SCHOOLS

The horrors of the Indian residential schools are by now well-known historical facts, and they have certainly found purchase in the Canadian consciousness in recent years. Growing awareness of the fallout of the residential schools eventually prompted the following apology from then prime minister Stephen Harper in 2008: "Today, we recognize that this policy of assimilation was wrong, has caused great harm and has no place in our country. The government of Canada sincerely apologizes and asks the forgiveness of the aboriginal peoples of this country for failing them so profoundly. We are sorry."[1]

The apology, plus lawsuits from the survivors of the residential schools,[2] contributed to the formation of the Truth and Reconciliation Commission (TRC) of Canada in 2008. In its interim report, the TRC provided a detailed and vivid description of the horrors perpetrated within the schools. Children had their traditional clothing and ceremonial items taken away and their braided hair (which reflects sacred beliefs) forcibly cut on arrival. Staff frequently beat students for the most innocuous of actions, for speaking their traditional languages, or for observing their traditional cultures. Many staff members also frequently subjected the children to sexual abuse.[3]

The survivors also made it clear that there were repercussions far beyond their own immediate attendance at the schools, resulting in a phenomenon known as intergenerational trauma. Indigenous children who attended the residential schools were left without the skills or qualifications to pursue livelihoods, with low self-esteem as Indigenous persons, in an angry and traumatized state of being, and vulnerable to substance abuse, violence, and other behavioural issues. Those children would take out their pain and problems on those nearest to them, their own family members. The next generation of children would be subjected to physical and sexual violence in abusive home environments and therefore develop the same issues as the previous generation. And so the seeds planted by the residential schools pass on trauma from one generation to the next.[4] In 2015, the TRC released its final reports, which detailed and chronicled the harms inflicted by the residential schools as well as exploring ways to address the social fallouts that have been left behind. The TRC also made it clear that Canada as a nation-state has an ongoing responsibility to try to redress those fallouts.[5]

One of those fallouts is the persistent crisis of Indigenous over-incarceration in Canada. Estimates as of 2016 are that Indigenous inmates amount to 27 percent of provincial and territorial inmates and 28 percent of federal inmates, despite Indigenous Peoples amounting to only 3 percent of the overall population.[6] The focus of this book will be on the ongoing ties between the enduring traumas caused by the residential schools and Indigenous over-incarceration.

Residential schools and intergenerational trauma are certainly not the only contributors to Indigenous over-incarceration. There is, for example, "racial profiling," the practice of assigning to particular racial groups negative stereotypes that infer increased propensity toward criminal behaviour so as to justify increased surveillance. The practice is by now well known.[7] Official public inquiries have confirmed that Canadian police forces have engaged in discriminatory practices against Indigenous Peoples, including increased surveillance on the basis of race.[8] A 2008 study by Carol LaPrairie found that Indigenous persons are seven times more likely than non-Indigenous persons to be identified as offenders by the police,[9] demonstrating a culture that countenances a lack of respect for Indigenous Peoples.

Residential schools are also part of the larger picture of Canadian colonialism against Indigenous Peoples. Other colonial processes included military conquest[10] or the acquisition of Indigenous land bases through treaties.[11] These processes have led to economic dispossession, which has contributed to Indigenous poverty, and that in turn contributes to Indigenous over-incarceration. Another colonial process has been the disproportionate apprehension of Indigenous children from their families by child welfare authorities, which may also contribute in turn to Indigenous over-incarceration.

The residential school system may not be the only harmful process of colonization that fuels Indigenous over-incarceration — but it has been and continues to be a critical cause behind Indigenous incarceration and is arguably the most critical factor of all. It is likely that for almost every Indigenous person who ends up incarcerated, residential schools will form an important part of their background, even for those who did not themselves attend the schools. The harm that the schools have caused and continue to generate provides vivid and crucial links between Canadian colonialism and Indigenous over-incarceration. The TRC made numerous recommendations, termed Calls to Action, and several of those were specifically directed toward remedying Indigenous over-incarceration (as we will see in Chapter 5). Several years have passed since the TRC final reports were issued — yet we have seen little progress with either implementing the Calls to Action or addressing Indigenous social conditions.

The other reason for focusing on residential schools is that they are a subject over which mainstream Canadians continue to exhibit denial and a refusal to acknowledge responsibility. The extent to which Canadians understand intergenerational trauma suffered by Indigenous Peoples, and the degree to which they are willing to support reconciliation, remains unclear even years after the release of the final reports. One survey report suggested that many Canadians are quite supportive of reconciliation,[12] while another suggested that support was stronger in the central and eastern provinces while weaker in the western provinces, where problems such as Indigenous over-incarceration are especially acute.[13]

And yet there remains cause for concern that least a substantial portion of the Canadian population may dismiss residential schools as a thing of the past for which present-day Canadians have no responsibility. For example, former senator Lynn Beyak has publicly defended the residential schools as "well-intentioned" and having had positive impacts that have been overshadowed by the negative depictions of the TRC. She even went as far as publishing over a hundred letters supportive of her viewpoints on her official website, with many of those letters espousing frankly racist descriptions of Indigenous Peoples as freeloaders trying to milk their traditional cultures and political correctness for even more handouts.[14] Her son, a city councillor named Nick, went as far as to say that his mother's viewpoints were supported by the majority of Canadians.[15]

An Angus Reid poll in 2018 indicated that 53 percent of the 2,500 Canadians it surveyed felt that Canada spends too much time apologizing for residential schools, and 53 percent felt that Indigenous Peoples should fully integrate into mainstream Canadian society without any special legal considerations or status.[16]

In a Facebook chatroom for RCMP members only, several blatantly racist comments were found. These included: "There comes a time when someone needs to stand up to these spoiled children and tell them to just f— off" and "There comes a time when we have apologized more than enough and compensated enough." In response to a First Nation in British Columbia refusing to evacuate during wildfires, there were comments like "what an ignorant bunch of clowns," "You can't fix stupid" and "You can … just let the fire do its thing." When a female Indigenous RCMP officer indicated that residential schools were not just a thing of the past as she herself had been a student at one, she heard back in reply: "Does an end date exist? Or are my great-grandchildren expected to continue to reconcile?"[17]

It is perhaps telling that the former head of the TRC, Murray Sinclair, felt the need to explain why Indigenous Peoples simply cannot "get over it" with respect to residential schools. He indicated that just as Americans cannot forget 9/11 so easily, or how Western democracies celebrate the sacrifices of war veterans during Remembrance Day, Indigenous Peoples similarly cannot simply be expected to forget about the schools.[18]

Chapter 2 of the book builds on these themes, but with reference to very different ways of viewing crime. One view is that crime is simply a moral choice by an offender to do wrong, and the state is therefore justified in punishing the offender. It turns out that many, if not most, Canadians seem to ascribe to this viewpoint — which in turn fuels law-and-order policies that justify mass incarceration, with an inordinately harsh effect on disadvantaged minorities such as Indigenous Peoples. Reducing crime to moral choices implicitly also allows a denial of past injustices by the Canadian state, such as the residential schools, as having any role in Indigenous over-incarceration.

An alternate viewpoint sees crime as a reaction by the offender to adverse personal and social circumstances that law-abiding persons may not have to worry about. This viewpoint may demand viewing an offender in a more compassionate and sympathetic light, demanding that we search for alternatives to incarceration in addressing harmful behaviour. Prison abolition is an emerging school of thought that explores fundamental questions about the organization of society and how society responds to harmful behaviour by its own members. A common thread throughout prison abolition approaches is a striving for the very nearly complete abandonment of incarceration as a criminal sanction. Its theories are based on the conclusion that the vast majority of crimes are better explained as reactions to personal and social stresses than as isolated moral choices. Prison abolition as a concept was developed by Black American scholars who focused on the over-incarceration of Blacks in the United States.[19]

A key endeavour of this book is to adapt notions of prison abolition in ways that are distinctive to the circumstances and needs of Indigenous Peoples in Canada. Indigenous over-incarceration describes incarcerating Indigenous people at rates that are disproportionate to their representation in the overall Canadian population. The term itself may hold out the unfortunate suggestion that incarcerating Indigenous Peoples at rates comparable to non-Indigenous Canadians is reasonable. But I want to go further than that. I envision a future where incarceration becomes almost completely unnecessary for Indigenous Peoples. And that means an extensive search for alternatives to incarceration, including preventative programming, Indigenous approaches to justice that resemble restorative justice, and improving correctional programming.

There is no question that residential schools have left behind a dreadful social legacy. Empirical evidence is mounting to prove that the schools have left multiple generations of Indigenous Peoples in poorer overall health,[20] with poorer mental health and increased depressive symptoms,[21] and more likely to contemplate or commit suicide.[22]

A key part of this book in Chapters 3 and 4 is to disprove the skeptics and establish strong connections between the residential schools and the ongoing problem of Indigenous over-incarceration. Numerous empirical studies prove that certain social conditions — like poverty, exposure to child welfare apprehension, and growing up in an abusive or unstable home environment — will increase crime and recidivism in communities, Indigenous or non-Indigenous. Residential schools, through their physical and sexual abuse of students and by neglecting student education and thus contributing to Indigenous poverty, have ensured that deplorable social conditions conducive to crime have persisted in Indigenous communities generation after generation. Many reported decisions from the Canadian legal system see judges confirming that these factors can be tied back to the residential schools and that they played a strong role in Indigenous accused getting charged with Canadian criminal offences. Residential schools may not be the only causal factor behind Indigenous over-incarceration, but there is no mistaking that the problem would not be anywhere near the magnitude it is today, if at all, but for the schools.

Chapter 5 explores what is meant by *reconciliation*, a term that itself has been subject to significant debate. The understanding of reconciliation that will be advanced here is that Canada must accept responsibility for the social problems left behind by residential schools, with concrete actions and policies that go far beyond any verbal apologies. This book envisions two stages of reconciliation. First is a transitory phase in which Canada must accept responsibility by acting in genuine partnership with Indigenous Peoples themselves in pursuing a comprehensive set of actions and policies that will undo the harmful social legacy of residential schools. The transitory phase occurs largely within a state-administered framework. The hope here is that the transitory phase can eventually give way to revitalized Indigenous legal orders that can administer themselves with a substantial independence from the Canadian state. Note that the transitory phase may be necessary to begin, as full Indigenous self-determination can never be an immediate overnight realization. The transitory phase envisions Indigenous Peoples growing their capacity and ability to administer over time, to the point that they can manage their own Indigenous legal orders.

Chapter 6 explores the current legal and political status quo, concluding that it comes nowhere close to what is needed for reconciliation. Civil compensation for the students of the residential schools does nothing to address the ongoing destructive social forces that the residential schools set in motion. There have been efforts to address the harms caused by residential schools through social programming. But these initiatives tend to be inadequate and are subject to oscillating priorities, especially as governments change after elections. The Aboriginal Healing Foundation, for example, operated for a little over twelve years before being forced to close its doors.

The Canadian criminal justice system remains fundamentally committed to deterrence and retribution through incarceration. Its actors, such as judges or lawyers, frequently acknowledge the influence of residential schools in bringing Indigenous accused into its courts. There are now in fact legal principles that require judges and lawyers to account for the circumstances of Indigenous accused and to seriously consider alternatives to prison for Indigenous Peoples. But the judges typically end up falling back on deterrence and retribution to justify incarceration, as the fundamental orientation of the justice system obliges them to do so. Prison abolition advocates have criticized American law-and-order policies as accomplishing a new form of segregation through incarceration, punishing Black people for being Black. That condemnation strikes a chord for the discussions in this book as well. The routine operation of the Canadian criminal justice system becomes an exercise in incarcerating Indigenous Peoples for being Indigenous. It places the blame squarely on Indigenous Peoples, with little if any interrogation into the Canadian state's culpability in Indigenous over-incarceration.

Even if Indigenous Peoples obtain self-determination, the next natural question is what to do with it. Chapters 7 to 11 consider in detail what kind of initiatives are necessary for true reconciliation. A comprehensive resolution is one that attempts to address Indigenous over-incarceration at all possible points in time that can lead to Indigenous persons being subjected to imprisonment. Chapter 7 explores a greater investment in preventative and social programming that will build and mould healthier Indigenous communities so as to minimize to the maximum possible extent the need for any "after the fact" responses in the criminal justice system.

Chapter 8 canvasses arguments in favour of Indigenous justice initiatives that parallel restorative justice. Chapter 9 explores arguments that raise concerns about the ability of restorative justice to realize its objectives, such as the potential for power abuses, questions of whether it actually lowers crime in comparison to the standard justice system, and whether restorative justice can truly motivate offenders to accept responsibility and reform behaviour.

Chapter 10 explores paths forward for Indigenous justice, specifically in ways that respond to the critiques raised in Chapter 9. Procedural protections can be designed into restorative justice initiatives to prevent power abuses, although the efficacy of restorative justice programming may depend on the willingness to invest real resources into such frameworks, as a form of justice reinvestment. I also explore methods of accountability that are rooted in Indigenous cultures. The transitory phase certainly implies expanding the reach of restorative justice beyond the minimal range of less serious offences to which the state can comfortably apply restorative justice. If we can move beyond the transitory phase to fully realized Indigenous legal orders, those legal systems have their ways of instilling accountability and responsibility that are different from Western reliance on incarceration. Indigenous legal orders can then use Indigenous approaches to justice for an even greater range of behaviours than those expected during the transitory phase of state partnership. I argue that it is possible to mould mainstream public opinion to become more supportive of alternatives to incarceration, thereby avoiding concerns that Indigenous justice initiatives would only amount to co-opted appendages of the state.

Chapter 11 starts by recognizing that, even while trying to minimize the need for incarceration, there may be a select few offences that are so serious (e.g., murder) or a select few offenders who are so dangerous that Indigenous communities themselves may not see any reasonable alternative to prison. Furthermore, the transitory phase suggests that lessening reliance on incarceration will itself be a long-term project that can take years or even decades. The chapter therefore examines the development of culturally appropriate correctional programs that will facilitate parole and reintegration for Indigenous inmates, as well as Indigenous-specific risk assessment instruments that will increase Indigenous inmates' access to needed programs and services. We now begin the discussions by examining different ways of viewing crime.

Notes

1   CBC Digital Archives, "A long-awaited apology for residential schools," June 11, 2008 <cbc.ca/archives/entry/a-long-awaited-apology-for-residential-schools>.

2   *Blackwater v. Plint* [2005] 3 S.C.R. 3, 2005 SCC 58 <scc-csc.lexum.com/scc-csc/scc-csc/en/item/2239/index.do>.

3   Truth and Reconciliation Commission of Canada, *Truth and Reconciliation Commission of Canada: Interim Report* (Winnipeg: Truth and Reconciliation Commission of Canada, 2012), 5.

4   Truth and Reconciliation Commission of Canada, *Interim Report*, 6; Peter Menzies, "Developing an Aboriginal Healing Model for Intergenerational Trauma," *International Journal of Health Promotion and Education* 46, 2 (2014); Lloyd Hawkeye Robertson, "The Residential School Experience: Syndrome or Historic Trauma," *Pimatisiwin* 4, 1 (2006).

5   Truth and Reconciliation Commission of Canada, *Honouring the Truth, Reconciling for the Future*. (Winnipeg: Truth and Reconciliation Commission of Canada, 2015).

6   Julie Reitano, *Adult Correctional Statistics in Canada, 2015–2016* (Ottawa: Statistics Canada, 2017), 5.

7   David Tanovich, "Using the Charter to Stop Racial Profiling: The Develop-

ment of an Equality-Based Conception of Arbitrary Detention," *Osgoode Hall Law Journal* 40, 2 (2002); Scot Wortley and Julian Tanner, "Data, Denials, and Confusion: The Racial Profiling Debate in Toronto," *Canadian Journal of Corrections* 45, 3 (2003); Scot Wortley and Julian Tanner, "Inflammatory Rhetoric? Baseless Accusations? A Response to Gabor's Critique of Racial Profiling Research in Canada," *Canadian Journal of Corrections* 47, 3 (2005).

8   Alvin Hamilton and Murray Sinclair, *The Justice System and Aboriginal People: The Report of the Aboriginal Justice Inquiry* (Winnipeg: Indigenous Justice Inquiry, 1991); Justice David H. Wright, *Report of the Commission of Inquiry into Matters relating to the Death of Neil Stonechild* (Saskatoon: Commission into Matters relating to the Death of Neil Stonechild, 2004). See also Elizabeth Comack, *Racialized Policing: Aboriginal People's Encounters with the Police* (Winnipeg: Fernwood Publishing, 2012).

9   Carol LaPrairie, "The Neighbourhood Context of Urban Aboriginal Crime," *Canadian Journal of Corrections* 50, 5 (2008).

10   Although Canada did not fight wars against Indigenous Peoples as often as the United States, they did use military subjugation on occasion. A particularly notorious example was the defeat of the Rebellion of 1885 involving Métis and Cree groups. See Olive Patricia Dickason, *A Concise History of Canada's First Nations* (Don Mills: Oxford University Press, 2006), 234–47; James R. Miller, *Skyscrapers Hide the Heavens: A History of Indian-White Relations in Canada* (Toronto: University of Toronto Press, 2000), 202–11.

11   For a historical overview of the numbered treaties in the western provinces, see J.R. Miller, *Skyscrapers Hide the Heavens*, 216–24; Dickason, *A Concise History of Canada's First Nations*, 173–87.

12   Reconciliation Canada, *The Canadian Reconciliation Landscape: Current Perspectives of Indigenous Peoples and Non-Indigenous Canadians* (Vancouver: Reconciliation Canada, 2017).

13   Tides Canada, *Canadian Public Opinion on Indigenous Peoples* (Vancouver: Tides Canada, 2016).

14   Andrew Russell, "Sen. Lynn Beyak Publishes 'Outright Racist' Comments about Indigenous People on her Website," *Global News*, January 5, 2018.

15   Jorge Barrera, "Sen. Lynn's Son, a City Councillor, Says Conservative Leadership Cowed by Political Correctness" CBC *News,* January 5, 2018.

16   Angus Reid Institute, *Truths of Reconciliation: Canadians Are Deeply Divided on How Best to Address Indigenous Issues* (Vancouver: Angus Reid Institute, 2018).

17   Trina Roache, "Indigenous People Described as 'Lazy,' 'Racists' in Another RCMP Facebook Site," APTN *National News,* April 30, 2018 <aptnnews. ca/2018/04/30/indigenous-people-described-as-lazy-racists-in-another-private-rcmp-facebook-site/>.

18   "How Senator Murray Sinclair Responds to Why Don't Residential School Survivors Just 'Get Over It'," *The Current,* CBC Radio, April 4, 2017.

19   Angela Davis, *Abolition and Democracy: Beyond Empire, Prisons, and Torture* (New York: Seven Stories Press, 2005); Michelle Alexander, *The New Jim Crow: Mass Incarceration in the Age of Colorblindness* (New York: The New Press, 2020).

20   Sylvia S. Barton et al., "Health and Quality of Life of Aboriginal Residential School Survivors," *Social Indicators Research* 73 (2005); Charles Brasfield, "Residential School Syndrome," *British Columbia Medical Journal* 43, 2 (2001).

21   Amy Bomby, Kimberly Matheson, and Hymie Anisman, "The Impact of Stressors on Second Generation Indian Residential School Survivors," *Transcultural Psychiatry* 48, 4 (2011).

22   Brenda Elias et al., "Trauma and Suicide Behavior Histories among a Canadian Indigenous Population: An Empirical Exploration of the Potential Role of Canada's Residential School System" *Social Science and Medicine* 74 (2012).

2

DIFFERENT VIEWS OF CRIME

THEORETICAL CONSTRUCTIONS OF CRIME

One way to view crime is as a moral choice or rationale on the part of the perpetrator. According to this view, the offender weighs the benefits of committing the crime (e.g., financial gain, emotional catharsis through revenge) alongside the probabilities of either getting caught and punished or getting away with it. Perceptions of greater benefits along with more optimistic estimations of being able to get away it can result in the choice to commit a crime. Perceptions of decreased benefits along with more pessimistic evaluations of being caught and given a severe punishment can inform a decision to not to commit a crime.[1] Understanding crime squarely as the offender's choice serves to validate the subsequent punishment as a deserved expression of condemnation.[2]

An alternative view of crime may require a degree of empathy or sympathy with the offender, proposing that offenders and the crimes they commit are, to a very real degree, products of the social environments in which they grew up and negative life experiences that are tied to those environments.[3] This alternative view asks that we move beyond seeing an offender as just a bad person who needs to be punished and instead as a complicated human being who offended in reaction to negative circumstances and experiences that a privileged law-abiding person may not have had to face.

Prison abolition theories exhibit a strong and principled preference for constructions of crime and incarceration that consider societal factors rather than focusing on moral choice. Their view is that the mass incarceration of Black people is far more the product of the social conditions that many Blacks are forced to face rather than morally deficient choices. Angela Davis in particular condemns the mass incarceration of

Black people, including the "war on drugs," as intentionally racist policy. Focusing solely on what an incarcerated Black person did, and avoiding the difficult questions of why that person did what he or she did, allows the state to conveniently avoid any responsibility for enduring racial inequalities. Placing blame on incarcerated Black persons themselves allows the state to push difficult questions of racism and inequality under the table, and it becomes an exercise in criminalizing Black people for simply being Black.[4] Abolitionists argue that redirecting resources to build healthier communities is by far the better route to lowering crime versus emphasizing moral condemnation through incarceration.[5]

I would argue that similar reasoning is required with respect to Indigenous Peoples. Colonialism has forced numerous adverse conditions on Indigenous Peoples, with residential schools being an especially destructive node. This has resulted in many Indigenous Peoples suffering stresses like poverty, poor mental health, racial discrimination, and intergenerational domestic and sexual violence. These are stresses that many, if not most, non-Indigenous Canadians do not have to worry about. Tied to colonialism, these are also the societal factors that drive Indigenous over-incarceration. Linking these stresses to residential schools will be the subject of Chapters 3 and 4.

Canada has an ongoing responsibility to address this situation, which it created through colonialism and through residential schools in particular. Applying standard criminal sentencing law to Indigenous Peoples who get charged with Canadian criminal offences frequently amounts to focusing on what Indigenous people did to get charged, with either minimal or no acknowledgement of the aforementioned social stresses. Over-incarceration of Indigenous Peoples in effect becomes an exercise in blaming Indigenous Peoples themselves, and it implicitly absolves Canada, as a state built on colonialism, of its responsibility for creating the conditions that have led to Indigenous over-incarceration. The application of sentencing law in ways that amount to systemic racism is a focus of Chapter 6.

The moral choice and societal factors constructions are fundamentally different theoretical views on the nature of crime. But they are not just theoretical constructions. They also, as previously suggested, compete with each other in the real world to shape the course of criminal justice policy toward Indigenous Peoples. How the theoretical constructions clash with each other in trying to shape policy is the subject of the next section. It turns out that the "crime as a choice to be punished" construction overwhelmingly wins over the social factors construction.

CONSTRUCTIONS OF CRIME AND JUSTICE POLICY

It is necessary to first explain the basic structure of Western criminal justice systems. Publicly elected legislators have a primary role in the creation and shaping of criminal law. The primary piece of federal criminal legislation that has been passed by Parliament is the *Criminal Code of Canada*.[6] It defines most of the recognized criminal offences in Canada and provides minimum (e.g., fines) and maximum (e.g., number of years in prison) ranges of sentences for those offences.

Judges and lawyers engage with that law when accused people are charged and prosecuted in individual cases for committing criminal offences. If the accused is found guilty after a trial, or pleads guilty, the accused's defence lawyer argues for a more lenient sentence while the Crown prosecutor typically argues for a more severe sentence. It falls to an independent and impartial judge to decide what the sentence will be.[7]

The *Criminal Code* also provides judges with objectives that they must address when passing sentences. One of its provisions calls for denouncing unlawful conduct, deterrence, separating offenders from society where necessary, rehabilitating offenders, reparations to victims for harm done, promoting "a sense of responsibility in offenders," and the "acknowledgement of the harms done to victims and the community" as objectives of sentencing.[8] One can sense competition between the different constructions of crime even within this list of sentencing objectives. The denunciation of unlawful conduct and the promotion of responsibility objectives in particular recognize the crime-as-choice construction. The rehabilitation objective potentially recognizes the social factors construction.

The judiciary in turn articulates legal principles that interpret the *Criminal Code* and provide guidance for sentencing. Aggravating factors are facts that, if accepted as true by a sentencing court, make the offence more serious and therefore justify a more severe sentence. Such factors include repeating the offence after having been convicted of it in the past or harming an especially vulnerable victim (e.g., an elderly person or a child). Mitigating factors are facts that, if accepted as true by a sentencing court, make the offence less serious and thereby justify a less severe sentence. Examples here include accepting responsibility by pleading guilty, having a traumatic past that explains the accused's behaviour, and apologizing to the victim.[9] Some mitigating factors recognize the social factors construction and try to give it legal force through a reduction of sentence where merited. Aggravating factors, on the other hand, recognize the crime-as-choice construction and give it legal force through more severe sentences.

While it may be that judges can employ the social factors construction, their capacity to do so is limited. Legislators set the range of sentences that can be applied for any given offence, so judicial use of aggravating and mitigating factors has to remain within that range. These legislative limits on sentencing options is also the point where the crime-as-choice construction exerts a tangible pull on criminal justice policy.

Voting publics in Western democracies often demand hefty prison terms. Public opinion surveys in the 1990s have indicated that approximately 80 percent of voters in Australia, Canada, England, the Netherlands, and the United States felt that existing sentences were too lenient.[10] Sometimes the public demand for stiffer sentences is also fuelled by a perceived need to get tough on particular categories of crime. A frequent political response to crimes that gain public notoriety for being prevalent and/or serious is to increase imprisonment terms for those offences. Examples enacted by the Liberal government of Jean Chrétien in 2005 included street racing, auto theft,[11] and possessing or trafficking in crystal meth.[12]

A federal Department of Justice report indicated that at least two thirds of Canadians supported the approach of Stephen Harper's Tory government, elected in 2007, of increasing both police presence and crime sentences.[13] The Tory government did indeed embark on a course of increased incarceration with the intention of securing voter support. Bill C-10 received royal assent on March 13, 2012, with this public statement provided as justification:

> Canadians want and deserve to feel safe in their homes and communities, and this means that dangerous criminals need to be kept off our streets. Our Government is committed to ensuring that criminals are held fully accountable for their actions and that the safety and security of law-abiding Canadians comes first in Canada's judicial system. We will continue to fight crime and protect Canadians so our communities are safe places for people to live, raise their families and do business.[14]

Note the appeals to feeling safe and secure from crime. The pursuit of public safety as extolled in the public statement depends largely on the use of mandatory minimum sentences, which judges cannot lessen. Bill C-10 includes mandatory minimums for several sexual offences against children, ranging from thirty days to one year when the Crown proceeds by summary conviction, and one to five years when the Crown proceeds by indictment.[15] Mandatory minimums are also legislated for various drug offences, like trafficking, exporting, and possession with intent to either traffic or export, ranging from six months to two years. Those mandatory minimums can increase from one year to three years if certain aggravating factors are proven, such as the offence occurring in prison or near a school, being for the benefit of organized crime, involving the threat of violence or use of weapons, or presenting a health or safety hazard.[16]

Certain offences were no longer eligible for a conditional sentence (i.e., incarceration served through house curfew) under Bill C-10. These include offences that prescribe a maximum sentence of fourteen years or more (e.g., manslaughter, aggravated assault) and offences punishable by ten years or more and in which the Crown proceeds by indictment (e.g., assault causing bodily harm). They also include any of prison breach, sexual harassment, sexual assault, kidnapping, trafficking in persons, abduction of a person under fourteen years, theft over $5,000, motor vehicle theft, break and enter, unlawfully being in a dwelling, and arson for a fraudulent purpose, when the Crown proceeds by indictment.[17]

It is obvious that politicians often see justice policy as a valuable commodity that allows them to get elected. Pushing a law-and-order platform is perceived to win votes. Publicly advocating for alternative methods of dealing with crime is frequently seen as risking voter support. An effect of this political reality is that empirical research that provides insights as to the nature of crime and what can effectively reduce crime can become marginalized. Other areas of policy see governments relying extensively on empirical research and efficacy evaluations in formulating policy. Wildlife conservation policies, for example, are often the products of consultations with biologists, biochemists, and other environmental experts. Criminal justice policies that emphasize "law and order" go against that grain because ignoring the experts is often perceived to be the better route to electoral success.[18]

So, what empirical insights do criminal justice experts have to offer?

A great deal of research conducted by criminologists validates the social factors construction of crime. In criminology, testing theories of crime relies on an experimental group drawn from an initial sample and a comparison group. For example, suppose that the theory is that poverty increases the occurrence of property crime — those who live in poverty are more likely to commit property crimes than those who do not live in poverty. The criminologist looks for crime rates among members of the experimental group who live below the poverty line. The criminologist then compares those rates to rates from the comparison group, which consists of people who live above the poverty line. If the experimental group does have statistically significant higher rates of property crime than the comparison group, the criminologist can then conclude that poverty does increase the likelihood of property crime. It is not to say that everyone who lives in poverty will commit crime, but it will still significantly increase the probability of crime such that any differences between experimental and comparison groups cannot be dismissed as mere chance.[19] This kind of conclusion is what is known as a criminogenic effect.

Many studies produced by criminologists conclude not only that there are many societal factors that are behind offending behaviour, but that justice policies are likely to fail if they insist on longer prison sentences without considering those societal factors.[20] The preponderance of empirical evidence offered by social scientists, which is further detailed in Chapters 3 and 4, seems to validate the social factors construction of crime.

Anthony Doob, now professor emeritus of criminology at the University of Toronto, argues that governments prior to Harper's Tories had at times made tough-on-crime policies to garner votes. But Doob concludes that the Tory government's law-and-order agenda amounted to touting tough-on-crime schemes to gain electoral support while completely devaluing empirical research on criminal justice, to levels that were unprecedented.[21] Doob also unequivocally assesses Harper's policies as choosing the moral choice construction over the social factors construction: "The Harper policies involve much more than increased penalties. Rather, they represent an explicit attempt to create divisions among Canadians: offenders are not the product of social circumstances but are inherently bad people who should be permanently distinguished from law-abiding citizens."[22]

People who believe in the moral choice construction often exhibit a tendency to view explanations offered by social factors construction as "sob stories" or excuses meant to avoid accountability and deserved punishment. That tendency often results in derisive commentary in cases where an accused is perceived to have received a lesser punishment than what is "deserved," including cases involving Indigenous accused persons with traumatic pasts. Alain Bellemare, a Cree man from Quebec, was convicted of aggravated assault for inflicting multiple cigarette burns on an unidentified five-year-old girl, his stepdaughter.[23] He did not attend residential school himself, but both sets of his grandparents had. He grew up in a physically abusive home environment that been passed through generations, from his grandparents to his parents. He received fifteen months instead of the four years that the Crown prosecutor requested. Judge Guy Lambert noted the social circumstances distinctive to Indigenous Peoples when passing a relatively lenient sentence on Bellemare.[24]

The comments sections on news stories of sentencing cases often convey the dismissal of "sob stories" and "lame excuses," and the Bellemare case was no different. A sample of comments include:

- "Must be nice to get a pass based solely on your ethnic background."

- "So he never attended a residential school, nor did his parents but he gets a coupon to burn people? What a load of garbage. Wish there was a way to get rid of these activist judges."

- "Absolutely ridiculous sentencing. Just because the abuser suffered abuse it should not diminish his purposed and knowing role of abuse on the innocent 5 year old. He should have been sentenced to the fullest extent of the law period!"

- "The judge's ruling reflects the mindless repeating mantra of the judicial elite in Canada that aboriginal crime is forgiven by white guilt."[25]

Some of the comments expressed outrage over the perceived lack of justice for the victim herself:

- "Horrendous injustice to this victim … that helpless young girl … big mistake … way too lenient [sic]."

- "I'm absolutely sickened. There is no excuse for this sort of behaviour. My heart breaks for this girl who suffered this terrible abuse and gets no justice."

- "What about this little girl? What about her? Who is looking out for HER? Where is her justice??"[26]

It is easy in the moment to get caught up in a dichotomy of the accused as the wrongdoer to be punished and sympathy for the victim at the same time. Yet this case illustrates what is meant by intergenerational trauma, how abuse and trauma can pass from one generation to the next. What is in store for the young girl if one takes the time to think matters through? One would always hope that she finds healing and lives a good life afterward. But a hard, honest, and reasoned appraisal may conclude that she herself, inheriting abuse from Bellemare as he did from previous generations, may in her own turn become angry and traumatized. And she may in turn end up harming those around her. It is certainly not a long-term result that anyone would want. But it must be recognized as a distinct possibility, maybe even a probability. How would the people who always view crime as a moral choice then see this girl if she does end up harming somebody else? When does today's heartbreak become tomorrow's "sob story" and "lame excuse"? One of the online commentators even anticipates that possibility, while remaining dismissive: "So if the poor child grows up to become a child abuser, i guess she too will get a pass. We all carry wounds from childhood, some more than others of course, but personal responsibility and the expectation that we will behave in a moral fashion seems to be lacking here."[27]

Many people seem inclined to see crime as a moral choice to be punished. It is understandable, because people fundamentally want to feel safe as they go about their lives. But it can also lead to an inflexible and stubborn unwillingness to see crime as a reflection of social circumstances when it may be merited. And that includes cases involving Indigenous persons with traumatic pasts that trace back generations to residential schools. Non-Indigenous persons have often been dismissive toward any tangible connection between residential schools and ongoing Indigenous social problems. Enough people adhere to the moral choice construction so as to sustain criminal justice policies that are often driven by law-and-order agendas. And that extends to an uncritical insistence on punishing Indigenous accused through standard incarceration sentences without any critical interrogation into whether those policies will fail to lessen Indigenous crime or even make matters worse.

A fundamental position of this book is that standard punitive policies cannot continue to be applied to Indigenous people affected by the social legacies left behind by residential schools. Those policies will at best do nothing to address the passing of trauma from one generation to the next in Indigenous communities, and at worst they will aggravate those problems. But the first step in setting out that position is to address the denial that there is any connection between residential schools and ongoing Indigenous social problems. And that begins by setting out in detail how residential schools, through their abuse of students, planted the seeds of intergenerational trauma in Indigenous communities.

Notes

1   Thomas Lougran et al., "Can Rational Choice be Considered a General Theory of Crime? Evidence from Individual-Level Panel Data," *Criminology* 54, 1 (2016).

2   Jean Hampton, "The Moral Education Theory of Punishment," in R.G Frey and Christopher B. Morris (eds.), *Liability and Responsibility: Essays in Law and Morals* (New York: Cambridge University Press, 1991) 377.

3   Marvin Krohn, James Massey, and William Skinner, "A Sociological Theory of Crime and Delinquency: Social Learning," in Edward Morris and Curtis Braukmann (eds.), *Behavorial Approaches to Crime and Delinquency* (New York: Plenum Press, 1997), 455.

4   Angela Davis, "Race and Criminalization: Black Americans and the Punishment Industry," in Toni Morrison (ed.), *The House That Race Built* (New York: Vintage Books, 1997), 264.

5   David Scott, *Against Imprisonment: An Anthology of Abolitionist Essays* (Sherfield on Loddon, Great Britain: Waterside Press, 2018), 200–2.

6   *Criminal Code, Revised Statutes of Canada* 1985, c. 46 <laws-lois.justice.gc.ca/eng/acts/c-46/>.

7   "Overview of Sentencing," The Criminal Law Notebook <criminalnotebook.ca/index.php/Overview_of_Sentencing>.

8   *Criminal Code*, s. 718.

9   *R. v. McDonnell*, 1997 SCC 389.

10   Andrew Ashworth and M. Hough, "Sentencing and the Climate of Opinion," *Criminal Law Review* (1996): 780–81.

11   "Cotler to Table Bills Inspired by Cadman," *Vancouver Sun*, September 28, 2005, A1.

12   Jonathan Fowlie, "Liberals to Ramp Up War on Meth," *Vancouver Sun*, December 12, 2005, A1.

13   Alberta Currie et al., *The 2007 National Justice Survey: Tackling Crime and Public Confidence* (Ottawa: Department of Justice Canada, 2007). See also Karin Stein, *Public Perception of Crime and Justice in Canada: A Review of Opinion Polls* (Ottawa: Department of Justice Canada, 2001).

14   "Statement by the Government of Canada on the Royal Assent of Bill C-10,"
     Government of Canada <canada.ca/en/news/archive/2012/03/statement-gov-
     ernment-canada-royal-assent-bill-c-10-832089.html>.
15   "Legislative Summary of Bill C-10: An Act to Enact the Justice for Victims of
     Terrorism Act and to Amend the State Immunity Act, the Criminal Code, the
     Controlled Drugs and Substances Act, the Corrections and Conditional Re-
     lease Act, the Youth Criminal Justice Act, the Immigration and Refugee Protec-
     tion Act and other Acts," Library of Parliament <lop.parl.ca/sites/PublicWeb-
     site/default/en_CA/ResearchPublications/LegislativeSummaries/411C10E>.
16   Library of Parliament, "Legislative Summary of Bill C-10."
17   Library of Parliament, "Legislative Summary of Bill C-10."
18   David Garland, *The Culture of Control: Crime and Social Order in Contempo-
     rary Society* (Oxford: Oxford University Press, 2001), 142–43.
19   Gennaro F. Vito, Jeffrey R. Maahs, and Ronald M. Holmes, *Criminology: Theo-
     ry, Research, and Policy* (London: Jones & Bartlett Publishers, 2006), 11.
20   See, for example, Mark Halsey, "Child Victims as Adult Offenders: Fore-
     grounding the Criminogenic Effects of (Unresolved) Trauma and Loss," *British
     Journal of Criminology* 58, 1 (2018), 7.
21   Anthony Doob, "The Harper Revolution in Criminal Justice Policy ... and
     What Comes Next," *Policy Options*, May 4, 2015 <policyoptions.irpp.org/mag-
     azines/is-it-the-best-of-times-or-the-worst/doob-webster/>.
22   Anthony Doob, "The Harper Revolution."
23   Suzanne Colpron, "La torture impunie," *La Presse*, April 16, 2016 <lapresse.ca/
     debats/201604/13/01-4970734-la-torture-impunie.php>.
24   Graeme Hamilton, "'Collateral Victim' of Residential Schools Gets 15 Months
     for Burning Child 27 Times with Cigarette, Lighter," *National Post*, April
     7,   2016   <nationalpost.com/news/canada/collateral-victim-of-residential-
     schools-gets-15-months-for-burning-child-27-times-with-cigarette-lighter>.
25   "Lingering Effect of Damage Done by Residential School Had to Be Taken into
     Account When Determining Sentence, Judge Says," *National Post*, Facebook,
     April 6, 2016 <facebook.com/NationalPost/posts/10154109638944595>.
26   *National Post*, "Lingering Effect of of Damage."
27   *National Post*, "Lingering Effect of of Damage."

3

THE SEEDS OF INTERGENERATIONAL TRAUMA

STORIES AND STUDIES OF TRAUMA

I will for the next two chapters use a certain methodology to substantiate the connections between residential schools, the operation of Canadian sentencing law, and Indigenous over-incarceration.

The first part of the methodology reviews numerous case law excerpts where Canadian judges have recognized the presence of factors in the accused's background that can be tied back to residential schools, and they further recognized that these factors had a role in the accused getting caught up in the justice system. This chapter will cover risk factors that originated in the abuses suffered by those who directly attended the residential schools, although in many instances these risk factors continue to make themselves felt for years after the schools themselves closed. These factors include physical and sexual abuse by school staff, racism in the schools and afterward, the erosion of traditional Indigenous cultures, and the development of substance addictions and mental health problems in response to the abuse. The next chapter focuses on risk factors that have spread intergenerationally following the initial abuses perpetrated within schools.

The case law review mentions the crimes with which the accused were charged and what sentences they received. It will not be hard to notice that terms of incarceration were used in the clear majority of cases. Deterrence and retribution were given higher priority in the vast majority of cases, and a legal preference for the moral choice construction certainly becomes evident.

There is a third aspect to the methodology. The factors described in the sentencing cases are recognized as causally linked to crime not just by lawyers and judges, but in the social sciences as well. Those studies will be summarized to provide additional proof that social factors tied to the abuse of residential school students increased the likelihood that they would go onto harmful behaviour after leaving those institutions. The case law narrative excerpts provide a microcosmic view of the problems, while the social science studies empirically validate the link between the residential schools and Indigenous over-incarceration.

The purpose of this particular chapter is to demonstrate that the residential schools planted the seeds for Indigenous over-incarceration by directly harming the students. That in turn led to abandoning those students in a severely damaged state where they were susceptible to harming those around them and spreading the damage throughout their communities. The passing of harm to future generations is the focus of the next chapter.

VICTIMIZED IN THE RESIDENTIAL SCHOOLS

There are many cases where judges have recognized that having directly attended residential schools has been a contributing factor to offending behaviour.[1] It has been noted that sometimes the child was abused in residential schools, while remaining in their birth parents' home would have been comparatively much more positive. Judge Rounthwaite noted in a case of driving under the influence that the accused enjoyed a loving environment when he returned to his birth parents at night, but was frequently strapped while attending residential school during the day.[2] Justice Burrows noted in *R. v. Tootoosis*, where the accused received two years plus three years' probation for possession of child pornography and improper storage of a firearm: "Mr. Tootoosis told the probation officer who prepared the Presentence Report that he experienced verbal, physical and psychological abuse when, as a child, he attended a residential school as a day student. He gave a positive description of his childhood experiences in his own home."[3] In *R. v. M.A.G.*, where the accused was designated a long-term offender after a series of violent offences, Justice Chicoine writes: "[M.A.G.] attended a residential school at age 13. He recalls being physically abused, and specifically regrets that his father would sometimes leave his children at the school over the weekend, when incidents of abuse would get worse."[4]

Sometimes the abuse was especially degrading and humiliating. A Saskatchewan case, which involved an application to have the accused designated a dangerous offender subject to indefinite incarceration, noted that the accused as a child was arrested for shoplifting. The RCMP brought him back to his residential school, where he was "stripped naked and beaten with a steel brush on his buttock until blood was drawn."[5]

There are numerous cases of Indigenous accused being prosecuted for offences and where their backgrounds included both physical and sexual abuse by residential school staff.[6] In *R. v. Patrick*, where the accused was sentenced to five years for sexual assault, Justice Steinberg notes how complaining about the abuse led to retaliation by school staff:

> He was taken from his family home and placed, for a number of years, in a northern isolated residential school. There, he was sexually abused for a number of years. He complained about the abuse and, for his troubles, was beaten by the people with whom he laid his complaints. He has subsequently developed a severe alcohol problem.[7]

Anger and self-loathing are frequently expected in cases like these. Another case from Saskatchewan involving a dangerous offender application noted that the accused became an "angry, impulsive, dangerous man" who had been "acting out his anger against others for many years" and also "on certain occasions attempted to hurt himself."[8] A Yukon Court of Appeal case that sentenced three and a half years for offences related to intoxicated driving noted that the accused as well as his siblings had suffered years of physical and sexual abuse in Lower Post Residential School in British Columbia. The accused blamed the school for both the suicide of his brother and the early death of his sister through chronic alcoholism.[9]

Then there are instances where members from multiple generations of the same family, including an accused, suffered abuse in residential schools.[10] Sometimes both intergenerational trauma and multiple generations having been in residential schools are present in background circumstances. A Northwest Territories case that saw the accused receive three and a half years for two counts of sexual assault described how his mother, his maternal grandparents, and his father all attended residential schools. The father was himself abusive toward his family members, including the accused. The Territorial court was not surprised that the accused became violent in his own turn and dependent on alcohol.[11]

ABUSE ALL AROUND: SCHOOL AND HOME

There are also cases where accused were abused both within a residential school as well as in a dysfunctional family environment. Sometimes it was physical abuse both inside and outside the school. One example is *R. v. Cote*, where the accused received two years less a day for aggravated assault, and he had been physically abused by his mother as well as by residential school staff.[12] Another example is *R. v. Francouer*, where the female Indigenous accused was abused in residential schools with belts and yardsticks and then later ended up in a string of abusive intimate relationships. We see in the latter case both harsh physical discipline in residential school and then pairing with abusive partners afterward. Her sentence was one year plus two years' probation for assault with a weapon.[13]

Sometimes the accused suffers physical and sexual abuse while in residential school and then is subjected to physical abuse once he or she returns home. A Saskatchewan Provincial Court case noted that the accused had amassed at least forty prior convictions, many of them for violent offences, before being designated a dangerous offender. He had been physically abused by both his father and several of his siblings. Attending the Lebret Residential School for eight months led to physical and sexual abuse.[14] A British Columbia case noted that the accused had been physically and sexually abused in a residential school for eight years. Returning to his family home meant physical abuse by his father. He was sentenced to two years and three years' probation for sexual assault.[15] Another Saskatchewan case saw the accused sentenced to two years less a day plus three years' probation for theft and uttering threats. Justice Gunn noted: "Joey says he was physically abused by his mother when he was in her care. Joey went to the residential school in Lebret when he was about 8 years of age. He asserts that he was physically and sexually abused while in Lebret and that he ran away from the school on more than one occasion."[16]

An Ontario case saw the accused receive two years less a day for aggravated assault. She suffered physical abuse through strapping in residential school but was sexually violated after returning to a dysfunctional home environment.[17] Another Saskatchewan case noted that the accused was abused in the Lebret Residential School for three and a half years. He returned home and was sexually abused by multiple family members.[18]

Then there are cases where the accused experienced both physical and sexual abuse in residential school and in the family home.[19] A Yukon case involved an Indigenous woman who was physically and sexually abused in residential school. She was then sexually abused by an uncle several times after her return home, as well as by numerous male visitors to her home. One of her earlier assault victims reminded her of her mother, who was emotionally abusive toward her. She developed a habit of physically abusing her male partners after they passed out from alcohol, to project her anger over the sexual abuse that she previously suffered. She was sentenced to fourteen months for assault causing bodily harm.[20]

SUBSEQUENT SUBSTANCE ABUSE

Substance abuse (drugs or alcohol) is also recognized as a risk factor for criminal behaviour. A meta-analysis of thirty studies in 2008 found that in the aggregate, drug users were three to four times more likely to offend than non-drug users.[21] Studies since have continued to affirm that drug and/or alcohol abuse significantly raises the risks of recidivism for many offences, including crimes committed while incarcerated,[22] sexual offences,[23] domestic violence offences,[24] and juvenile delinquency.[25]

It should therefore not be surprising that many court cases have recognized that substance abuse was at once both a reaction to having been victimized in residential schools and a contributor to subsequent criminal behaviour.[26] A Saskatchewan case noted that the accused was sexually abused by a residential school staff member when he was ten years of age, and that staff member threatened to kill him should he ever tell anyone. Judge Kalmakoff observed that the accused's addiction to alcohol that started in his teen years was a result of being unable to cope with the memories of the sexual abuse. He also had seventy-two prior convictions before being sentenced to nine years for impaired driving causing death.[27]

A Yukon case, where the accused was sentenced to two years for driving under the influence, saw an expert witness conclude that alcohol abuse was a way to cope with painful memories of having been abused in residential schools:

> In summary, alcohol abuse has been a long-term maladaptive coping mechanism by which Mr. Joe has 1) blocked out knowl-

edge, feelings, and memories related to the residential sexual abuse and 2) released his inhibitions and preoccupations related to fears of criticism, rejection, and embarrassment as well as feelings of inadequacy and inferiority.[28]

Another case, in which the accused was sentenced to three and a half years for impaired driving, noted that the accused began drinking almost immediately after leaving the residential school where he had been sexually abused. Judge Tomkins of the Saskatchewan Provincial Court noted that the alcoholism was to block out painful memories of the abuse, and that any crime the accused committed occurred when he was angry and intoxicated at the same time.[29]

Sometimes the damage is so extensive that despite periods of sobriety, relapse becomes frequent. A Yukon Territorial Court noted that the accused had experienced a period of "extensive involvement with the criminal justice system between 1961 and 1986." He underwent residential treatment and stayed sober from 1986 to 1998, even becoming a substance abuse counsellor. However, he relapsed after 1998 and was given a nine-month conditional sentence and three years' probation for driving under the influence.[30]

It is to be expected that substance abuse will in turn lead to other self-destructive behaviours. A Saskatchewan Court of Queen's Bench case noted that the accused suffered years of physical and sexual abuse in a residential school. She started sniffing gasoline at age nine, starting drinking alcohol at age twelve, starting using marijuana at age fifteen and opiates at age seventeen. Her substance abuse problems became such that she would use instantly use drugs or alcohol whenever it was available. And when it was not available with enough frequency, she would take to petty theft crimes and street prostitution to support her habits.[31]

It should also not be surprising that receiving a residential school settlement payment can actually make substance abuse problems worse. We see this comment from a Saskatchewan case where the accused was convicted of manslaughter: "In 2004, shortly after Mr. Stonechild received a portion of his residential school settlement, he lapsed back into his addictive behaviours — behaviours that led to more run-ins with the criminal law."[32] Another Saskatchewan case provides an example that is quite ironic. An expert witness noted that the accused managed to overcome his substance abuse problems and had been clean for several years.

Participating in legal proceedings to obtain a residential school settlement ending up bringing memories of abuse to the fore and resulted in a
relapse to alcohol. The accused received a two-year conditional sentence
for driving under the influence.[33]

MENTAL HEALTH

Being at risk for mental health problems stemming from abuse while
young also increases the risk for involvement with the criminal justice system. An American study involving 5,501 children placed with
ninety-two child welfare agencies nationwide found that mental health
problems stemming from abuse while young made arrest six times more
likely.[34] A study was done by the Aboriginal Healing Foundation based
on 127 Aboriginal persons in British Columbia who were litigating residential school claims. Ninety-three of those cases indicated prognoses
of mental health problems, and some of the percentages were quite substantial. They included 21.1 percent for major depression, 26.3 percent
for substance abuse disorder, 20 percent for dysthymic disorder, and
64.2 percent for post-traumatic stress disorder.[35]

And there is an apparent connection to criminal history as well. Sixty-
two of those 127 case files had criminal histories, with significant percentages of those 62 for murder (4.8%), sexual offences (51.6%), possession of weapons (4.8%), assault (54.8%), robbery (8.1%), theft (24.2%),
drug offences (11.3%), and driving offences (64.5%).[36] A Saskatchewan
case, where the accused was sentenced to eighteen months for driving
under the influence and other charges, noted that the accused had been
physically and sexually abused in a residential school. He became dependent on alcohol and cocaine and ended up under the care of a psy-
chiatrist for anxiety at a correctional centre.[37]

RACISM IN AND OUTSIDE OF RESIDENTIAL SCHOOLS

While residential schools were a brutal implementation of a fundamentally racist policy, Indigenous Peoples have over generations experienced
racism both within and outside of the school. Murray Sinclair said in
a radio interview that generations of Canadians, both before and after
residential schools, have been raised to believe "that Indigenous people
were inferior, that they were unclean, that they were pagans."[38] Racial
discrimination has been recognized as risk factor for offending behav-

iour. For example, a study compared African-American men who experienced racial discrimination (e.g., racial slurs, racial profiling by police, having been physically attacked over race) to subjects who had not experienced racial discrimination. Those who reported higher discrimination committed crimes of intimate partner violence more often (28%) in comparison to those who reported lower discrimination (16%). The difference was also significant for crimes involving street violence (32.7% to 27.8%).[39] A US study by Monica Martin and others found that Black youth who had experienced personal discrimination (e.g., racial slurs, racial attacks) had significantly increased probabilities for general delinquency (e.g., property crimes) and for violent delinquency.[40] Another US study by Anthony Hoskin found that Black youth who perceived fellow students as being prejudiced had significantly increased probabilities of violent offending.[41]

Similar studies have not been carried with reference to Indigenous populations in Canada. Nonetheless, it is not difficult to find at least anecdotal evidence of Indigenous persons experiencing racism both within and without residential schools.[42] An Ontario manslaughter case saw a female Indigenous accused sentenced to twenty-seven months for manslaughter. She experienced sexual abuse as a child, in addition to racism and bullying during her elementary school years. One particularly humiliating incident involved one of her few friends inviting her to a sleepover, only for the friend's parents to close the door on her. She was left alone to try and find her own way back home in the dark. Two men drove her back home after noticing her.[43]

Some cases see authorities in mainstream schools treating later generations of Indigenous students in a manner that cannot be told apart from how residential schools treated earlier generations of Indigenous children. In an Ontario case where the accused received nine years for sexual assault and robbery, it was noted that the accused was often subjected to racial slurs during his school years. In particular, he was kicked out of a high school for breaking a vice-principal's nose in response to being called a "wagon burner."[44] In an Alberta case, where the accused received a global sentence of seven and a half years for violent sexual offences, the accused had previously faced racial slurs on a daily basis. The principal had also shaken him by his shirt in front of the rest of the class while calling him a "fucking Indian," while the rest of the kids laughed at him.[45]

Sometimes racism made the mainstream school environment so intolerable that Indigenous students were unable to complete their education — and that in turn can exacerbate other contributing factors like poverty. In a Saskatchewan case, where the accused was sentenced to nine months for attempted robbery, Justice Martinez noted that overt racism from the teachers became so severe that he ended up avoiding school altogether. He had only completed Grade 8 by the time he was convicted.[46] An Ontario case saw the accused sentenced to life imprisonment without parole eligibility for ten years for second-degree murder. He had been subjected to constant racist bullying by both students and teachers during his early school years. Fighting back led to school discipline without repercussions for the other students. He only lasted a few days in high school before dropping out for odd labour jobs. He eventually slid into substance abuse and life on the streets.[47]

Sometimes the racism can indeed instill anger to such a degree that it leads to a pattern of violent offending. The accused in a Saskatchewan case received a global sentence of seven years for numerous offences, including multiple counts of violence, and after a lengthy criminal record that included many assaults and previous robberies. Justice Elson of the Saskatchewan Court of Queen's Bench noted that after years of having to fight racist bullies in school, he ended up dropping out before the end of Grade 10.[48] An Alberta case saw the accused designated a dangerous offender following numerous violent offences, including violent abuse of several intimate partners. Justice Romaine of the Alberta Court of Queen's Bench noted:

> The appellant also attended non-residential schools at various times, experiencing racism and abuse in that setting as well. He stated of his childhood on the reserve: "We were taught not to trust white people. Stick with your kind. If I stick with my kind, I stick with the trauma, but if I stick with the white people, I have to deal with all the bullies and racism." However, experiencing his family being outcasts on the reserve also made him cynical about his Indigenous culture — having otherwise received only a "smattering of Siksika teachings, religious teachings from his churchgoing grandmother."[49]

Note the dilemma, described in the excerpt, between either enduring racism outside of Indigenous settings or enduring abuse inside a traumatized Indigenous community. The passage also indicates another factor — the erosion of Indigenous cultures.[50]

LOSS OF CULTURE

Residential schools have also had a very significant role in the loss of traditional culture and knowledge, including customary laws that could have acted as a positive mechanism of social control and restraint against criminal behaviour. This has often had profound consequences for contemporary Indigenous communities. As Carol LaPrairie explains with reference to the James Bay Cree:

> Residential schools, the decline of traditional activities, the emergence of the reserve system which binds people together in unnatural ways, and the creation of band government which locates power and resources in the hands of a few have dictated the form of reserve life across the country and have profoundly affected institutions such as kinship networks, families, as well as the unspoken rules of behaviour in traditional societies. The lack of respect for others, and the absence of shame about one's bad behaviour and about harming another or the community were, to many Cree for example, the most troubling aspects of contemporary life.[51]

Harald Finkler also attributes the dramatic rise in crime and disorder among the Inuit in the Canadian north to the erosion of traditional methods of social control and their displacement by Western institutions.[52]

Several cases have noted that the obliteration of Indigenous culture as a result of residential schools represented the loss of a positive force in an accused's life and may have contributed to their getting charged with offences.[53] An Ontario case noted that residential schools resulted in parents not being able to pass down intergenerational cultural values. Alcohol abuse was instead what was passed on, as a destructive replacement.[54] One case in particular saw the accused sentenced to one year of jail for aggravated assault and possession of a dangerous weapon. Justice Lacelle of the Ontario Superior Court of Justice made linkages between residential schools, the loss of culture, the accused's problems, and social dysfunction in his Mohawk community:

The *Gladue* evidence confirms that because of that history the Mohawk community has suffered from tragedy, abuse, violence and alcoholism. A shattered cultural identity and fractured social support systems have been the result for families and individuals. As noted by the author of the PSR addendum, "these factors increased the likelihood of difficulties for the subject throughout his life." They have contributed to the social problems experienced by Mr. Hall.[55]

Residential schools' replacement of eroded traditional cultures with far worse alternatives reverberates in another British Columbia case where the accused was charged with having sexual relations with a person under the age of consent. The relationship with his own cousin started when he was sixteen years old and she was ten. She became pregnant by age thirteen. The sentencing report noted that the Alberni Residential School led at the same time to both the loss of traditional cultural values in the Tseshaht First Nation in British Columbia and an increase in substance abuse. The latter in turn led to increased promiscuity among the very young after the loss of traditional values that regulated sexual relations, as well as a loss of appropriate sexual boundaries between young persons.[56]

DEFICIENT PARENTING

Many studies have verified a correlation between poor parenting styles, such as those marked by a lack of parental monitoring or discipline, or those marked by hostility and rejection toward the children, and juvenile delinquency. In 2009, a meta-analysis of 161 studies found that parental skills are significantly tied to juvenile delinquency.[57] The meta-analysis found that parental neglect, rejection, hostility, or combinations thereof may increase juvenile delinquency rates by 10 percent to 13 percent. On the other hand, adequate parental monitoring was found to have reduced juvenile delinquency by 9 percent to 12 percent.[58] More studies since then have continued to find correlations between juvenile delinquency and parental neglect[59] or lack of parental monitoring[60] or lack of effective parent-adolescent communication[61] or verbal abuse.[62]

The connection between parenting skills and subsequent juvenile delinquency has been noticed by Canadian courts as well.[63] Some cases have provided to-the-point observations that the accused's parents did not learn adequate parenting skills as a result of residential schools and thus were unable to provide adequate guidance to the accused.[64] Other cases have noted that residential schools disrupted the intergenerational transmission of parenting skills so that not only did the accused offend as a result of inadequate parental supervision, but so did the accused's parents previously, back through generations to the ancestors who first attended residential school.[65]

The lack of parenting skills is often mixed with other problems as well. Parents openly abusing drugs and alcohol in front of their children, including the accused when he or she was younger, has been seen in several cases.[66] In a British Columbia case where the accused received two years plus three years' probation for driving under the influence, armed robbery, and obstructing a police officer, we see alcoholism alongside parental neglect:

> In addition to the battle with alcohol, Mrs. B. struggled as she became a young mother to her three boys, of whom the accused is the youngest. She has described the residential experience, understandably, as having deprived her of the opportunity to learn from her own mother how to raise her sons. She has told professionals involved in working with the accused that she was not a good mother. She was an alcoholic for thirty years and drank while pregnant with the accused. It is apparent that the accused grew up in an impoverished and neglectful environment.[67]

Another British Columbia case saw the accused receive three years' probation for possession of fentanyl with intent to traffic. It was an example where the accused just could not find a suitable living arrangement. He was apprehended by social services from his father, a residential school survivor who became an alcoholic. But the foster home was not any better — a Caucasian woman who suffered from mental illness and was addicted to drugs.[68] A Manitoba case notes that both of the accused's parents had been in both residential schools and foster homes. All seven children, including the accused, had been apprehended multiple times by social services due to parental neglect and alcoholism. The Manitoba Court of Queen's Bench notes that the parents were "incapable of parenting" and the entire family was "in crisis." The accused received twenty-nine months in youth custody for manslaughter.[69]

Sometimes is it not just parental neglect but also setting a negative example that will inform the accused's offending behaviour as an adult. An Alberta case noted that the accused's mother and all of his grandparents suffered abuse in residential schools. He was left with multiple caregivers, many of whom not only openly abused drugs and alcohol, but also trafficked in illegal drugs for livelihoods. He received three years' probation for trafficking heroin and fentanyl.[70]

Sometimes parental abuse and parental neglect go together.[71] A British Columbia Provincial Court case describes a very horrific scenario. The father was abusive. The mother, herself a residential school survivor, attempted to douse the father with boiling water and served three years for attempted murder as a result. She also attempted suicide numerous times, including once directly in front of the accused while he was still an infant. He was also apprehended from her home numerous times due to alcohol abuse and neglect. He received a two-year intensive supervision and custody order for criminal negligence causing death along with property offences.[72] A Manitoba case noted that the accused's father was strapped regularly by the principal during his stay in a residential school. The father became in his own turn physically abusive toward the accused. Both the father and the mother became alcoholics and frequently left the accused unsupervised as a child. Justice Sandhu of the Manitoba Provincial Court commented that "[t]he damage inflicted by the systemic abuse of aboriginals in the residential school system echoes through time."[73]

Sometimes poor parenting can make its way across multiple generations. A Yukon case noted that the accused as a child always ended up in a setting marked by alcoholism and neglect, whether it was his own mother or his grandparents who were supposed to be babysitting him. He was sentenced to ninety-six days followed by two years' probation in relation to aggravated assault and other charges.[74]

One Quebec case has noted that the problem may go far beyond the individual accused to reflect problems that are pervasive in the community itself. The accused received time served plus nine years and four and a half months for multiple charges. Judge Chabot explained:

> As a judge, I have presided over court sessions in Mistissini for almost six years. I make no pretense of having a full extent of knowledge in Cree matters, but I am aware of a number of things that might have played a role in the unique background of the

Cree nation. I keep in mind for instance, that many people were forced to attend residential schools. As a result, many struggle with exercising their parental responsibilities since they did not have a model, having practically been raised far from their own parents.[75]

It should be obvious that many among the first generations of Indigenous children who attended residential schools were harmed in ways that resulted in lasting damage for them. That damage was severe enough to lead to criminal behaviour that was in turn harmful to those around them. In this way, residential schools planted the seeds for widespread trauma and destructive behaviour in Indigenous communities, which in turn has become a key cause of Indigenous over-incarceration. The next chapter substantiates these linkages, explaining how the trauma inflicted on the first generations of residential school students has percolated down through subsequent generations and resulted in lasting social trauma for Indigenous Peoples.

Notes

1   *R. v. Charles*, 2009 BCPC 448, para. 2; *R. v. Kendi*, 2009 BCPC 1066; *R. v. D.(G.)*, 2005 ONCJ 10045; *R. v. G.E.W.*, 2014 BCSC 2597; *R. v. Wuttunee*, 2012 ABPC 348; *R. v. Scott*, 2014 SKQB 379; *R. v. Ahpay*, 2018 SKQB 147; *R. v. A.J.A. and J.A.F.*, 2018 BCPC 50.

2   *R. v. Craigan*, 2007 BCPC 1362, para. 4.

3   *R. v. Tootoosis*, 2010 ABQB 574, para. 10.

4   *R. v. M.A.G.*, 2006 SKQB 313, para. 28.

5   *R. v. Daniels*, 2008 SKQB 349, 10–12.

6   *R. v. Stonechild*, 2010 SKQB 458; *R. v. R.H.L.*, 2005 SKPC 9; *R. v. Johnnie*, 2009 YKSC 42.

7   *R. v. Patrick*, 2002 BCPC 648, para. 5.

8   *R. v. Bunn*, 446 Sask. R. 184 (C.A.), para. 11.

9   *R. v. Joe*, 2017 YKCA 13, para. 9.

10 *R. v. Sam*, 2005 YKSC 2, para. 12; *R. v. Maineville*, 2015 ONCJ 1931; *R. v. Awasis*, 2016 BCPC 219; *R. v. Linklater*, 2005 ONSCJ 518; *R. v. Silversmith, 2008 ONSC 60168*, para. 24.

11 *R. v. McLeod*, 2012 NWTSC 26.

12 *R. v. Cote*, 2005 SKQB 508, para. 8.

13 *R. v. Francouer*, 2009 ONCJ 4399, para. 9.

14 *R. v. Redwood*, 2006 SKPC 663, para. 18–19.

15 *R. v. Williams*, 2010 BCPC 436, para. 13–14.

16 *R. v. Keewatin*, 2009 SKQB 58, para. 58.

17 *R. v. Whiskeyjack*, 2008 ONCA 800, para. 13 and 23.

18 *R. v. S.C.*, 2009 SKQB 272, para. 5.

19   *R. v. Good*, 2012 YKCA 12, para. 4; *R. v. Bird*, (2014) 440 Sask. R. 131 (Q.B.), 30.

20   *R. v. Smith*, 2004 YKTC 14, para. 15. See also *R. v. M.L.B.*, 2004 SKPC 136, para. 32. The case was stayed to avoid multiple convictions from the same inci dent, in compliance with the rule in *R. v. Kineapple* [1975] 1 S.C.R. 729.

21   Trevor Bennett, Katie Holloway, and David Farrington, "The Statistical Association between Drug Misuse and Crime: A Meta-Analysis," *Aggression and Violent Behavior* 13 (2008).

22   Simone Lambert, "Substance Abuse and Prison Recidivism: Themes from Qualitative Interviews," *Journal of Addictions & Offender Counselling* 31, 1 (2010), 10.

23   Jan Looman and Jeffrey Abracen, "Substance Abuse among High-Risk Sexual Offenders: Do Measures of Lifetime History of Substance Abuse Add to the Prediction of Recidivism over Actuarial Risk Assessment Instruments?" *Journal of Interpersonal Violence* 26, 4 (2011), 683

24   David Hirschel, Ira Hutchinson, and Meaghan Shaw, "The Interrelationship between Substance Abuse and the Likelihood of Arrest, Conviction, and Re-Offending in Cases of Intimate Partner Violence," *Journal of Family Violence* 25, 1 (2010), 81.

25   Solomon Osho and Monique Grant, "Substance Abuse of Repeat Juvenile Offenders: An Empirical Investigation," *European Journal of Social Science* 19, 4 (2011), 492.

26   *R. v. Battaja*, 2010 YKTC 192; *R. v. E.K.*, 2012 BCPC 132; *R. v. O.S.*, 2005 BCPC 727; *R. v. Simon*, 2006 ABPC 21; *R. v. Langan*, 2010 SKPC 3; *R. v. McLeod*, 2006 YKTC 118; *R. v. Joe*, 2005 YKTC 21; *R. v. D.B.E.*, 2005 BCPC 2064; *R. v. Omeasoo* [2014], 5 W.W.R. 598, 2013 ABPC 328; *R. v. Ratt*, 2012 SKPC 154; *R. v. Steinhauer*, 2016 BCSC 1322; *R. v. Ballantyne*, 2012 SKPC 168; *R. v. Joe*, 2005 YKTC 21; *R. v. D.B.E.*, 2005 BCPC 2064; *R. v. Cody*, 2008 BCPC 428; *R. v. Laprise*, 2005 SKPC 80; *R. v. R.B.P.*, 2006 ONCJ 280.

27   *R. v. Okemahwasin* (2015) 79 M.V.R. (6th) 310 (Sask. P.C.), para. 10.

28   *R. v. Joe*, 2008 YKTC 65, para. 16.

29   *R. v. Obey*, 2013 SKPC 98, para. 15–17.

30   *R. v. Craft*, 2010 YKTC 127, para. 12.

31   *R. v. Moostoos*, 2017 SKQB 12, para. 15–17, 19.

32   *R. v. Stonechild*, 2017 SKQB 138, para. 25.

33   *R. v. M.L.W.*, 2004 SKPC 90, para. 8.

34   Dannia Southerland, Cecilia E. Casaneuva, and Heather Ringeisen, "Young Adult Incomes and Mental Health Problems among Transition Age Youth Investigated for Maltreatment during Adolescence," *Child and Youth Services Review* 31, 9 (2009), 947; Katerina Maniadaki and Efthymios Kakouros, "Social and Mental Health Profiles of Young Male Offenders in Detention in Greece," *Criminal Behavior and Mental Health* 18 (2008), 207.

35   *Mental Health Profiles for a Sample of British Columbia's Aboriginal Survivors of the Canadian Residential School System* (Ottawa: Aboriginal Healing Foundation, 2003), 51.

36   *Mental Health Profiles*, 46.

37   *R. v. D.S.*, 2010 SKQB 562.

38   "Lynn Beyak's Resignation Good for the Senate, Good for Canada, Says Senator Murray Sinclair," CBC, January 27, 2021 <cbc.ca/radio/thecurrent/the-current-for-jan-27-2021-1.5888592/lynn-beyak-s-resignation-good-for-the-senate-good-for-canada-says-sen-murray-sinclair-1.5889535?>.

39   Elizabeth Reed et al., "Experiences of Racial Discrimination & Relation to Violence Perpetration and Gang Involvement among a Sample of Urban African American Men," *Journal of Immigrant and Minority Health* 12, 3 (2010), 323.

40   Monica Martin et al., "The Enduring Significance of Racism: Discrimination and Delinquency Among Black American Youth," *Journal of Research on Adolescence* 21, 3 (2010), 662.

41   Anthony Hoskin, "Explaining the Link Between Race and Violence With General Strain Theory," *Journal of Ethnicity in Criminal Justice* 9 (2011), 56.

42   *R. v. D.M.G.*, 2006 NSPC 58, para. 14; *R. v. Kipling*, 2014 MBQB 27, para. 13.

43   *R. v. Jourdain*, 2016 ONSC 7890, para. 14.

44   *R. v. Corbiere*, 2012 ONSC 2405, para. 33.

45   *R. v. T.W.S.*, 2018 ABQB 870, para. 56.

46   *R. v. Laliberte*, 2017 SKPC 82, para. 60.

47   *R. v. Land*, 2013 ONSC 6526, para. 45–46.

48   *R. v. J.P.*, 2018 SKQB 96.

49   *R. v. Wolfleg*, 2018 ABCA 222, para. 85.

50   *R. v. Paulin*, 2011 ONSC 5027; *R. v. Cappo*, 2005 SKCA 134; *R. v. Tymiak*, 2012 BCCA 40; *R. v. Pauchay*, 2009 SKPC 35; *R. v. Leaney*, 2002 BCCA 67; *R. v. W.R.B.*, 2010 MBQB 102; *R. v. Shawn Curtis Keepness*, 2011 SKQB 293; *R. v. Renschler*, 2005 MBPC 53233; *R. v. Klymok*, 2002 ABPC 95; *R. v. R.L.*, 2012 MBPC 22; *R. v. Boisseneau*, 2006 ONSC 562; *R. v. Corbiere*, 2012 ONSC 2405; *R. v. Sharkey*, 2011 BCSC 1541; *R. v. Makela*, 2006 BCPC 320; *R. v. Loring*, 2009 BCCA 166; *R. v. B.S.*, 2018 BCSC 2044; *R. v. George*, 2012 ONCJ 756.

51   Carol LaPrairie, "Aboriginal Crime and Justice: Explaining the Present, Exploring the Future," *Canadian Journal of Criminology* 34 (1992), 287.

52   Harald Finkler, "Community Participation in Socio-Legal Control: The Northern Context," *Canadian Journal of Criminology* 34 (1992), 503.

53   *R. v. Raven*, 2007 MBPC 295; *R. v. Knight*, 2012 MBPC 52; *R. v. Big Sorrel Horse*, 2012 ABCA 327; *R. v. Sanderson*, (2015) 320 Man. R. (2d) 307.

54   *R. v. Silversmith*, 2008 ONSC 60168, para. 20–24.

55   *R. v. Hall*, 2017 ONSC 3003, para. 8.

56   *R. v. D.G.*, 2014 BCCA 84.

57   Matcheld Hoeve et al., "The Relationship between Parenting and Delinquency: A Meta-Analysis," *Journal of Abnormal Child Psychology* 37 (2009), 749.

58   Hoeve et al., "The Relationship between Parenting and Delinquency," 758.

59   Daniel Maughan and Simon Moore, "Dimensions of Child Neglect: An Exploration of Parental Neglect and its Relationship with Delinquency," *Child Welfare* 89, 4 (2010), 47; Matcheld Hoeve et al., "Maternal and Paternal Parenting Styles: Unique and Combined Links to Adolescent and Early Adult Delinquency," *Journal of Adolescence* 34, 5 (2011), 813; Wan-Yi Chen et al., "Child Neglect and Its Association with Subsequent Juvenile Drug and Alcohol Offense," *Child and Adolescent Social Work Journal* 28, 4 (2011), 273.

60   Ryan D. Schroeder et al., "Parenting and Adult Criminality: An Examination of Direct and Indirect Effects by Race," *Journal of Adolescent Research* 25, 1 (2010), 77.
61   Tanusree Moitra and Indrani Mukherjee, "Parent-Adolescent Communication and Delinquency: A Comparative Study in Kolkata, India," *Europe's Journal of Psychology* 8, 1 (2012), 74.
62   Sarah Evans, Leslie Simons, and Ronald Simons, "The Effect of Corporal Punishment and Verbal Abuse on Delinquency," *Journal of Youth and Adolescence* 41, 8 (2012), 1095.
63   *R. v. Daybutch*, 2016 ONCJ 595.
64   *R. v. Ominayak*, 2007 ABQB 447, para. 150; *R. v. Eustache*, 2014 BCCA 337, para. 8; *R. v. Paulette*, 2010 NWTSC 31.
65   *R. v. Dantimo*, 2009 ONSC 6627, para. 14; *R. v. Smith*, 2011 YKTC 62, para. 36.
66   *R. v. Addley*, 2012 ONSC 137, para. 49; *R. v. Jimmie*, 2009 BCCA 1284, para. 9.
67   *R. v. D.R.B.*, 2004 BCPC 47, para. 14–15.
68   *R. v. Porter*, 2017 BCPC 30, para. 87–88.
69   *R. v. C.L.K.*, 2009 MBQB 227, para. 9.
70   *R. v. Smallboy*, 2018 BCPC 383, para. 17–18.
71   *R. v. Charles*, 2009 BCSC 1928, para. 12.; *R. v. Michel*, 2012 NWTSC 17, para. 26; *R. v. Burwell*, 2017 SKQB 375.
72   *R. v. D.R.U.*, 2004 BCPC 120, para. 33.
73   *R. v. Abraham*, 2008 MBPC 14, para. 7.
74   *R. v. Quock*, 2015 YKTC 32.
75   *R. v. Brien*, 2011 QCCQ 15643, para. 29.

4

INTERGENERATIONAL TRAUMA AND CRIME

The first generations of residential school students returned to their communities angry, damaged, and traumatized. It was inevitable that many of them would harm Indigenous community members around them. And that harm itself results in more Indigenous persons, even if they did not themselves attend residential schools, becoming damaged and traumatized and prone to themselves harming those around them. Indigenous children are very often the most vulnerable victims of this cycle of harm, who, as they age, move toward harmful behaviour against others. That is at the heart of what is meant by intergenerational trauma.

The previous chapter demonstrated how the destructive seeds were planted in Indigenous communities by the abuse that occurred within the residential schools. This chapter details how the seeds sprouted widespread abuse and trauma in Indigenous communities, affecting Indigenous persons as many as two or even three or more generations removed the original generations of residential school students. The cycle has sustained itself well after the schools planted those seeds. That in turn means that the routine application of Canadian sentencing law, in combination with the social legacy of residential schools, results in a particularly harsh form of systemic discrimination in the form of Indigenous over-incarceration.

I am of course cognizant that not everyone who went to residential schools or experienced intergenerational trauma went on to commit crimes. I also recognize the objection that crime, irrespective of background circumstances, still carries with it an element of personal choice. I will address these concerns more fully in Chapter 6. What I wish to emphasize for the time being is that the link between Indigenous over-incarceration and the social ramifications of residential schools is so strong that it cannot ignored or dismissed.

INTERGENERATIONAL DOMESTIC VIOLENCE

Many studies have found that domestic violence and home abuse are passed along generationally. Growing up in an abusive home environment increases the chances of children and adolescents later becoming involved in crime, including violent offences and drug-related offences.[1] One survey of 457 participants found that children who were exposed to domestic violence (36.8%), were themselves abused (41.7%), and were exposed to both (47.5%) had higher rates of committing of committing felony assault in comparison to those who had no exposure.[2]

An American study whose sample of 1,000 included Black, white, and Latino persons found that maltreatment experienced during adolescence also increased the probabilities of criminal behaviour. Percentages for late-adolescent criminality were 58.7 percent for general offending, 39 percent for violent offending, 30.4 percent for drug use, and 30 percent for arrest. Percentages come adulthood came to 63.9 percent for general offending, 26.9 percent for violent offending, 49.5 percent for drug use, and 32.7 percent for arrest.[3]

Research has shown that when male children witness the abuse of their mothers in the home, it significantly increases their later chances of becoming abusive toward their partners as well as their children. A psychology meta-analysis of several prior studies found that 60 percent of maritally violent men in the samples had reported family-of-origin violence, while 20 percent of maritally non-violent men reported family-of-origin violence.[4] A study that involved 1,099 adult males with histories of committing domestic abuse found that the frequency and severity of domestic violence correlated more strongly for those who witnessed domestic violence and those who were themselves physically abused in comparison to those were neither abused nor witnessed abuse (approximately 0.25). The correlation was even stronger for those who had both witnessed domestic violence and were themselves abused.[5] Greater exposure to violence as a child also meant greater likelihood of abusing their own children as adults.[6]

It may be that other social stresses enhance this phenomenon as well. One study was based on a sample of 205 domestic abusers, of which half were white, one third were Black, and nearly the remainder were Latino. The study found that taking the whole sample into consideration, witnessing parental abuse in the home as children was not significantly predictive of committing intimate partner violence as adults. Race did, however, have a significant impact on the results. Non-whites who witnessed parental abuse in their homes as children were three times more likely to engage in minor intimate partner abuse[7] and over five times as likely to engage in severe intimate partner violence.[8]

Jennifer Kwan, a mental health therapist in Edmonton, estimates that at least 65 percent of Indigenous people in Canada have been affected to some degree by family violence. She ascribes this rate to factors reflective of colonialism, such as poverty, unstable lifestyles, substance abuse, and gender inequality.[9]

Numerous cases note that where a male Indigenous accused was abused as a child by his father, he in turn became abusive toward his own family.[10] Other cases note an accused becoming an abuser after witnessing his father abusing his mother.[11] An especially pointed example comes from a Manitoba case where the accused was designated a dangerous offender in reaction to a domestic violence charge, which was the last offence on top of a lengthy previous criminal record. Being physically abused by family members for years, and witnessing physical violence against other family members, led the accused to believe that "physical violence was a normal form of discipline."[12] Justice Menzies of the Manitoba Court of Queen's Bench wrote, "As for domestic relationships, Moore regularly witnessed women being violently abused. Moore came to accept that physical abuse of women was normal. Moore expressed to Kolton that if he did not abuse his partner, she would think he didn't love her."[13]

Another study based on a survey that included almost 3,000 women also found that women could be at risk for violent behaviour later in life as well. The study summarized its results by using odds ratios, with an odds ratio over 1.0 indicating increased risk and an odds ratio less than 1.0 indicating decreased risk. Having been victimized by their father (1.15), having been victimized by their mother (1.35), and having witnessed domestic violence in the home (1.06) were all found to significantly increase the risk of women themselves becoming domestic abusers later in life.[14] That same study found that men (over 2,300 were included in the study) and women alike faced increased risk of also becoming abusers of their children as adults. The odds ratios were 1.13 for men previously exposed to mother-on-father violence, 1.21 for women abused by their mothers, 1.06 for women exposed to father-on-mother violence, and 1.13 for women exposed to mother-on-father violence.[15]

Sometimes the residential school experience can lead Indigenous women to become abusive toward their own children.[16] A British Columbia case noted that the accused's mother was abused by his father, and she in turn physically abused him. The accused was designated a dangerous offender following a lengthy violent record, the last case of which was an assault against his girlfriend.[17] A British Columbia case noted that the accused had as a child complained to his mother about being shivering cold after leaving a bathtub. His mother responded by burning him on a hot stove, and her friends and herself laughing at him over it. The accused was sentenced to forty-one months followed by a ten-year long-term offender supervision term for numerous and varied offences.[18]

Other cases note that it is the children who are abused by residential school survivors, with both parents acting as abusers, and those children get caught up in the justice system for offences other than domestic violence.[19] Sometimes abuse can lead to the accused adopting a lifelong pattern of violent behaviour.[20] A Saskatchewan case describes how the accused's brothers and father frequently beat each other during violent confrontations. There was even an instance where the father shot a firearm at one of the brothers. The accused himself was designated a dangerous offender following a lengthy record that included numerous violent offences.[21]

As mentioned, sometimes the abuse spans multiple generations — grandparents who were abused in residential schools in turn abused the parents, who in turn abused the accused.[22] An Alberta case noted that the accused's grandmother was a residential school survivor, while his father subjected both his siblings and him to extensive domestic violence. The court would normally have assessed thirty months for a serious assault but reduced it to twenty-one months in recognition of the accused's life experiences.[23] In an Ontario case, the accused was directly abused by the grandmother, who had attended a residential school. The grandmother verbally abused her by frequently calling her ugly and stupid. The grandmother also very frequently hit her with a fly swatter with the plastic flap removed. The accused was sentenced to two years less a day plus three years' probation for aggravated assault.[24]

Finally, Judge Singer of the Saskatchewan Provincial Court offered this reflection in reaction to a case of aggravated assault in which the accused had been physically abused by his mother, who herself had been physically abused in residential school:

In my experience, almost every time we see cases of horrific crime involving Aboriginal offenders, they are the actions of damaged individuals who were damaged as children due to neglect, poverty and deprivation, coupled with minimal opportunity for positive, socially-acceptable role models and education. In most cases, these can be traced back to the individual's own experience, or parents or loved ones in residential schools.[25]

And as we will see, it is not only physical abuse that gets spread from generation to generation. It is sexual abuse as well.

INTERGENERATIONAL SEXUAL ABUSE

Indigenous Peoples disproportionately experience sexual abuse. A 2014 study found that Indigenous persons experienced sexual violence at a rate (58 out of 1,000) that was substantially higher than the mainstream Canadian population (20 out of 1,000). The rates were even more disproportionate when gender was factored in: Indigenous women were much more likely to have been sexually assaulted (115 out of 1,000) than non-Indigenous women (35 out of 1,000). And there is reason to believe much of that abuse occurs in home or familial settings. The same report also found that Indigenous people were 1.4 times more likely to have been subjected to childhood maltreatment.[26]

When sexual abuse becomes endemic in Indigenous communities, it is not hard to anticipate that the abuse can spread across generations. A survey of 471 participants found that a youth who was abused by a female was 3.89 times more likely to subsequently abuse a female than a youth who was not abused by a female. A youth abused by a male was 6.05 times more likely to subsequently abuse a male. A youth abused by both males and females was 1.88 times more likely to subsequently abuse both males and females.[27] Another study involving 179 preadolescent girls found that girls were 3.6 times more likely to experience sexual victimization if the mother was herself sexually abused as a child.[28]

There are cases where the accused was personally abused in residential school and went on to perpetrate sexual abuse.[29] And some cases have seen the accused sexually abuse his own children after having been sexually abused in residential school.[30] One case, where the sentence was one year plus three years' probation for the accused sexually touching his daughter, saw Judge Ellan of the British Columbia Provincial Court provide this observation:

> Considering the effect of Mr. G's attitude to the offence, I consider that his background, in particular the sexual abuse he experienced, may have resulted in a blurring of the boundaries that would otherwise naturally prevail in a parental relationship. This may explain why Mr. G. has less ability to understand the effect of his actions toward his daughter than would an individual who had not himself been abused as a child.[31]

Sometimes sexual abuse in residential schools led to sexual abuse of extended family members, such as nephews and nieces.[32]

In other cases, the accused was on the receiving end of abuse from parents,[33] adoptive parents,[34] grandparents,[35] siblings,[36] or extended family members[37] who were themselves abused in residential school.

Sometimes parental neglect can lead to unsupervised environments where other community members who were previously strangers to the accused end up abusing the accused while he or she is a child. In a Saskatchewan case where the accused's mother was abused in residential schools and he was sentenced to five years for sexual assault and assault with a weapon, we read:

> Richard's mother used alcohol for much of her pregnancy with him, and he was raised in an environment where substance abuse and domestic violence was prevalent. Richard was repeatedly exposed to violence which occurred during his parents' house parties. He was sexually abused at the age of seven, once by a stranger and twice by a neighbour. The episodes of sexual abuse left Richard confused, ashamed and full of hate.[38]

Other cases have noted how sexual abuse can span generations, from grandparents to parents to children.[39]

POVERTY

Many studies have found a correlation between community poverty and higher crime rates.[40] This is apparently true even for the most serious of offences, including homicide.[41] Poverty and lack of employment opportunities have also been found to be positively correlated with gang membership.[42] Lack of education also increases the chances of falling into a life of crime.[43] Conversely, greater education and literacy decreases the chances of young people getting caught up in criminal lifestyles.[44] Poverty also increases domestic violence because it leaves battered women with fewer resources to obtain independence from abusive partners.[45]

There is plenty of empirical support for the fact that many Indigenous Peoples live in poverty. In 2005, the median income for Indigenous people was $16,752, while the median income for the non-Indigenous population was $25,955. One third of Indigenous households experienced food insecurity, and 14.4 percent experienced severe food insecurity. Non-Indigenous households experienced food insecurity at a rate of 8.8 percent. The survey found that 27.5 percent of Indigenous children lived in low-income households, in comparison to 12.9 percent of non-Indigenous children.[46] A 2016 study by the Canadian Centre for Policy Alternatives found that Indigenous children are twice as likely to live in poverty as non-Indigenous children. Poverty rates were 50 percent for First Nations children and 60 and for First Nations children living on reserve.[47] Data from Canada's 2016 census found that approximately 20 percent of Indigenous children over age fifteen had experienced food insecurity in the twelve months leading up to the survey.[48]

There is also empirical support for the assertion that poverty will affect the chances of Indigenous children succeeding later in life. Indeed, a study by Evelyne Bougie and Sacha Senechal found that residential school attendees were more likely to live in low-income households and to have experienced income insecurity. Indigenous children who came from higher-income households were more likely to be successful in school than Indigenous children from low-income households and were vulnerable to food insecurity.[49] Another study, by Robin Fitzgerald and Peter Carrington, found a strong statistical correlation between Indigenous persons residing in disadvantaged and impoverished neighbourhoods and Indigenous persons being over-represented in urban police-reported crime.[50]

A Saskatchewan case saw the accused sentenced to ninety days to be served intermittently followed by two years' probation. Judge Daunt of the Saskatchewan Provincial Court noted that poverty played a role as follows:

> Ms. Arcand is an aboriginal offender, so her individual circumstances include the post-colonial history of First Nations peo-

ple in this country.... In Ms. Arcand's case, it is not difficult to see why, when faced with financial problems, she might think she had fewer choices than a 21-year-old middle class college graduate who has a family with some financial resources. Ms. Arcand's immediate family is dysfunctional. Many of her peers live on the fringes of society. With that past history and present reality, it is easier to understand how Ms. Arcand might stray into the margins herself.[51]

Other cases have noted the accused committing offences of monetary gain, such as drug trafficking or property offences, in response to personal poverty.[52]

A British Columbia case saw the accused receive a conditional sentence of two years less a day plus three years' probation for failure to provide the necessities of life for her daughter. Judge Buller Bennett of the British Columbia Provincial Court noted:

Ms. C.O. has lived her life in poverty, isolation and violence. For the last ten years, if not longer, she has been disconnected from her family and traditions that are her sources of strength and support. She continues to live in poverty and violence. She is socially isolated with no one to call upon for help. Her home community still struggles with poverty, violence and offers few resources. Based on the evidence on sentencing, Ms. C.O. has had few realistic opportunities to change. In my view, the poverty, isolation and violence are precisely what brought Ms. C.O. to court.[53]

A case in the Alberta Court of Queen's Bench saw the accused sentenced to three years for manslaughter and break and enter. The court noted that the lengthy record that preceded the manslaughter charge included stealing money from other homes as a youth to provide for himself and his younger brother. The thefts later evolved into stealing to feed drug addiction.[54]

CHILD WELFARE

According to a report prepared by the First Nations Child and Family Caring Society, Indigenous children face child welfare apprehension rates far out of proportion compared to non-Indigenous children.

Substantiated child welfare investigation rates for physical abuse were 5.97 per 1,000 Indigenous children compared to 5.33 per 1,000 non-Indigenous children, 1.00 compared to 0.60 for sexual abuse, 32.33 compared to 4.98 for neglect, 6.77 compared to 3.07 for emotional maltreatment, and 11.24 compared to 5.87 for exposure to domestic violence.[55] The 2016 national census estimated that as of 2011, 48.1 percent of children up to age fourteen in the foster care system were Indigenous, despite representing only 7 percent of the general population of children up to age fourteen.[56]

It is more than reasonable to suggest that residential schools have a strong causal connection to this problem as well. Many of the facts described in the aforementioned cases would also constitute legal grounds for child welfare apprehension. For example, under s. 17(2) of Manitoba's *Child and Family Services Act*, grounds for when a child needs protection include abuse, potential for abuse, lack of supervision, and neglect of the child's physical needs.[57]

Being in the child welfare system is itself a risk factor for youth involvement in the criminal justice system. Instability of care home placements has been found to increase juvenile delinquency for children, males in particular. One study involving 278 Black American youth, for whom investigations of abuse or neglect were substantiated, found that 5 percent were delinquent, but 95 percent were not delinquent if there had only been one prior child welfare placement. Those percentages changed to 14 percent and 86 percent for two prior placements, and 15 percent and 85 percent for three or more placements.[58] A study of children who were substantiated as maltreated in Chicago and other Cook County suburbs found that maltreated children who were placed into care had a delinquency rate of 16 percent, compared to children who were not placed into care having a delinquency rate of 7 percent.[59] Another study of children in California's system found that children who were placed at least once in a group home were 2.5 times more likely to become delinquent compared to children who were placed in a foster home.[60] Placement instability has been found to be significantly predictive for adult criminality as well. A study based on 772 persons with histories of abuse or neglect prior to age twelve found that rates of adult arrest correlated with the degree of placement instability. The rates were 35 percent for no child welfare placements, 45.4 percent for one, 60 percent for two, and 76.3 percent for three or more.[61] A 2015 survey study of 432 participants aged eleven to seventeen found that youth with substantiated child welfare reports were more likely to have committed theft, more likely to carry a hidden weapon, and more likely to engage in drug use.[62] A 2018 study of 5,399 files of youth convicted for criminal offences (from 2003 to 2012) provided by the Quebec City Youth Centre found substantial linkages between child maltreatment combined with foster care placement and criminal behaviour. At least 68 percent of the sample were considered very high multi-offenders, a category that averaged fifteen prior convictions.[63]

As previously noted, residential school attendance by an accused's parents can lead the traumatized parents to in turn create an abusive and/or neglectful home environment.[64] And just like intergenerational trauma, as a Manitoba case recognized, trauma across generations can mean multiple generations affected by child welfare placement.[65] Many other cases have similarly noted such placements[66] or residential instability[67] as contributing factors. There are, moreover, instances where the child welfare system can compound the abuse. Some cases have noted that the accused as a youth was abused in a group home[68] or in an adoptive or foster home.[69] A British Columbia case noted that the accused, who received twenty-one months of youth custody for break and enter as well as robbery, had to be apprehended from his foster home because he was not being fed properly.[70]

SUBSTANCE ABUSE IN LATER GENERATIONS

Many studies have confirmed that alcohol and drug abuse in the home significantly increases the chances of substance abuse passing intergenerationally,[71] and many sentencing judges cannot help but notice as much.[72] We can see such intergenerational transmission of substance abuse, and its connections to residential schools, in a Prince Edward Island case where the accused was sentenced to eighteen months for possessing marijuana with intent to traffic. Justice Mitchell stated:

> Children, like Legere's mother, removed from their parents and culture, abused and belittled, often turn to substances such as alcohol to dull the pain. Legere's mother turned to alcohol. She was a mean alcoholic, and not a good mother. She was a product of that system. The pain and suffering that Legere suffered was a direct result of that system.[73]

A Yukon case noted that the accused's parents were residential school students but neither had been involved in the justice system. However, he had witnessed multiple fights and drinking parties as a young child. He started drinking at age seven and starting using drugs at nine. He received a ninety-day intermittent sentence for impaired driving.[74]

Several cases note how multiple family members, both immediate and distant, who were residential school survivors learned to cope through substance abuse. The accused in those cases were exposed to substance abuse at very early ages and subsequently became substance abusers caught up in the justice system.[75]

Then there are cases where one has been both a residential school survivor and exposed to substance abuse in the home as a child.[76] For example, a Saskatchewan case noted that the accused attended a residential school but was later apprehended from his parents because of their drug and alcohol addictions. He started using drugs at age nine. He was sentenced to life imprisonment and ineligible for parole for sixteen years for a second-degree murder he committed while he was intoxicated with both alcohol and ecstasy.[77]

Sometimes either physical or sexual abuse combined with substance abuse pass from generation to generation.[78] A sentencing report from a Manitoba case where the accused received a ninety-day intermittent sentence for impaired driving causing bodily harm, reads in part:

> The historical impact of colonization and of residential schools has affected the subject's family. There has been a devastating generational impact of lost culture and identity which continues to affect the subject and both the communities he feels connected to. Though they struggled to discuss some [of] the issues that highlight the colonization that their community has suffered through, the family disclosed generational struggles and it is clear that substance misuse has become a means to cope.[79]

The pervasiveness of substance abuse in turn leads to another fallout, explored in the next section.

FETAL ALCOHOL SPECTRUM DISORDER

A 2004 study of 418 patients diagnosed with fetal alcohol spectrum disorder (FASD) found that 60 percent of the sample had come into contact with criminal justice systems as suspects or as charged accused.[80] A 2011 Canadian study found that individuals with FASD were much more likely to be involved in the criminal justice system compared to those who did not have FASD: almost 90 percent for FASD subjects compared to 40+ percent for non-FASD subjects when it came to having any youth court history; almost 60 percent compared to less than 5 percent when it came to fifteen or more youth convictions; almost 90 percent versus almost 50 percent for a prior provincial jail term; and almost 30 percent compared to approximately 10 percent for fifteen or more adult convictions.[81] A 2019 study based on clinical diagnoses of eighty federal penitentiary inmates estimated that the rate of FASD ranged from 17.5 to 31.2 percent (if prenatal exposure to alcohol was confirmed) among the correctional population, where FASD among the general Canadian population was estimated at 2 to 5 percent.[82] There are presently no recent comprehensive empirical studies that set out the prevalence of FASD among Indigenous Peoples compared to non-Indigenous people across Canada. The studies that exist are dated, regional in their focus, and with small sample sizes.[83]

Indigenous accused suffering from FASD has, however, been a distinctly noticeable problem in the Canadian criminal justice system. Indeed, some cases have also traced the problem back to residential schools.[84] A British Columbia case where the accused received a year of youth custody for sexual touching represents an example where residential school abuse led to FASD for a third-generation family member:

> There is no doubt that the subject has been affected by the history of colonialism and the residential school system that his grandparents were victims of ... indeed his mother's drinking allegedly resulted in his FAS diagnosis which could be a direct link to personality traits that make J. difficult to manage in the community ... unfortunately, J. presents as difficult and hostile and does not take responsibility for his actions.[85]

Given that residential school abuse has spanned generations, it should not be surprising that there may be cases where an accused was both a residential school survivor and inherited FASD from a prior generation of residential school survivors.[86] A Yukon Territorial Court case saw the accused sentenced to six months and three years' probation for armed robbery, failure to attend court, and breach of recognizance. Judge Heino Lilles made explicit connections between residential schools and FASD.[87] The Yukon Court of Appeal confirmed the original sentence, as well as the connections made by Judge Lilles:

> The evidence is clear that Mr. Charlie suffers from the effects of FAS and that the effect is serious, although potentially not as serious as was thought at the time of sentencing before Lilles T.C.J. Nonetheless, the FAS effects are directly linked to his parents' forced placement in a residential school. Specifically, the FAS is the product of Mr. Charlie's mother consuming high levels of alcohol during her pregnancy, which consumption of alcohol is linked to her experience in the residential schools.[88]

This chapter has thus far outlined numerous intergenerational risk factors. What if Indigenous accused are experiencing several of them at once?

MULTIPLE TRAUMAS

These problems can be multilayered. A study by Carter Hay and colleagues argues that community poverty exacerbates the effects that unstable family environments have on levels of crime. In their study of 1,423 youth files, family environmental problems — based on a variety of measures, such as weak supervision and coercive discipline — were found to result in a significant increase in crime levels. If community poverty was present in a youth file, it could raise the effects of family problems by 36 percent. Conversely, reducing community poverty was found to instead reduce the effects of family problems on crime levels.[89] Preeti Chauhan and N. Dickon Reppucci's study asserts that poverty, coupled with exposure to violence while young — whether while growing up in an abusive environment or witnessing it first-hand, has been shown to increase propensity toward juvenile violence.[90] Poverty has been found to increase the probability of substance abuse, and both in turn increase the probability of criminal behaviour.[91] A study of more than 61,000 inmates in Texas found that inmates who had both a mental disorder and a substance abuse problem had higher recidivism rates (based on percentage comparison) than inmates who had only a mental health disorder or a substance abuse problem.[92]

Even two or three of the aforementioned risk factors can increase crime and recidivism at rates higher than just one risk factor acting alone. Now imagine, for a moment, all of these risk factors being present at once, and on a pervasive scale, in Indigenous communities. This is precisely what residential schools have done, to force upon so many Indigenous Peoples a multitude of social stresses that present a powerful push toward lives of crime. It is no wonder that the problem of Indigenous over-incarceration has reached the magnitude that it has.

Residential schools may not be the only explanation for Indigenous over-incarceration. For example, joining an Indigenous gang in itself may have a certain social appeal for many Indigenous youth today.[93] But it is also no exaggeration to say that residential schools have arguably been the most crucial causative factor behind the issue of Indigenous over-incarceration. The problem would be nowhere near its current extent, if at all, were it not for the schools having introduced on a massive scale multiple social stresses into Indigenous communities that have persisted from generation to generation. Annie Yessine and James Bonta's study, based on comparing Indigenous youth under probation in Manitoba with non-Indigenous youth, argues that Indigenous youth are incarcerated far disproportionately to their representation in the population because they come from disadvantaged social backgrounds that include poverty, unstable family settings, and negative peer associations (e.g., youth gangs).[94]

James Waldram interviewed many Indigenous federal inmates in the Regional Psychiatric Centre in Saskatoon, the Saskatchewan Penitentiary, and the Stony Mountain Penitentiary and Rockwood Institution, both in Winnipeg, in his study. Many inmates in their interviews attributed their incarceration to various factors, including severe poverty, racial persecution, having been violently and/or sexually abused in their home environments, loss of connection to their cultures, loss of positive self-esteem as Indigenous persons, and substance abuse.[95]

There are indeed many cases where courts have recognized that Indigenous accused have acted out after having suffered through a multitude of traumas in the course of their lives.[96] Some of those cases involve accused who were residential school survivors and experienced multiple traumas after leaving the schools.[97] Sometimes multiple traumas get passed onto the children of residential school survivors.[98] What is perhaps truly telling is that some cases note that the accused suffered virtually all of the risk factors discussed previously. That becomes a true indictment of what residential schools have done to their survivors and have passed on to subsequent generations of Indigenous people.[99] At times the factors have together become so powerful that it has led to a lifelong pattern of offences and eventually to a Crown application to have the accused subjected to indefinite detention as a dangerous offender.[100] And when numerous individuals have these problems, it stands to reason that entire communities will be severely damaged from the fallout.

AT A COMMUNITY LEVEL

Judges, while not having the training of a criminologist or sociologist, can just as well notice that social stresses have often reached epidemic proportions in the communities of their court's Indigenous accused.[101] In an Ontario case, where the accused was sentenced to eight years for manslaughter, we read how widespread poverty made for an unsafe community:

> Quoting directly from the presentence report.... "The people of Cat Lake have suffered from the impact of various government policies and practices and the aftermath of the residential school legacy." Cat Lake suffers many problems. The most significant of which is extreme levels of poverty. This poverty has spawned a high risk environment where the residents suffer physical and sexual violence and experience the damaging effects of rampant substance abuse.[102]

Judge Chabot noted in a Quebec case — where the accused was sentenced to four and a half years for assault, assault causing bodily harm, and uttering threats — how residential schools led to community-wide deterioration in parenting skills:

> I keep in mind for instance, that many people were forced to attend residential schools. As a result, many struggle with exercising their parental responsibilities since they did not have a model, having practically been raised far from their own parents.
>
> I am also aware that people strive to maintain their roots,

their ancestral lifestyle and values alive, that many young people, by quitting school early, have not developed their full potential, that alcohol abuse and violence are not part of ancestral values of the Cree Nation.[103]

A British Columbia case file observed how residential schools took away the positive from — and infused the negative into — Aboriginal communities:

> The observation is made and I confirm that it is recognised that the residential school experience has had a lasting impact on many aboriginal families. Apart from being isolated from a normal family environment, many of the people attending these schools found themselves disconnected from their cultures and traditions. Many lacked parenting role models and many experienced cruelty and abuse.[104]

Numerous cases have recognized that intergenerational trauma and sexual abuse can infect entire communities.[105] The accused was convicted of sexual touching and sexual luring of a minor in a British Columbia case, but sentencing itself was adjourned following a *Charter* application. The sentencing report relates how intergenerational sexual abuse became so prevalent in the community that it had become normalized:

> The impacts of colonization and residential school are still impacting the community. There are many families that are direct survivors of the residential school system and the foster care system ... their community, like many others, has suffered from the impacts of colonialism, including displacement, Indian residential school, foster care, substance abuse, poverty, violence and sexual abuse. There are high rates of death and violence in the community. [J.S.] reports that their community has high rates of sexual abuse which is often underreported; she stated that this "condones the behaviour and teaches young men that it is okay."[106]

Substance abuse is also a serious problem in many Indigenous communities: surveys have indicated that 74 to 77 percent of Indigenous Peoples feel that it is an issue in their communities, while 33 percent feel that it is a problem in their homes or a problem for a family member.

Additionally, 25 percent admit to personally having a drinking problem.[107] Indigenous Peoples are also hospitalized for substance abuse problems at rates that far exceed those of non-Indigenous persons.[108] Rates of cannabis use were 27 percent among Indigenous adults, 48 percent for Indigenous youth aged fifteen to seventeen, and 15 percent for Indigenous youth aged twelve to fourteen.[109]

As was previously noted, substance abuse has very often been a response to either residential school abuse or intergenerational trauma. It should not be surprising that numerous court cases have recognized as much, in addition to how substance abuse has infected entire communities.[110] A Manitoba case saw the accused sentenced to twelve years for manslaughter. It was noted that in the accused's First Nation, "25% of Aboriginal children between the ages of 5 and 12 are gasoline inhalant abusers."[111] An Ontario case saw the accused receive a curative discharge for numerous intoxicated driving offences. Dr. Brenda Restoule, a clinical psychologist, appeared as an expert witness. She indicated that substance abuse across multiple generations becomes a way to cope with the multiple traumas introduced into Indigenous communities by residential schools:

> One of the most damaging aspects of the residential school experience on survivors has been their resulting incapacity to develop healthy parenting values and practices with which to help their own children during their developmental stages. Dr. Restoule explained that in this way the traumas are transmitted onto the next generation and the negative patterns, including alcohol dependence, continue. She said that to view an individual's life story, it is necessary to determine how residential trauma has impacted the family and to understand that person's capacity for resiliency.[112]

In an Ontario case where the accused was sentenced to three years and three months for impaired driving causing death, the court noted that the accused's grandparents, parents, and siblings alike were residential school survivors. The accused herself had experienced emotional, physical, and sexual abuse multiple times within her home environment, and she subsequently developed substance abuse problems.[113] Justice Whalen commented:

I do not doubt that these factors have had great adverse effect in the formation of her character, views and propensities. Those same antecedents, however, have made her resistant to many of the ordinary social and regulatory norms that must be respected and maintained for social co-existence, peace and progress in any society, no matter the race, colour or cultural origin.[114]

It is undeniable that residential schools have been the most crucial underlying reason behind the problem of Indigenous over-incarceration — it is easy enough to identify the problem. The focus must now turn to exploring ways forward as part of reconciliation. As it turns out, though, Indigenous reconciliation is itself a subject of debate.

Notes

1   Emily Salisbury, Kris Henning, and Robert Holdford, "Fathering by Partner-Abusive Men: Attitudes on Children's Exposure to Interparental Conflict and Risk Factors for Child Abuse," *Child Maltreatment* 14, 3 (2009), 232.

2   Cindy Sousa et al., "Longitudinal Study on the Effects of Child Abuse and Childrens' Exposure to Domestic Violence, Parent-Child Attachments, and Anti-social Behavior in Adolescence," *Journal of Interpersonal Violence* 26, 1 (2011), 122.

3   Carolyn A. Smith, Timothy O. Ireland, and Terrence B. Thornberry, "Adolescent Maltreatment and its Impact on Young Antisocial Behavior," *Child Abuse & Neglect* 29, 10 (2005), 1106.

4   Catherine Daysol and Gayla Margolin, "The Role of Family-of-Origin Violence in Men's Marital Violence Perpetration," *Community Psychology Review* 24, 1 (2004), 99.

5   Amy Murrell, Karen Christoff, and Kris Henning, "Characteristics of Domestic Violence Offenders: Associations with Childhood Exposure to Violence," *Journal of Family Violence* 22, 7 (2007), 528. See also Patrick Lussier, David P. Farrington, and Terrie E. Moffitt, "The Abusive Man? A 40-year Prospective Longtitudinal Study of the Development Antecedents of Intimate Partner Violence," *Criminology* 47, 3 (2009), 741; Katherine Pears and Deborah Capaldi, "Intergenerational Transmission of Abuse: A Two-Generational Prospective Study of an At-Risk Sample," *Child Abuse & Neglect* 25, 11 (2011), 1439. For a study based on a Vancouver sample of 1,249, see Marilyn Kwong et al., "The Intergenerational Transmission of Relationship Violence," *Journal of Family Psychology* 17, 3: (2003), 288.

6   Murrell, Christoff, and Henning, "Characteristics of Domestic Violence Offenders," 528.

7   Jennifer Wareham, Denise Paquette Boots, and Jorge M. Chavez, "A Test of Social Learning and Intergenerational Transmission among Batterers," *Journal of Criminal Justice* 37, 2 (2009), 168.

8   Wareham, Boots, and Chavez, "A Test of Social Learning and Intergenerational

Transmission among Batterers," 169.

9   Jennifer Kwan, "From Taboo to Epidemic: Family Violence Within Aboriginal Communities," *Global Social Welfare* 2, 1 (2015), 1.

10   *R. v. Rossi*, 2011 ONCJ 14665, para. 31. See also *R. v. Knowlton*, 2005 ABPC 29; *R. v. Whitehead*, 2008 SKPC 90; *R. v. Sutherland*, 2010 ONCJ 103.

11   *R. v. R.J.N.*, 2016 YKTC 55.

12   *R. v. Moore*, 2016 MBQB 116, para. 27.

13   *R. v. Moore*, para. 31.

14   Richard Heyman and Amy Smith, "Do Childhood Abuse and Interparental Violence Lead to Adulthood Family Violence?" *Journal Marriage and Family* 64, 4 (2002): 868–69.

15   Heyman and Smith, "Do Childhood Abuse and Interparental Violence," 868.

16   *R. v. Patrick*, 2017 BCPC 223; *R. v. Tourville*, 2011 ONSC 1897.

17   *R. v. Tom*, 2017 BCSC 452, para. 34–38.

18   *R. v. Jeurrisen*, 2014 BCSC 1718.

19   *R. v. Jackpine*, 2012 ONSC 158; *R. v. McCements*, 2012 YKTC 34; *R. v. O.N.M.*, 2011 BCPC 97; *R. v. Napesis*, (2014) 580 A.R. 380; *R. v. E.W.*, 2016 SKQB 226; *R. v. Creighton*, 2016 ABPC 83; *R. v. Neapetung*, 2017 SKPC 43; *R. v. Bailey*, 2017 BCCA 389; *R. v. M.E.W.*, 2011 BCPC 267; *R. v. Snake*, 2010 ONSC 10891; *R. v. Lennie*, 2012 NWTC 21; *R. v. Ost*, 2017 MBPC 26; *R. v. Alkenbrack*, 2011 BCPC 424; *R. v. C.M.J.*, 2005 BCPC 2351.

20   *R. v. Caissey*, 2008 BCPC 716; *R. v. M.(O.N.)*, 2011 BCPC 1097.

21   *R. v. Badger*, 2009 SKQB 418, para. 418. For another, similar example that also led by dangerous offender status, see *R. v. Moise*, 2017 SKQB 372.

22   *R. v. E.M.Q.* 2015 BCSC 201; *R. v. Harry*, 303 Man. R. (2d) 39 (C.A.); *R. v. Knott*, 2012 MBQB 105; *R. v. T.F.J.*, 2010 SKPC 88; *R. v. Cardinal*, 2017 ABCA 396.

23   *R. v. Okimaw*, 2016 ABCA 246.

24   *R. v. Pawis*, 2006 ONCJ 6297, para. 38–41.

25   *R. v. Neapetung*, para. 48; see also *R. v. I.W.S.*, 2014 ONSC 791.

26   Samuel Perreault, *Criminal Victimization in Canada, 2014* (Ottawa: Statistics Canada, 2015), 17.

27   David Burton, "Male Adolescents: Sexual Victimisation and Subsequent Sexual Abuse," *Child and Adolescent Social Work Journal* 20, 4 (2003), 277.

28   Laura McCloskey and Jennifer Bailey, "The Intergenerational Transmission of Risk for Sexual Abuse," *Journal of Interpersonal Violence* 15, 10 (2000), 1109.

29   *R. v. Nippi*, (2015) 471 Sask. R. 210 (Q.B.); *R. v. J.C.*, 2013 NWTSC 88; *R. v. W.D.*, 2017 NWTSC 16; *R. v. J.O.*, 2007 QCCQ 716; *R. v. R.T.O.*, 2012 ABPC 130.

30   *R. v. H.G.R.*, 2015 BCSC 68, para. 6.

31   *R. v. W.R.G.*, para. 34.

32   *R. v. G.F.*, 2018 BCCA 339.

33   *R. v. Chanalquay*, 2015 SKCA 141; *R. v. White*, 2013 BCCA 44; *R. v. Land*; *R. v. R.L.W.*, 2011 BCSC 1363.

34   *R. v. D.W.J.*, 2012 BCPC 15, para. 6–7.

35   *R. v. Doolan*, 2018 BCPC 28; *R. v. Boucher*, 2015 ONSC 3326.

36   *R. v. Elliott*, 2013 BCPC 270; *R. v. B.E.B.*, 2011 MBQB 255, para. 10.

37   *R. v. Killitkee*, 2011 ONSC 12404.

38   *R. v. Wolfe*, 2016 SKQB 16, para. 22–23.

39   *R. v. R.J.N.*, 2011 BCPC 159; *R. v. Hansen*, 2014 BCSC 625; *R. v. Gilbert*, 2006 NSPC 522; *R. v. Touchie*, 2015 BCSC 1833.

40   Some of the most recent ones include Marc Hooghe et al., "Unemployment, Inequality, Poverty and Crime: Spatial Distribution Patterns of Criminal Acts in Belgium, 2001–06," *British Journal of Criminology* 51, 1 (2011), 1; Kaaryn Gustafson, "The Criminalization of Poverty," *Journal of Criminal Law and Criminology* 99, 3 (2009), 643; Ricardo Sabates, "Educational Attainment and Juvenile Crime: Area-Level Evidence Using Three Cohorts of Young People" *British Journal of Criminology* 48 (2008), 395; Scott Atkins, "Racial Segregation, Concentrated Disadvantage, and Violent Crime," *Journal of Ethnicity in Criminal Justice* 7 (2009), 30; Patricia F. Case, "The Relationship of Race and Criminal Behavior: Challenging Cultural Explanations for a Structural Problem," *Critical Sociology* 34 (2008), 213; Songman Kang, "Inequality and Crime Revisited: Effects of Local Inequality and Economic Segregation on Crime," *Journal of Population Economics* 29, 2 (2016), 593.

41   Some of the most recent studies on this include David E. Eitle, Stewart J. D'Alessio, and Lisa Stolzenberg, "Economic Segregation, Race, and Homicide," *Social Science Quarterly* 87, 3 (2006), 638; Jessenia M. Pizarro and Jean Marie McGloin, "Explaining Gang Homicides in Newark, New Jersey: Collective Behavior or Social Disorganization?" *Journal of Criminal Justice* 34, 2 (2006), 195; William Alex Pridemore, "A Methodological Addition to the Cross-National Empirical Literature on Social Structure and Homicide: A First Test of the Poverty-Homicide Thesis," *Criminology* 46, 1 (2008), 133.

42   Richard Spano, Joshua D. Frielich, and John Bolland, "Gang Membership, Gun Carrying, and Employment: Applying Routine Activities Theory to Explain Violent Victimization Among Inner City, Minority Youth Living in Extreme Poverty," *Justice Quarterly* 25, 2 (2008), 381.

43   Sabates, "Educational Attainment and Juvenile Crime," 172.

44   James S. Vacca, "Crime Can Be Prevented if Schools Teach Juvenile Offenders to Read," *Children and Youth Services Review* 30, 9 (2008), 1055.

45   Shelby A.D. Moore, "Understanding the Connection between Domestic Violence, Crime, and Poverty: How Welfare Reform May Keep Battered Women from Leaving Abusive Relationships," *Texas Journal of Women and the Law* 12 (2003), 451; Diane M. Purvin, "Weaving a Tangled Safety Net: The Intergenerational Legacy of Domestic Violence and Poverty," *Violence against Women* 9 (2003), 1263; Hind Khalifeh et al., "Intimate Partner Violence and Socioeconomic Deprivation in England: Findings From a Cross-Sectional National Survey," *American Journal of Public Health* 103, 3 (2013), 462.

46   Chantal Collin and Hilary Jensen, *A Statistical Profile of Poverty in Canada* (Ottawa: Parliamentary Information and Research Service, 2009), 16–18.

47   David MacDonald and Daniel Wilson, *Shameful Neglect: Indigenous Child Poverty in Canada* (Ottawa: Canadian Centre for Policy Alternatives, 2016), 10–11.

48   *First Nations People, Métis and Inuit in Canada: Diverse and Growing Populations* (Ottawa: Statistics Canada, 2016), 11.

49   Evelyne Bougie and Sacha Senechal, "Registered Indian Children's School Success and Intergenerational Effects of Residential Schooling in Canada," *International Indigenous Policy Journal* 1, 1 (2010), 1.

50   Robin Fitzgerald and Peter Carrington, "The Neighbourhood Context of Urban Aboriginal Crime," *Canadian Journal of Criminology* 50, 5 (2008), 523.

51   *R. v. Arcand*, 2014 SKPC 12, para. 11.

52   *R. c. Amitook*, 2006 QCCQ 2705; *R. v. Kaiwatum*, 2003 SKCA 57; *R. v. Koe*, 2004 NWTSC 82; *R. v. Carson Day*, 2010 ONSC 1874.

53   *R. v. C.G.O.*, 2011 BCPC 145, para. 61.

54   *R. v. Isadore*, 2016 ABQB 83.

55   Nico Trocme et al., *Understanding the Over-Representation of First Nations Children in Canada's Child Welfare System: An Analysis of the Canadian Incidence Study of Reported Child Abuse and Neglect* (Ottawa: First Nations Child and Family Caring Society, 2006), 4.

56   Annie Turner, *Living Arrangements of Aboriginal Children Aged 14 and Under* (Ottawa: Statistics Canada, 2016), 7.

57   *Child and Family Services Act*, C.C.S.M. c. C80, s. 17(2).

58   Joseph Ryan, Mark Testa, and Fuhua Zai, "African American Males in Foster Care and the Risk of Delinquency: The Value of Social Bonds and Permanence," *Child Welfare* 87, 1 (2008), 129.

59   Joseph Ryan and Mark Testa, "Child Maltreatment and Juvenile Delinquency: Investigating the Role of Placement and Placement Instability," *Children and Youth Services Review* 27, 3 (2005), 227.

60   Joseph Ryan et al., "Juvenile Delinquency in Child Welfare: Investigating Group Home Effects," *Children and Youth Services Review* 30, 9 (2008), 1088.

61   Sarah DeGue and Cathy Spatz Widom, "Does Out-of-Home Placement Mediate the Relationship Between Child Maltreatment and Adult Criminality?" *Child Maltreatment* 14, 4 (2009), 350.

62   Susan Snyder and Rachel Smith, "Do Youth with Substantiated Child Maltreatment Investigations have Distinct Patterns of Delinquent Behaviors?" *Children and Youth Services Review* 58 (2015), 82.

63   Alain Marc et al., "The Thin Line between Protection and Conviction: Experiences with Child Protection Services and Later Criminal Convictions among a Population of Adolescents," *Journal of Adolescence* 63 (2018), 85.

64   *R. v. Payou*, 2012 NWTSC 34; *R. v. Ewenin*, 2009 SKQB 207; *R. v. C.A.P.*, 2009 BCSC 425; *R. v. Florence*, 2010 BCSC 1010; *R. v. Whitehead*, 2008 SKPC 90; *R. v. Villemaire*, 2009 YKTC 100; *R. v. Okemow*, 2009 SKPC 53; *R. v. Combes*, 2009 BCSC; *R. v. Nayneecassum*, 2008 SKPC 100; *R. v. Esquega*, 2009 ONSC 4522; *R. v. R.H.G.M.*, 2010 BCPC 434; *R. v. Nuvaqiq*, 2009 NUCJ 11; *R. v. Quock*, 2012 YKTC 49; *R. v. Lawson*, 2012 BCCA 508; *R. v. D.K.D.B.*, 2013 BCSC 2321; *R. v. Owen*, 2016 MBPC 12; *R. v. Broadfoot*, 2018 ONCJ 215.

65   *R. v. Kipling*, 2014 MBQB 27, para. 12. See also *R. v. Porter*, 2017 YKTC 13.

66   *R. v. Greene*, 2009 BCPC 359; *R. v. Ledesma*, 2012 ABPC 10; *R. v. Fineday*, 2007 SKPC; *R. v. Koe*, 2004 NWTSC 82; *R. v. Brossault*, 2009 BCSC 464; *R. v. Moc-*

casin, 2006 SKCA 5; *R. v. Benson*, 2011 NSSC 1337; *R. v. Ewenin*, 2009 SKQB 207; *R. v. Sisco*, 2008 ONCJ 12; *R. v. C.A.P.*, 2009 BCSC 425; *R. v. Florence*, 2010 BCSC 1010; *R. v. Whitehead*, 2008 SKPC 90; *R. v. Villemaire*, 2009 YKTC 100; *R. v. Okemow*, 2009 SKPC 53; *R. v. Combes*, 2009 BCSC; *R. v. Nayneecassum*, 2008 SKPC 100; *R. v. S.A.C.*, 2005 BCPC 688; *R. v. Esquega*, 2009 ONSC 4522; *R. v. R.H.G.M.*, 2010 BCPC 434; *R. v. Nuvaqiq*, 2009 NUCJ 11; *R. v. Quock*, 2012 YKTC 49; *R. v. Lawson*, 2012 BCCA 508; *R. v. D.K.D.B.*, 2013 BCSC 2321; *R. v. Owen*, 2016 MBPC 12; *R. v. Broadfoot*, 2018 ONCJ 215.

67 *R. v. Rae*, 2010 ONCJ 3491; *R. v. Makela*, 2006 BCPC 320; *R. v. Michael*, (2014) 121 O.R. (3d) 244.

68 *R. v. Kudlak*, 2011 NWTSC 29; *R. v. L.M.W.*, 2007 SKQB 265; *R .v. Auger*, 2013 ABPC 180; *R. v. Stewart*, 2016 BCSC 2577; *R. v. J.E.R.*, 2012 BCPC 103.

69 *R. v. Mercier and Peterson*, 2004 BCPC 333; *R. v. Ewenin*, 2009 SKQB 207; *R. v. Leaney*, 2002 BCCA 67; *R. v. Penny*, 2010 NBCA 350; *R. v. J.L.C.*, 2012 BCSC 623.

70 *R. v. J.F.*, 2012 BCSC 780, para. 63.

71 David C. Kerr et al., "Intergenerational Influence on Early Alcohol Use: Independence from the Problem Behavior Pathway," *Development and Psychopathology* 24, 3 (2012), 889; Elizabeth Handley and Laurie Chassin, "Intergenerational Transmission of Alcohol Expectancies in a High-Risk Sample," *Journal of Studies on Alcohol and Drugs* 70, 5 (2009), 675; Justine Campbell and Tian Oei, "A Cognitive Model for the Intergenerational Transference of Alcohol Use Behavior," *Addictive Behaviors* 35, 2 (2010), 73; Stefan Belles, "Parental Problem Drinking Predicts Implicit Alcohol Expectancy in Adolescents and Young Adults," *Addictive Behaviors* 36, 11 (2011), 1091; Terence Thornberry, Marvin Krohn, and Adrienne Freeman-Gallant, "Intergenerational Roots of Early Onset Substance Abuse," *Journal of Drug Issues* 36, 1 (2006), 1; Eloise Dunlap et al., "Mothers and Daughters: The Intergenerational Reproduction of Violence and Drug Use in Home and Street Life," *Journal of Ethnicity in Substance Abuse* 3, 2 (2004), 21.

72 *R. v. Geetah*, 2015 NUCJ 10; *R. v. Finlay*, 2016 BCCA 299; *R. v. Marchand*, 2014 BCSC 2554; *R. v. Rodrigue*, 2015 YKTC 5; *R. v. VanEindhoven*, 2013 NUCJ 30; *R. v. Cornell*, 2014 YKSC 54; *R. v. Manyshots*, 2018 ABPC 17; *R. v. McMaster*, 2017 ABPC 49; *R .v. Letandre*, 2016 MBQB 91; *R. v. Klondike*, 2014 NWTSC 28; *R. v. Ryle et al.*, 2013 MBQB 33; *R. v. Gargan*, 2015 NWTSC 62; *R. v. Swampy*, 2018 MBPC 16.

73 *R. v. Legere*, 2016 PECA 7.

74 *R. v. Allen*, 2012 YKTC 36, para. 8–9.

75 *R. v. Bertrand*, 2011 NWTSC 38; *R. v. Akan*, 2012 BCPC 31; *R. v. T.B.M.*, 2012 BCSC 286; *R. v. S.C.L.*, 2014 BCCA 336; *R. v. Whitefish and Ferguson*, 2009 BCPC 73; *R. v. Kelly*, 2014 NWTSC 67.

76 *R. v. G.(C.)*, 2011 NWTSC 57.

77 *R. v. Worm*, 2009 SKQB 122, para. 120. Sixteen years parole ineligibility for second-degree murder.

78 *R. v. Souvie*, 2018 ABCA 148; *R. v. Nelson*, 2012 BCPC 348; *R. v. Johnson*, 2012 YKTC 73; *R. v. S.D.C.*, 2013 ABCA 46; *R. v. Eli*, 2015 BCSC 926; *R. v. Okemow*,

2016 MBQB 240.

79   *R. v. Anderson*, 2016 MBQB 28, para. 15.

80   Ann P. Streissguth et al., "Risk Factors for Adverse Life Outcomes in Fetal Alcohol Syndrome and Fetal Alcohol Effects," *Developmental and Behavioral Pediatrics* 25, 4 (2004), 228.

81   Patricia MacPherson and Albert Chudley, *Fetal Alcohol Spectrum Disorder: Screening and Estimating Prevalence in an Adult Federal Correctional Population* (Ottawa: Correctional Service of Canada, 2011).

82   Kaitlyn MacLachlan et al., "Prevalence and Characteristics with Fetal Alcohol Spectrum Disorder in Corrections: A Canadian Case Ascertainment Study," bmc *Public Health* 19, 1 (2019), 1.

83   See Michael Pacey, *Fetal Alcohol Syndrome & Fetal Alcohol Spectrum Disorder Among Aboriginal Canadians: Knowledge Gaps* (Prince George: National Collaborating Centre for Aboriginal Health, 2010), 17.

84   *R. v. Dayfoot*, 2007 ONCJ 4674; *R. v. Cardinal*, 2015 BCSC 2536; *R. v. Brass*, 2013 MBPC 40; *R. v. F.A.B.*, 2014 BCSC 1293; *R. v. Manyshots*, 2018 ABPC 17; *R. v. Green*, 2013 ONSC 423; *R. v. George*, 2010 ONSC 617.

85   *R. v. W.*, 2010 BCPC 36, para. 31.

86   *R. v. Wycotte*, 2010 BCPC 463.

87   *R. v. Charlie*, 2012 YKSC 5, para. 6 and 9.

88   *R. v. Charlie*, 2015 YKCA 3, para. 32.

89   Carter Hay et al., "The Impact of Community Disadvantage on the Relationship between the Family and Crime," *Journal of Research in Crime and Delinquency* 43, 4 (2006), 326.

90   Preeti Chauhan and N. Dickon Reppucci, "The Impact of Neighbourhood Disadvantage and Exposure to Violence on Self-Report of Antisocial Behavior among Girls in the Juvenile Justice System," *Journal of Youth and Adolescence* 38 (2009), 401; see also Richard Spano, Craig Rivera, and John Bolland, "The Impact of Timing of Exposure to Violence on Violent Behavior in a High Poverty Sample of Inner City African American Youth," *Journal of Youth and Adolescence* 35 (2006), 681.

91   Alison Ritter and Jennifer Chalmers, "The Relationship between Economic Conditions and Substance Abuse and Harms," *Drug and Alcohol Review* 30, 1 (2011), 1. This is a summary of past research on the correlation.

92   Jacques Baillargeon et al., "Risk of Reincarceration among Prisoners with Co-Occurring Severe Mental Illness and Substance Abuse Disorders," *Administration and Policy in Mental Health and Mental Health Services Research* 37, 4 (2010), 367.

93   Kathleen Buddle, "Urban Aboriginal Gangs and Street Sociality in the Canadian West: Places, Performances and Predicaments of Transition," in Heather A. Howard and Craig Proulx (eds.), *Aboriginal Peoples In Canadian Cities: Transformations and Continuities* (Waterloo: Wilfred Laurier University Press, 2007), 171.

94   Annie K. Yessine and James Bonta, "The Offending Trajectories of Youthful Aboriginal Offenders," *Canadian Journal of Criminology* 51, 4 (2009), 435. See also Dane Hautala, Kelly Sittner, and Les Whitbeck, "Prospective Childhood

Risk Factors for Gang Involvement among North American Indigenous Adolescents," *Youth Violence and Juvenile Justice* 14, 4 (2016), 390.

95 James Waldram, *The Way of the Pipe* (Peterborough: Broadview Press, 1997), 44. For a thesis study that focused more specifically on the tie between residential schools and over-incarceration, based on interviews with six Aboriginal offenders in a federal prison, see Michael Gauthier, "The Impact of the Residential School, Child Welfare System and Intergenerational Trauma Upon the Incarceration of Aboriginals" (MEd Thesis, Queen's University, 2010).

96 *R. v. Moosomin*, 2010 SKQB 182; *R. v. Lindley*, 2006 BCCA 380; *R. v. Osmond*, 2011 ONSC 4124; *R. v. Glen Bannon*, 2011 ONSC 3000; *R. v. R.C.L.*, 2012 BCPC 53; *R. v. Ashkewe*, 2010 ONSC 6723; *R. v. Ross*, 2011 ONCJ 182; *R. v. O.(C.G.)*, 2012 BCCA 560; *R. v. Kudlak*, 2011 NWTSC 29; *R. v. B.L.F.*, 2012 BCPC 92; *R. v. Tippeneskum*, 2011 ONCJ 219; *R. v. D.D.P.*, 2012 ABQB 229; *R. v. Jackson*, 2012 ABCA 154; *R. v. D.A.H.*, 2010 BCPC 313; *R. v. Piapot*, 2011 SKQB 470; *R. v. Pelkey*, 2012 BCSC 815; *R. v. Knight*, 2012 MBPC 52; *R. v. J.P.*, 2011 SKQB 7; *R. v. C.L.W.*, 2007 SKPC 54; *R. v. Whalen*, 2010 ONCJ 501; *R. v. S.L.N.*, 2010 BCSC 405; *R. v. Sandfly*, 2010 SKPC 39; *R. v. Cardinal*, 2013 YKTC 30; *R. v. Biwer*, 2017 BCCA 424; *R. v. Power*, 2016 NSSC 198; *R. v. McCook*, 2015 BCPC 1; *R. v. Morrisseau*, 2017 ONCJ 307; *R. v. Schell*, 2015 ONSC 6013; *R. v. McNab*, 2018 SKQB 64; *R. v. Sutherland-Cada*, 2016 ONCJ 650; *R. v. Lundgren*, 2016 ABPC 138; *R. v. Paul*, 2016 ABPC 113; *R. v. A.E.*, 2017 ONSC 511.

97 *R. v. W.J.L.*, 2005 BCPC 572; *R. v. D.S.*, 2010 SKQB 262.

98 *R. v. Johnny*, 2015 BCSC 615; *R. v. Kwandibens*, 2008 ONCJ 5557; *R. v. Sellars*, 2018 BCCA 195; *R. v. Gabriel*, 291 Man. R. (2d) 291; *R. v. Sunshine*, 359 BCAC 295.

99 *R. v. N.R.R.*, 2011 MBQB 90; *R. v. Zapra*, 2009 NFLDSC 280.

100 *R. v. Shanoss*, 2013 BCSC 2335; *R. v. Papin*, 2013 ABPC 46.

101 *R. v. Klondike*, 2012 NWTSC 28; *R. v. T.(J.J.)*, 2010 MQBQ 216; *R. v. N.H.*, 2009 NSPC 36; *R. v. Moonias*, 2013 ONCJ 126; *R. v. S.F.*, 2015 BCPC 441.

102 *R. v. Wesley*, 2013 ONSC 7197, para. 7.

103 *R. c. Brien*, 2011 CQ 14350, para. 29–30; see also *R. v. Nagotchi*, 2005 ONCJ 37; *R. v. Saunders*, 2009 ONCJ 3732; *R. v. Watts*, 2016 ABPC 57.

104 *R. v. Blind*, 2008 BCPC 43.

105 *R. v. Cafferata*, 2009 YKTC 95; *R. v. Edgar*, 2014 BCPC 20; *R. v. Firingstoney*, 2017 ABQB 343; *R. v. Hans*, 2016 BCPC; *R. v. Blaney*, 2018 BCSC 2401.

106 *R. v. B.S.*, 2018 BCSC 2044, para. 38.

107 *The Human Face of Mental Health and Mental Illness in Canada, 2006* (Ottawa: Public Health Agency of Canada, 2006), 168.

108 Health Canada, First Nations and Inuit Health Branch, Pacific Region, "A Statistical Report on the Health of First Nations in British Columbia" (Ottawa: Health Canada, 2001), Appendix A: Figures, Charts and Tables [unpublished]; J.C. Cardinal et al., "First Nations in Alberta: a Focus on Health Service Use" (Edmonton: Alberta Health and Wellness, 2004) [unpublished].

109 Health Canada, "A Statistical Report on the Health of First Nations in British Columbia," 167.

110 *R. v. Audy*, 2010 MBQB 55; *R. v. Van Bibber*, 2010 YKTC 49; *R. v. H. (T.D.J.)*,

2011 BCPC 3619; *R. v. Tom*, 2012 YKTC 55; *R. v. Edgar*, 2014 BCPC 20; *R. v. Nayneecassum*, 2015 SKPC 172; *R. v. Whitehead*, 2017 BCSC SKQB 263

111 *R. v. R.(N.R.)*, 2011 MBQB 190, para. 17.

112 *R. v. Daybutch*, 2016 ONSC 595, para. 28–32.

113 *R. v. Niganobe*, 2008 ONSC 54322, para. 34–36.

114 *R. v. Niganobe*, para. 74. See also *R. v. S.O.*, 2005 BCPC 3868.

5

RECONCILIATION SO FAR

WHAT IS MEANT BY RECONCILIATION

What does reconciliation mean in the context of Indigenous-state relations? The Royal Commission on Aboriginal Peoples in 1996 emphasized that reconciliation meant an equitable partnership and reciprocity between Canada and Indigenous Peoples.[1] The concept would receive at least nominal government support soon thereafter in the form of a "Statement of Reconciliation" made by the then minister of Indian and northern affairs, Jane Stewart, on January 7, 1998. The statement emphasizes that Canada must go beyond mere rhetoric and work toward addressing the social problems of Indigenous Peoples through concrete actions. The statement also stresses that Canada and Indigenous Peoples must work together to address problems through an equitable partnership that involves a genuine sharing of power, not a paternalistic top-down imposition.[2]

Other academic commentary on reconciliation tends to resonate with the Royal Commission and the "Statement of Reconciliation."[3] Michael Murphy, professor of political science with the University of Northern British Columbia, states:

> Reconciliation speaks to the past, present, and future of Aboriginal-state relations in Canada. Perhaps nowhere was this message more clearly articulated that in the final report of the Royal Commission on Aboriginal Peoples ... the commissioners recommended an honest and open confrontation with the history of colonization, concrete measures to address the contemporary legacy of injustice, and the forging of a new relationship built on the foundations of mutual recognition, respect, and trust.[4]

Brian Rice and Anna Snyder, professors of political science and conflict resolution studies, respectively, with the University of Winnipeg, emphasize that true reconciliation means a willingness to engage in meaningful cooperation with Indigenous Peoples — and that means a willingness to share power. They explain:

> In order for reconciliation to occur, the process must reflect the mutual interests of the parties involved. Without power-sharing in decision-making, a constructive outcome from the reconciliation process is unlikely. A destructive outcome results from one party imposing decisions made unilaterally with little or no consideration for the interests and needs of the other party.[5]

David MacDonald, political science professor with the University of Guelph, likewise suggests that reconciliation involves a genuine sharing of power and decision-making with Indigenous Peoples. That sharing of power should not only increase the space for Indigenous processes and institutions, but Canadian institutions may themselves become fundamentally altered from what they previously had been in a process he calls "syncretic democracy."[6]

The idea of reconciliation as it is often articulated has not been universally accepted. Taiaiake Alfred, the former director of the Indigenous Governance program at the University of Victoria, is of the view that the only satisfactory resolution for Indigenous Peoples is for them to become their own completely independent polities, separate from Canada.[7] He also views reconciliation without being preceded by massive restitution of land and economic resources as "an emasculating concept, weak-kneed and easily accepting of half-hearted measures of a notion of justice that does nothing to help Indigenous Peoples regain their dignity and strength."[8] Glen Coulthard, political science professor with the University of British Columbia, is likewise concerned that reconciliation carries with it the danger of empowering the state to maintain the status quo of continued colonialism, to the detriment of Indigenous Peoples.[9]

Both scholars view reconciliation as part of a larger colonial project — the politics of recognition. The politics of recognition may include rhetoric that superficially recognizes past colonial injustices and the need for progress. It may include some concessions in decision making and power to Indigenous Peoples, but these will be minimal. Social and power structures remain fundamentally colonial in the end. And the politics of recognition, through the deployment of surface rhetoric and minimal concessions, only serves to entrench continued colonialism. Both scholars also see a cognitive trap for Indigenous participants in that process. Their participation, and any minimal concessions that are gained, may convince the Indigenous participants that they are moving toward progress on behalf of Indigenous Peoples. But the politics of recognition ultimately becomes a process of co-optation. Indigenous participants mistake entrenched colonialism for Indigenous empowerment and decolonization.[10]

Dale Turner, Anishinaabe professor of political science with the University of Toronto, offers a counterargument. Turner's book, *This Is Not a Peace Pipe: Towards a Critical Indigenous Philosophy*, precedes the final reports of the TRC and Coulthard's work, but it does critique Alfred's work.[11] A key starting point of his is that the presence of the Canadian state is a reality from which Indigenous people cannot unilaterally extricate themselves. He states: "For better or worse, it is predominately non-aboriginal judges and politicians who have the ultimate power to protect and enforce aboriginal rights, and so it is important to find a justification of them that such people can recognize and understand."[12] Turner's vision of the way forward is for Indigenous intellectuals and philosophers, as "Word Warriors," to advance Indigenous perspectives within the discourses of Canadian legal and political spaces. The hope is that by truly convincing Canadian leaders of the merits of Indigenous alternatives, the legal and political relationship with the state can be realigned in ways that allow Indigenous Peoples to end colonialism and move forward.[13] Turner sees Alfred's theories as inadequate. A refusal to participate in the state discourses means the state continues to unilaterally construct Indigenous rights in ways that are detrimental, restrictive, and unchallenged.[14]

Coulthard has in turn critiqued Turner's theory. He argues that Turner does not adequately describe how engaging the state through Word Warriors would work in practice. The state itself can continue to hold the monopoly over the normative discourses that Turner hopes can become sites of transformation. He therefore sees Turner's conceptions as another ineffectual example of participating in the politics of recognition.[15]

Coulthard advocates for resurgence and direct action instead of negotiation within the politics of recognition. Resurgence means recovering past Indigenous values and cultural practices and putting them into contemporary practice in ways that revitalize present-day Indigenous communities.[16] Direct action means action undertaken at the initiative of Indigenous Peoples that is less cooperative and more confrontational in seeking to upset the colonial status quo. Examples include, but are not necessarily limited to, blockades that deny corporate resource industries access to Indigenous lands, as well as the nationwide protest movement that was known as Idle No More.[17] Coulthard sees at least three justifications for direct action. First, it is action undertaken by Indigenous Peoples themselves that attempts an immediate disruption of the power imbalance inherent in colonialism. Second, it encourages Indigenous Peoples to free themselves from internalized colonialism, which, for Coulthard, is a fundamental prerequisite for enduring change. Third, it can be reconstitutive and reconstructive for Indigenous communities in ways that encourage resurgence instead of submission to colonialism.[18] So, who is right? What is the best way forward? These are certainly loaded and yet important questions. I will venture that I find being a Word Warrior, as Turner conceptualizes the term, preferable with respect to addressing Indigenous over-incarceration and all the enduring social harms that are tied to it. The reasons for that preference will be explained at the end of this chapter. For now it is time to canvass the specific Calls to Action offered by the TRC with respect to justice and consider how they fit into theoretical perspectives on reconciliation.

THE CALLS TO ACTION AND INDIGENOUS JUSTICE

Law societies regulate the conduct and professional standing of lawyers called to the bar, and their mandates include both the discipline of lawyer misconduct as well as lawyers' continuing legal education. At least two of the Calls to Action focus on legal education: Call to Action 27 requests that law societies provide training in cultural competency, including knowledge and understanding of the effects of the residential schools and intergenerational trauma. Call to Action 28 calls on law schools to provide at least one course that focuses on Indigenous Peoples and the law and includes cultural competency training.[19]

Additionally, Call to Action 30 calls on the government of Canada to commit to eliminating Indigenous over-incarceration within the next decade and to provide yearly reports setting out progress toward that objective. Call to Action 31 requests that the federal government provide stable and consistent funding for Indigenous programming that provides alternatives to incarceration for Indigenous accused. Call to

Action 32 calls for amendments to the *Criminal Code* that would allow judges to depart from mandatory minimum sentences in cases involving Indigenous accused. Calls to Action 33 and 34 urge more lenient sentencing and the provision of resources and services for Indigenous accused with FASD.[20]

Calls to Action 35, 36, and 37 call on the federal government to provide more Indigenous healing lodges and halfway houses; these should be sufficiently resourced so that they can provide effective services for those Indigenous accused who become incarcerated.[21] Call to Action 38 asks for a commitment to eliminate Indigenous over-representation in youth justice custody.[22]

Call to Action 39 requests the publication of data setting out the extent of the criminal victimization of Indigenous Peoples. Call to Action 40 calls for full provision of programs and services for Indigenous victims of crime.[23] Call to Action 41 called for a public inquiry into the disproportionate victimization of Indigenous women and girls.[24] This call was eventually realized through the National Inquiry into Missing and Murdered Indigenous Women and Girls.[25]

Finally, Call to Action 42 calls on Canadian governments to recognize and implement Indigenous justice systems "in a manner consistent with the Treaty and Aboriginal rights of Aboriginal peoples, the Constitution Act, 1982, and the United Nations Declaration on the Rights of Indigenous Peoples, endorsed by Canada in November 2012."[26] The final report of the Commission calls for Canada to develop a Royal Proclamation of Reconciliation in consultation and partnership with Indigenous Peoples. This Royal Proclamation would recognize Indigenous Peoples as "full partners in Confederation," establish a nation-to-nation relationship between Indigenous Peoples and Canada, and would involve the "recognition and integration of Aboriginal laws and legal traditions."[27]

The work of the TRC is very important, there is no mistaking that. That is also not to say, though, that the TRC final reports should be above any criticism or questioning. There may be questions of whether efforts at reconciliation need to restrict themselves to the Calls to Action and whether we should ask ourselves whether the Calls to Action go too far or do not go far enough. Call to Action 42 calls for Indigenous self-determination over justice. The final report also calls for a Royal Proclamation of Reconciliation that idealizes the revitalization of Indigenous legal orders so that they enjoy the same recognition as the common law and civil law traditions. And yet several of the other Calls to Action describe initiatives that occur entirely within the existing Canadian criminal justice system. And those Calls to Action may indeed be examples of the politics of recognition about which Alfred and Coulthard are deeply concerned. Are there contradictions and inconsistencies within the Calls to Action themselves that need to be unpacked and resolved?

A criticism that is frequently made against existing restorative justice programs is that they represent the institutionalization of restorative justice by the state.[28] Similar criticisms have been made against Indigenous justice initiatives.[29] Chris Andersen argues that contemporary Indigenous justice initiatives in Canada reflect an effort by the Canadian political hegemony to contain Indigenous aspirations for greater control over justice within certain parameters that in substance leave the status quo intact. In other words, Andersen argues that Indigenous justice initiatives provide a medium that displays a veneer of community empowerment and accommodation of cultural difference. Andersen argues that it is, however, the Canadian state that provides the funding and therefore calls the shots and sets the parameters of the justice initiatives. Those parameters are that Indigenous accused must plead guilty or otherwise accept responsibility (for purposes of diversionary initiatives) and that the justice initiatives will usually only cover the less serious offences that the standard justice system would itself be willing to deal with by community-based sentences (e.g., probation, conditional sentence) anyway. The Canadian state thus accommodates Indigenous justice initiatives only to the extent that its own interests happen to converge with those of Indigenous communities. Once there is no longer that convergence — for example, when Indigenous communities may want to apply their own approaches to offences that the standard justice system would want to deal with by incarceration — then the accommodation will stop.[30]

Jesse Sutherland, now the director of a workplace consultancy called Intercultural Strategies, states: "A successful Indigenous Justice Strategy must go beyond participatory and indigenised justice processes. Rather, it must support healing and capacity building within First Nations' communities as well as endeavour to decolonize and repair the relationship with the Canadian state."[31] Alfred is even more scathing in his criticism. In his view, surface Indigenization leads some Indigenous participants to believe they are renewing Indigenous self-determination, when really they end up co-opted by the state apparatus. The status quo ends up perpetuated.[32] Can the seeming contradictions within the Calls to Action themselves be resolved? Is reconciliation a doomed enterprise?

RECONCILIATION MOVING FORWARD

The starting point that will be advanced here is that the Calls to Action present a good foundation on which to start reconciliation — but they should not be thought of as being the sole authority and voice on what reconciliation should be. Calls to Action 27 to 40 fundamentally envision Indigenous participation within the Canadian justice system itself. Call to Action 42 contemplates the operation of Indigenous legal orders as living viable alternatives to the state justice system. It would ultimately be at cross-purposes with Call to Action 42 if our efforts were to be limited to Indigenous programming within the Canadian justice system in ways that are consistent with Calls to Action 27 to 40 on an enduring basis. Canadian criminal law would continue to dictate the outcomes for Indigenous Peoples if that becomes the end result of reconciliation, and those outcomes will still frequently mean mass incarceration of Indigenous Peoples. The laws of Indigenous legal orders would have little effect on those adverse outcomes. So how do we unpack those contradictions and make reconciliation work for Indigenous Peoples when it comes to Indigenous justice?

Given the extent of cultural loss over decades, it may be unrealistic to expect, even if Indigenous communities were to be suddenly granted full determination over justice, that they would overnight be able to exercise that self-determination in such a meaningful and proficient way as though no disruption had ever occurred. The recovery of traditional laws that have been disrupted or fallen into disuse is itself a process that takes time.[33] Adapting and implementing those laws and traditions for contemporary use in a changed world must itself be a process that also requires time. And indeed, the Royal Commission on Aboriginal Peoples argues that Indigenous Peoples gaining control over criminal justice would not be an overnight affair. There would have to be a transitory phase wherein Indigenous communities would have to remain in partnership with the standard justice system. As Indigenous communities become more capable and more accustomed to administering justice, they can gradually assume full control and self-determination over that process.[34]

This transitory phase would mark the implementation of Calls to Action 27 to 40. It would admittedly involve a great deal of what we have seen before, such as sentencing circles and Indigenous restorative justice programs in partnership with the Canadian justice system. And continuing with these kinds of initiatives does amount to being a "Word Warrior" as described by Turner. But it does not mean contentment with the status quo.

Call to Action 42 is the ultimate destination that is sought after the transitory phase. John Borrows argues that the depiction of Canada as founded by two legal traditions, common law and civil law, is inaccurate because it fails to recognize Indigenous legal traditions as a third and equally important legal foundation for the formation of Canada. And giving effect to that recognition also demands that Indigenous Peoples have the freedom to apply their own laws and traditions in addressing their own needs.[35] The revitalization of Indigenous legal orders by and for contemporary Indigenous communities is far from an idle fantasy that could be colloquially called a "pie in the sky." It is an endeavour that is being actively pursued as an emerging academic field by law professors such as Val Napoleon, Hadley Friedland,[36] and Tracey Lindberg.[37] But it is not just a field of academic study. The University of Victoria has started the world's first joint degree in both common law and Indigenous legal orders. It instructs students in common law but also the principles of multiple Indigenous legal orders, with the intention that at least some of the program's graduates will use their knowledge to aid in the revitalization of Indigenous legal frameworks.[38] The University of Victoria also has the Indigenous Law Research Unit, which has a team of dedicated researchers who assist Indigenous communities in the reclamation of their past laws for contemporary use and adaptation.[39] The University of Alberta has an equivalent program that is operated as a partnership between its Faculty of Law and its Native Studies Department, the Wahkohtowin Law and Governance Lodge.[40]

I argue that there are benefits to be realized through adapting Indigenous legal orders for contemporary use. What is envisioned here will in fact align with prison abolition, but in ways that are particular to the experiences and needs of Indigenous Peoples in Canada. One emphasis of prison abolition is the massive reinvestment of resources away from police and prisons and toward building healthier communities that minimize the need for responses based on criminalization and punishment. Chapter 7 will focus on preventative programming, but with a particular emphasis on undoing the enduring harms perpetrated on Indigenous communities by colonialism.

This book also advocates increasing the use of alternative sanctions and methods of accountability instead of incarceration. The state justice system typically only allows restorative justice alternatives for a minimal range of the least serious offences. Prison abolition envisions applying those alternatives to a far greater range of offences, and this is emphasized in the increasing transitory-phase use of restorative justice programs alongside the mainstream justice system, as embodied in Calls to Action 27 to 40. But what I envision is that as time goes by, as Indigenous communities will hopefully gain greater capacity and experience in managing themselves so that alternatives grounded in Indigenous legal orders can be applied to nearly every form of behaviour that could be deemed sanctionable.

There is, of course, the objection that the destination, the revival of Indigenous legal orders, would be unattainable in the way that I suggest because the transitory phase would only amount to getting nowhere by participating in the politics of recognition. What form of direct decolonizing action would be possible when it comes to Indigenous Peoples and criminal justice? The obvious goal is for Indigenous Peoples to unilaterally resolve disputes in their own communities without the involvement of any actors from the Canadian justice system.

A dissertation by Leslie Jane McMillan, now an anthropology professor with St. Francis Xavier University, documents how members of the Membertou First Nation in Nova Scotia often tried to use their local newsletter as a vehicle to resolve various matters without reporting them to the police. Sometimes a person who had an item stolen from him or her would publish a request to return the item with no questions asked and a promise to not report matters to police. Sometimes Elders or other community members would express concerns about a particular type of crime (e.g., vandalism) becoming prevalent in the community and admonishing the community at large to harken back to Mi'kmaw teachings of respect and responsibility. The newsletter was at other times, by way of mentioning incidents that were known in the community, used to prompt discussion and informal management of conflicts and issues.[41]

The problem with this form of direct action is that it is happenstance in the absence of any justice programming partnership between Indigenous communities and the state system. It is, absent any Indigenous justice programs, dependent on avoiding Canadian police becoming aware of the underlying incidents to begin with. If Canadian police do become aware of a criminal incident in an Indigenous community, then they will as a matter of course charge any perpetrators with an offence recognized under the *Criminal Code*. The Canadian justice system then holds onto it and deals with it in accordance with the principles of Canadian law, not the legal principles or preferences of the Indigenous community.

A telling observation was provided by Justice Bychok during the *Itturiligaq* case with respect to how many cases play out in Inuit communities:

> As I explained in *Anugaa*, this court travels to all 25 of our territory's far-flung and remote communities. Many months may pass in the smallest hamlets between court sittings. By the time cases are dealt with in court, many parties have already reconciled and have moved on with their lives. Resentment and stress are triggered when the justice system insists these proceedings continue to a legal resolution. Resentment, stress and anger often arise when offenders are sent to jail outside the community against the express wishes of the victim, family and sometimes the community.[42]

The reason I prefer the Word Warrior approach articulated by Turner is that it enlarges the space for Indigenous legal principles to operate free of interference from the Canadian state. It tries to attain that space by building an understanding with the state that certain matters that once were under state administration will now be handled by Indigenous communities. It tries to overcome the limitations of the direct-action approach by obviating the need to keep Indigenous processes that are unapproved by the state concealed from the eyes of the state, and it does so by trying to gain a new understanding with the state. Direct action in such circumstances can only ever be at best happenstance and cannot hope to enact fundamental change.

It must be acknowledged that Alfred's and Coulthard's objections remain valid and relevant. It could be that trying to enlarge the space for Indigenous legal orders by acquiring an understanding with the state will be just more of the same, making little if any progress by participating in the politics of recognition. I am in my own way just as dissatisfied with the status quo as Alfred and Coulthard. But I end up in my search for ways forward preferring a different direction. It is perhaps a testament to just how lopsided matters are between Indigenous Peoples and Canada as a colonial state that it is easier for Indigenous theorists to point out perceived flaws with each other's approaches than to find ways that can truly move matters forward. That is not to say we should give up doing so, either.

The next chapter examines the status quo against which Indigenous Peoples find themselves, a status quo that reinforces colonialism and produces Indigenous over-incarceration as a matter of course. That status quo is a state justice system that is fundamentally committed to mass incarceration for a wide breadth of criminal offences, while offering some programs or initiatives directed specifically at ameliorating Indigenous over-incarceration and the residential school's legacy. As we will see, those initiatives fall well short of any sort of partnership that involves an equitable sharing of power consistent with Calls to Action 27 to 40 — and still less consistent with implementing Indigenous legal orders in a fashion that meets Call to Action 42. It is a status quo that, to acknowledge Alfred's and Coulthard's criticisms, offers only minimal concessions to Indigenous perspectives on justice through the politics of recognition. It is also the status quo against which the Word Warrior approach must try to make its mark.

Notes

1   Royal Commission on Aboriginal Peoples, *People to People, Nation to Nation: Highlights from the Report of the Royal Commission on Aboriginal Peoples* (Ottawa: Ministry of Supply and Services Canada, 1996), 14, 648–55.

2   Schedule N to the *Indian Residential Schools Settlement Agreement* (May 8, 2006).

3   Paul Chartrand, "Towards Justice and Reconciliation: Treaty Recommendations of Canada's Royal Commission on Aboriginal Peoples (1996)," in *Honour Among Nations?: Treaties and Agreements with Indigenous Peoples* (Carlton, Victoria: Melbourne University Publishing Ltd., 2004), 120; Kiera L. Ladner, "Negotiated Inferiority: The Royal Commission on Aboriginal People's Vision of a Renewed Relationship," *American Review of Canadian Studies* 31, 1/2 (2001), 241.

4   Michael Murphy, "Civilization, Self-Determination, and Reconciliation," in Annis May Timpson (ed.), *First Nations, First Thoughts: The Impact of Indigenous Thought in Canada* (Vancouver: ubc Press, 2009), 251.

5   Brian Rice and Anna Snyder, "Reconciliation in the Context of a Settler Society: Healing the Legacy of Colonialism in Canada," in Aboriginal Healing Foundation (ed.), *From Truth to Reconciliation: Transforming the Legacy of*

Residential Schools (Ottawa: Aboriginal Healing Foundation, 2008), 46.

6   David MacDonald, "Reconciliation after Genocide in Canada: Towards a Syncretic Model of Democracy," *AlterNative: An International Journal of Indigenous Peoples* 9, 1 (2013), 60.

7   Taiaiake Alfred, *Peace, Power, Righteousness* (London: Oxford University Press, 2008).

8   Taiaiake Alfred, "Restitution is the Real Pathway to Justice for Indigenous Peoples," in Gregory Younging, Jonathan Dewar, and Mike DeGagné (eds.), *Response, Responsibility and Renewal: Canada's Truth and Reconciliation Journey* (Ottawa: Aboriginal Healing Foundation, 2009), 181.

9   Glen Coulthard, *Red Faces, White Masks: Rejecting the Colonial Politics of Recognition* (Minneapolis: University of Minnesota Press, 2014).

10   Alfred, *Peace, Power, Righteousness*, 80–88; Coulthard, *Red Faces, White Masks*, 151–59.

11   Dale Turner, *This Is Not a Peace Pipe: Towards a Critical Indigenous Philosophy* (Toronto: University of Toronto Press, 2006).

12   Turner, *This Is Not a Peace Pipe*.

13   Turner, *This Is Not a Peace Pipe*.

14   Turner, *This Is Not a Peace Pipe*.

15   Coulthard, *Red Faces, White Masks*, 46–47.

16   Coulthard, *Red Faces, White Masks*, 156–57.

17   Coulthard, *Red Faces, White Masks*, 159–63.

18   Coulthard, *Red Faces, White Masks*, 166.

19   "Truth and Reconciliation Commission of Canada Calls to Action," Government of British Columbia <www2.gov.bc.ca/assets/gov/british-columbians-our-governments/indigenous-people/aboriginal-peoples-documents/calls_to_action_english2.pdf>, 3.

20   "Truth and Reconciliation Commission of Canada Calls to Action," 3–4.

21   "Truth and Reconciliation Commission of Canada Calls to Action," 4.

22   "Truth and Reconciliation Commission of Canada Calls to Action," 4.

23   "Truth and Reconciliation Commission of Canada Calls to Action," 4.

24   "Truth and Reconciliation Commission of Canada Calls to Action," 4.

25   National Inquiry into Missing and Murdered Indigenous Women and Girls, *Reclaiming Power and Place: The Final Report of the National Inquiry into Missing and Murdered Indigenous Women and Girls* (Ottawa: National Inquiry into Missing and Murdered Indigenous Women and Girls, 2019).

26   "Truth and Reconciliation Commission of Canada Calls to Action," 4.

27   Truth and Reconciliation Commission of Canada, *Truth and Reconciliation Commission of Canada: Interim Report*, 252–53.

28   Barbara Hudson, "The Institutionalisation of Restorative Justice: Justice and the Ethics of Discourse," *Acta Juridica* 56 (2007).

29   Juan Tauri, "An Indigenous Commentary on the Globalisation of Restorative Justice," *British Journal of Community Justice* 12, 2 (2014).

30   Chris Andersen, "Governing Indigenous Justice in Canada: Constructing responsible individuals and communities through 'tradition,'" *Crime, Law and Social Change* 31 (1999). See also Paul Havenmann, "The Indigenization of

Social Control in Canada," in Robert A. Silverman and Marianne O. Neilson (eds.), *Indigenous Peoples and Canadian Criminal Justice* (Toronto: Harcourt, Brace & Co., 1992), 113.

31 Jessie Sutherland, "Colonialism, Crime and Dispute Resolution: A Critical Analysis of Canada's Indigenous Justice Strategy" (October 2002) <mediate. com/articles/sutherlandJ.cfm>.

32 Alfred, *Peace, Power, Righteousness,* 70.

33 Hadley Friedland and Val Napoleon, "Gathering the Threads: Developing a Methodology for Researching and Rebuilding Indigenous Legal Traditions," *Lakehead Law Journal* 1, 1 (2015), 17.

34 William D. Coleman, *Bridging the Cultural Divide* (Ottawa: Royal Commission on Aboriginal Peoples, 1996), 175–76.

35 John Borrows, *Canada's Aboriginal Constitution* (Toronto: University of Toronto Press, 2010).

36 Friedland and Napoleon, "Gathering the Threads."

37 Tracey Lindberg, *Birdie* (New York: Harper Collins, 2015).

38 University of Victoria, Faculty of Law, "jd/jid Program Overview" <uvic.ca/law/admissions/jidadmissions/jid-courses.php>.

39 University of Victoria, Faculty of Law, "Indigenous Law Research Unit (ilru)" <uvic.ca/law/about/indigenous/indigenouslawresearchunit/index.php>.

40 University of Alberta, "Wahkohtowin Law and Governance Lodge" <ualberta. ca/wahkohtowin/index.html>.

41 Leslie Jane McMillan, "Koqqwaja'ltimk: Mi'kmaq Legal Consciousness," PhD diss., University of British Columbia, 2002, 289–92.

42 *R. v. Itturiliqaq,* 2018 NUCJ 31, para. 120.

6

THE STATUS QUO IS
NOT RECONCILIATION

This chapter surveys responses by the Canadian state with respect to the residential schools up until now. Two of those responses have been specifically focused on the residential schools and their aftermath. Then there are "responses" that arise, not so much with residential schools' legacy specifically in mind, but through the routine operation of the Canadian criminal justice system. Although criminal justice policy is theoretically applied in an equal fashion to everyone, to a very real extent, it responds to residential schools' legacy by blaming Indigenous Peoples themselves for the social fallouts.

THE SETTLEMENT AGREEMENT

A class-action lawsuit is a civil lawsuit where multiple plaintiffs with the same grievances against the same defendant(s) can have their claims for compensation addressed all in the same case. A class-action lawsuit was brought forward in 2005 on behalf of any Indigenous persons who attended residential schools from January 1, 1920, to December 31, 1996.[1] The end result was the negotiated Residential Schools Settlement Agreement in 2005. The agreement provided $1.9 billion for survivors of the residential schools.[2]

The idea behind the settlement is corrective justice, monetary compensation for a past wrong suffered. Certainly the need to vindicate the harms suffered by residential school survivors in some form is necessary. Standing almost entirely on its own, however, a one-time cash settlement is far from an adequate response.[3] There are pretty compelling and underlying reasons behind Indigenous over-incarceration, and almost all of those reasons can be traced back to one extent or another to residential schools. The obvious reason for the inadequacy of civil payouts alone is because they do nothing to address the underlying causes of Indigenous crime.[4] An armed robbery case from British Columbia, for example, noted that the accused, who was sexually abused in residential schools, only ended up using his settlement money to fuel his existing drug addiction.[5]

In fact, there are also instances in which a residential school payout can make matters worse. In Fort Simpson, Northwest Territories, there have been at least four deaths that are thought to be brought on by alcohol abuse that accelerated after receipt of settlement monies.[6] Another case also found an accused guilty of manslaughter committed against a girlfriend during a drinking binge that was in anticipation of receiving settlement money.[7]

THE ABORIGINAL HEALING FOUNDATION

The Aboriginal Healing Foundation (AHF) was a charitable foundation established on March 31, 1998, with the mandate to financially support other non-profit organizations and projects in providing therapeutic services to Indigenous persons suffering the effects of residential school physical and sexual abuse. Those therapeutic services could address problems such as mental health, a lack of parenting skills, substance abuse, and counselling for sexual harm. It received an initial grant of $350 million for allocation. It received an additional $125 million under the terms of the Settlement Agreement.[8]

However, the Harper Tories, less than two years after his government's official apology, decided not to renew funding for the foundation in their 2010 budget. The result was that numerous organizations that received funds from the foundation to provide therapeutic services to troubled Indigenous persons either had to shut down completely or lay off staff in order to stay operational.[9] The foundation was certainly a demonstrable response specifically to the social legacy of residential schools. But the decision to end it after a mere twelve years, and the absence of any effort to renew the foundation since its closure, signals that dealing with the long-term damage wrought by residential schools is not a long-term priority for the Canadian state. Marie Ingram, who had been the director of the Cambridge Bay Community Wellness Centre in Nunavut, puts the closure of the foundation in perspective as follows:

> We saw 190 clients here last month that we won't see next month. Just because our funding stops, the needs don't stop. Right now, I'm just trying to find funding, anywhere and ev-

erywhere.... People should be telling their government that we need this money. They created the social problems here. They should know they take a lot longer to fix.[10]

I will now review how the criminal justice system, in its routine operation, responds to Indigenous accused who end up in the system by reason of having been affected in one fashion or another by the legacy of residential schools.

THE PROBLEM WITH DETERRENCE

Recall that Canadian sentencing law has several objectives, some of which contradict each other. Rehabilitation is one of those objectives, but sentencing decisions tend to give greater priority to deterrence. This extends to cases involving Indigenous accused who have had traumatized lives and that would otherwise strongly suggest the need for rehabilitative programming. Some cases recognize the trauma that has been created by the schools but nonetheless emphasize deterrence as the primary consideration.[11] A Northwest Territories Supreme Court case saw the accused, who struggled with alcoholism to cope with an impoverished and neglectful home life, receive two years less a day for aggravated assault. Here is an excerpt from that case, which focused on deterrence:

> But the law is also clear that when it comes to serious crimes of violence, there are limits to how taking those factors into account can impact the ultimate sentencing decision. The importance of having communities that are free from violence exists in aboriginal communities as much as it does in non-aboriginal communities. The need to discourage people from escalating fights by introducing weapons into them is as important in aboriginal communities as it is in non-aboriginal communities.[12]

A British Columbia Supreme Court case provides another example where the sentencing judge felt pulled in different directions. The accused was sentenced to four years for manslaughter and had suffered neglect, intergenerational domestic abuse, intergenerational sexual abuse, and substance abuse.[13] Madam Justice Griffins described the tension inherent in her task:

I also have to consider Ms. Taniskishayinew's life. Her life has been so full of trauma imposed upon her that it is likewise impossible to consider any sentence imposed on her as "fair." What has happened in Ms. Taniskishayinew's life is unfair because I recognize that Ms. Taniskishayinew's history has been greatly influenced by what our society has done to the Indigenous communities through the degradations and deprivations imposed by colonization and the residential school system.

The law is a blunt tool in such a sad case. Nevertheless, Indigenous communities deserve the protection of the law just as much as other non-Indigenous communities.[14]

Certainly Canadian judges are obliged by their oath of office to apply Canadian criminal law to all criminal cases that come to their dockets, including the cases of Indigenous accused that involve residential schools. And since Canadian law places a premium on deterrence, so judges must emphasize that in their decisions. This practice does, however, seem to assume that individual Indigenous accused and the communities they come from can respond to the message of deterrence. Legal doctrine aside, this assumption is highly dubious when it is subject to empirical validation. Classical criminological theory holds that the effectiveness of deterrence rests on three essential components: the certainty that a punishment will be assessed as a consequence of committing a crime, the swiftness with which the punishment will be assessed afterward, and the severity of the punishment itself.[15] The efficacy of each component has been called into question to one degree or another.

Some scholars argue that there is a profound lack of empirical evidence to support any claim that increasing the severity of sentences will enhance general deterrence.[16] What little research that has been done to assess the effects of sentence severity on general deterrence has not demonstrated a correlative relationship between the two.[17] Other research has also not demonstrated a strong link between incarceration, representing a more severe punishment than non-carceral alternatives, and specific deterrence of offenders who served time.[18] It has also been frequently argued that the prospect of jail will often have no deterrent value for certain persons. These include people in disadvantaged circumstances who lack legitimate opportunities and therefore have little if anything to lose by committing crimes, as well as those who are socialized into, and whose livelihoods depend on, criminal lifestyles.[19] Criminal sanctions may also lack deterrent effect on those who act out impulsively, in a moment of enflamed emotion, [20] or those who assess that they can commit crimes without getting caught.[21] Deterrence may also decrease for some people who envision and desire tangible benefits to themselves from committing crime. (e.g., money).[22]

This is not to say that deterrence is entirely a hollow shell. Some studies argue that it is the certainty and swiftness that *something* will be meted out to a criminal as a consequence of committing an act, rather than the particular severity of that *something* (e.g., length of the prison term), that has any real deterrent value.[23] Silvia Mendes, political science professor with the University of Minho, qualifies this to an extent. She suggests that the *something* still has to be at least significant if certainty and swiftness are to truly realize any deterrent potential. Otherwise, the mere fact of a certain and swift arrest, sans a meaningful sanction, will not have much persuasive value for prospective criminals.[24] Be that as it may, the deterrent value provided by certainty and swiftness may be reduced in some contexts. Some studies have shown that certainty and swiftness may have little impact on substance-abuse crimes.[25] Certainty and swiftness may also lose deterrence for repeat offenders[26] and certainly for repeat drug offenders.[27] Negative peer associations can likewise undermine the deterrent value of certainty and swiftness, either because those peer associations can encourage criminal behaviour or because knowledge that social peers have committed crimes and gotten away with it can encourage a risk assessment that optimistically minimizes the fear of getting caught and convicted.[28] Neither severity nor certainty have been found sufficient to deter domestic batterers from re-offending.[29] Critics suggest that not only is the deterrent value of imprisonment questionable, but also that imprisonment makes matters worse.

David Cayley, a former documentary broadcaster for CBC Radio, argues that prison life involves harsh conditions that harden inmates. Placing a convict among other convicts creates conditions whereby a convict has to harden himself, and be willing to commit violent acts without hesitation, in order to survive and convince the other convicts to leave him alone. Prisons have countercultures where the conventional rules of society are turned upside down. Defiance, lack of respect for authority, and violent behaviour become the norms. Once a person has done enough time, the painful effects of being separated from society wear off. Convicts frequently become acculturated and habituated into prison life so that they are unable to adapt to life outside of prison and even prefer to remain behind bars.[30] This has been verified to some degree by empirical studies that have demonstrated that imprisonment increases the probability of offender recidivism in comparison to offenders given a suspended sentence,[31] even for those offenders who previously had a high stake in conforming to societal norms and avoiding arrest.[32] Another study adds, "Although complete data on recidivism in Canada are not publicly available, studies suggest that the majority of ex-prisoners reoffend, typically within two years. Illicit drug use is a key, modifiable risk factor for recidivism."[33]

This worsening effect has also been observed among Indigenous inmates, at least in an anecdotal sense, if not empirically. Rupert Ross, a former Crown prosecutor who worked in Indigenous communities in Ontario, describes one of his personal conversations this way:

> In that regard, I remember an Aboriginal woman at a justice conference complaining about the use of jail. She felt that jail was a place where offenders only learned to be more defiant of others, more self-centred, short-sighted and untrusting. Further, because they had so many daily decisions taken away from them, she felt that their capacity for responsible decision making was actually diminished, not strengthened.[34]

Judge Heino Lilles stated:

> Jail has shown not to be effective for First Nation people. Every family in Kwanlin Dun [the Yukon] has members who have gone to jail. *It carries no stigma and therefore is not a deterrent. Nor is it a "safe place" which encourages disclosure, openness, or healing.* The power or authority structures within the jail operate against "openness." An elder noted: "jail doesn't help anyone. A lot of our people could have been healed a long time ago if it weren't for jail. Jail hurts them more and then they come out really bitter. In jail, all they learn is "hurt and bitter."[35]

Jail does temporarily assure public safety by separating the offender from society for the duration of the prison term. Mark Carter, law professor with the University of Saskatchewan, states: "The benefits of incapacitation, such as they are, are the only guarantees."[36] The problem is that those terms are usually temporary. There remains the potential danger that the offender has been worsened by the experience of imprisonment, with significant post-release probabilities for reoffending.[37] Jo-Anne Fiske, professor of gender studies with the University of Lethbridge, did a consultative study of the Lake Babine First Nation in British Columbia with the assistance of their chief, Betty Patrick, in 2002. They argue that incarceration can "aggravate rather than alleviate" social tensions in small Indigenous communities. Their consultations with members of the First Nation led them to believe that imprisoning violent or sexual offenders can leave the community feeling unsafe after the offenders are released.[38]

Prisons are also some of the best recruiting grounds for street gangs.[39] This phenomenon is particularly worrisome among Indigenous Peoples, as recent studies have found that the same social forces that fuel intergenerational trauma and over-incarceration also encourage Indigenous youth to enter gangs.[40] Many Indigenous inmates check in already as members of existing Indigenous gangs within prison walls, or as prime candidates for recruitment.[41] The Criminal Intelligence Service of Canada describes the origins of Indigenous gangs as follows:

> In Alberta, Aboriginal-based gangs that once existed primarily in prisons for protection purposes have now recognized the financial benefit of trafficking hard drugs (e.g., cocaine) on reserves. Many of the gangs have ready access to weapons, including firearms, that has resulted in a number of incidents of violence.[42]

Mark Totten, a research consultant based in Ontario, estimates that "twenty-two percent of known gang members are Indigenous, and that there are between 800-1000 active Indigenous gang members in the Prairie provinces."[43] He argues that sending Indigenous youth to prison will only entrench them in further into criminal lifestyles, precisely because of prison gang structures.[44]

Recall that residential schools have injected into Indigenous communities many social problems and risks. Many of these social factors are also recognized as capable of weakening deterrent strategies. Many Indigenous Peoples find themselves in social circumstances where deterrence, whether it is dependent on certainty, swiftness, or severity, has little value. These include crimes fuelled by poverty, substance abuse, intergenerational trauma, negative peer association (e.g., gangs), and domestic violence.

PUNISHMENT AS RETRIBUTION

Some cases recognize that the accused was affected negatively by the residential school system but nonetheless stress the harm that the accused caused others in order to justify a custodial sentence. A Northwest Territories case saw the accused sentenced to twenty-six months for possession of cocaine with intent to traffic. The accused did come from an unhealthy home environment on account of previous generations of family members going through residential schools. Nonetheless, during sentencing, Justice Schuler emphasized the harm that could potentially result in the accused's own Indigenous community, especially to local children, as a result of trafficking cocaine.[45]

An Ontario Superior Court case saw the accused sentenced to three years for defrauding her own First Nation. She had been both sexually abused in residential school and raped by several older men afterward. The court nonetheless justified the sentence on the basis that Indigenous communities "expect that their leaders conduct themselves with the highest degree of integrity, in the same fashion as what is expected of non-aboriginal leaders by their citizens."[46] Other cases emphasize the need for the accused to accept personal responsibility, such as in a Northwest Territories Supreme Court assault case. In handing down the year-long sentence, Justice Vertes acknowledged that the accused was abused in the Grollier Hall residential school, but added that "there had been plenty of opportunities for this man to try to come to grips with his difficulties, whatever they may be; and, frankly, by the age of 38, he has to look at himself and take responsibility for his life."[47] A Yukon Territorial case saw the accused receive two years for assault of a peace officer, common assault, and breach of recognizance. He had been violently abused in both residential school and at home. Justice Vertes nonetheless states: "He cannot continue to re-offend in a violent manner and rely on his aboriginal experience to excuse his conduct."[48]

There are also cases where the court downplays residential school trauma as a significant mitigating factor, even to the point of placing those who have been affected directly or indirectly by the schools as being on the same footing as non-Indigenous offenders. In a Saskatchewan Court of Queen's Bench case where the accused received three years for failure to provide the necessaries of life, the court noted: "Each of the accused spent time in homes and communities during their formative years where there was substance abuse, physical abuse and even sexual abuse."[49] The Court justified the sentence on the basis that, as middle-aged persons, they were still expected to know right from wrong.[50]

Then there is a British Columbia case where the accused received two years less a day for break and enter with intent to commit an indictable offence. The court acknowledged that the accused was abused by his father, who in turn had been abused in residential school. But the court insisted:

> At the same time, I am one of those who says that it is not sufficient to blame parents. There are lots of opportunities afforded every individual in this community to be a responsible citizen who contributes to the community. Each individual has that responsibility to do so and the failure to do so is going to result eventually in the deprivation of liberty.[51]

And finally, an accused received one year and two months for sexual assault in a Northwest Territories Territorial Court case. The court remarked:

> Mr. O. has many issues in his life, and I take that into account. He attended residential school and suffered abuse there; he also says that he suffered abuse in his own home and from his relatives when he was a child. There comes a time when it is difficult to continue to see a person as a victim, and this is when he repeatedly makes victims of others.[52]

These comments seem to sustain a legal fiction that has a questionable assumption. Whenever Canada prosecutes a crime, the style of cause is *Regina* (the Queen) versus the accused. This reflects the idea that when an accused has committed a crime, he or she has done something that threatens the good of the broader public, thus necessitating a public response from the head of state, the Crown. Thus, the Crown is doing no more than discharging its mandate to protect the public. This construction is perhaps legitimate if in fact the state has not had any responsibility for the crime itself. The construction is questionable, to say the least, when it comes to crimes committed by Indigenous persons that can be traced back to the residential schools. It is correct that some residential school survivors and some Indigenous persons affected by intergenerational trauma, racism, and poverty have never committed crimes, while others have inflicted severe harm on others around them. There is still some element of choice here. Nonetheless, it cannot be denied that the problem of Indigenous over-incarceration, and all the social problems of which over-incarceration is but a symptom, would be nowhere near today's magnitude, if existing at all, but for residential schools and their aftermath.

J. Andres Hannah-Suarez, a Crown prosecutor in Ontario, takes this a little further and argues that given the obvious social dispari- ties between Indigenous and non-Indigenous Peoples, punishment of Indigenous Peoples basically turns into punishing them for their lack of social luck. Retributive rationales for punishment thus lack rational or ethical justification.[53] It could be argued that at the very least, Canada as a nation-state has responsibility to address this problem if there is to be reconciliation. For the Canadian judicial system to cast all of the blame on Indigenous accused who act out after having been traumatized in the wake of residential school policy is implicitly to relieve the state of any culpability or responsibility. We have this insightful comment from Judge Cozens in *R. v. Elias*:

> In accepting responsibility for their role in causing such a nega- tive impact on First Nations individuals, their families and their communities, the Government of Canada implicitly should be seen as also accepting responsibility for ongoing participation in ameliorating the consequences of this impact on [aboriginal] individuals, their families and their communities. All too often it is in the criminal justice system where these negative impacts are to be found, not just in the victims of criminal activity but in the offenders who commit the crimes.
>
> It is not enough to apologize for harm done without making reparation for the harm. This reparation must reach beyond the payment of monies to former students of the residential schools. It must extend to how we treat [aboriginal] peoples involved in the criminal justice system, regardless of their role within it. Legislation designed to "get tough" on crime must not lose sight of the fact that the very individuals that suffered harm, either di- rectly or indirectly, perhaps as children of students of residential schools, may be the same individuals who are committing the crimes and who are, under such legislation, the individuals that the justice system will "get tough" on.[54]

It is important to note that there is a case where this type of argument had been explicitly invoked by an Indigenous accused. The accused in *R. v. Arcand* was convicted of sexual assault and kidnapping; he had also suffered severe physical and sexual abuse while in residential school.[55] The argument was that Harper's apology in 2008 was also implicitly an admission that by allowing the accused to be abused in residential school, "the Government is partly to blame for Mr. Arcand's criminal activity and that this was not given the proper consideration by the trial judge."[56] The Saskatchewan Court of Appeal dismissed the argument as follows: "At worst, this argument is specious and at best it says no more than the residential school abuse, as part of the *Gladue* factors, must be considered in sentencing."[57]

A similar argument surfaced in a Manitoba Court of Queen's Bench case where the accused had normalized violence against women in reaction to his own upbringing. Justice Menzies notes the defence counsel's argument but also provides his own reaction:

> The irony of having to protect society from someone who is the product of historical governmental policies is not lost on the court. However, the court must balance this historical dilemma with the need to protect the public. It cannot be forgotten that the vast majority of the victims in Moore's criminal behaviour were aboriginal people themselves.[58]

There is recognition that state misconduct can justify a reduction in the accused's sentence. For example, the Supreme Court in *R. v. Nasogaluak* recognized that a violation of an accused's *Charter* rights can warrant a reduction in sentence as a mitigating factor.[59] *Nasogaluak* also recognized that even state misconduct that does not amount to a *Charter* violation can justify a sentence reduction.[60] Of course, one could say that this concept typically involves police misconduct leading up to the arrest and may not contemplate historical state misconduct. But to foist all responsibility for crimes on Indigenous accused to justify their routine incarceration, while making absolutely no mention of the role of Canadian colonial policy in forming such an important part of the background, grossly oversimplifies matters and shears them of their full context. It is fair to question whether many of the Indigenous persons who get prosecuted and imprisoned would have ever committed any crimes but for the persistent legacy of residential schools. This oversimplification also implicitly absolves the state of any responsibility for the problem, so that it can thus continue to pursue a policy of extensive im prisonment while taking only minimal steps to address the social problems left behind by the schools. That falls far below Canada acting in a manner consistent with reconciliation.[61]

One could, however, persist with the contention that many Indigenous persons who were either residential school survivors or who were affected by intergenerational trauma have gone through their lives without having committed any crime. A study by Clemens Kronenberg, Isolde Heintze, and Guido Mehlkp of over 2,130 participants in Dreselden, Germany, gauged their willingness to commit either shoplifting or tax fraud. The study found that only respondents who did not feel constrained by moral norms engaged in a cost-benefit analysis of committing a crime (e.g., the likelihood of getting caught or getting away with it). Cost-benefit analyses were found to be completely irrelevant to individuals who had strongly internalized moral norms.[62] The mainstream justice system therefore continues to justify casting crime as a choice and not necessarily a compulsion towards criminal behaviour. Indigenous accused must therefore still be punished as a matter of measured retribution administered by the state. For example, in *R. v. Charlie*, where the accused was sentenced to almost two years for failing to comply with a breathalyzer demand, Judge Luther states: "The fact that Mr. Joe was horribly abused as a child in residential schools does not relieve him from responsibility for these offences. Nor, in my view, does it 'reduce his moral culpability,' in keeping with the jurisprudence.'"[63]

There is still more to the picture, though. A qualitative study from the Netherlands was based on interviews with forty-nine perpetrators of armed robberies between the ages of twelve and eighteen. The study argued that rational choice theory provides an overly simplistic view of crime, as it inadequately accounts for the often multifaceted decision-making processes that lead a person to commit a crime. Factors in decision making that emerged from the interviews that can cloud the view of rational choice theory include impulsivity (which has already been established by other studies as weakening deterrence), moral ambiguity, and expressivity.[64] In particular, the ability of an offender to impose moral ambiguity on his or her crime can provide a potent tilt in favour of seeing the offence through. And desperate social circumstances, such as lack of economic opportunity, can push people toward assigning moral ambiguity to actions that they would otherwise avoid or even themselves condemn.[65]

A study based on data obtained from the Federal Bureau of Investigation on property crime for the years 1982 to 1996 shows that risk factors for offending can follow a certain gradation.[66] Temporary unemployment did not have a statistically significant effect on property crime rates. What did have a statistically significant effect on property crime rates was unemployment lasting fifteen weeks or longer.[67]

I argue that the risk factors call into question not only the soundness of classical theories of deterrence, but also the soundness of an unrelenting application of retributive justifications for punishment. I do not mean to minimize the harm done to victims of crime, and I acknowledge that there is still some element of choice involved with engaging in criminal behaviour. But a number of key studies suggest that social risk factors have implications for how easy or difficult it is to make law-abiding choices. The Netherlands study indicates that personal distress and social conditions can encourage an offender to infuse his or her actions with moral ambiguity. The study based on FBI data indicates that even a single risk factor (e.g., lack of stable employment) can make the difference between a person committing a crime or abiding by the law. An implication that is hard to ignore is that the risk factors can make law-abiding choices more difficult than for someone who lives in an environment free of adverse social conditions. A non-Indigenous Canadian who lives above the poverty line in a stable home environment, with the resources and support to pursue educational and career opportunities, will have a comparatively easy time making choices that avoid prosecution under Canadian criminal law. The law-abiding choices will certainly be easier to make in comparison to an Indigenous person who has been devastated either by direct attendance in residential school or affected by intergenerational trauma and/or has had his or her life impacted by a multiplicity of historical state-sanctioned traumas and social stresses. It is not a stretch to say that choices to avoid criminal behaviour then become much more difficult to make, often to the point of seeming all but impossible for many Indigenous persons. While acknowledging that not everyone who has been affected by residential schools or intergenerational trauma has gone on to commit crimes, it is not unreasonable to suggest that such individuals succeeded in making what still amounted to comparatively

more difficult choices, perhaps showing remarkable strength of character and personality by doing so.

I again wish to stress that there is still the outstanding question of
whether many convicted Indigenous persons would ever have committed any crimes had it not been for the legacy of residential schools. The
Canadian state still has a responsibility for the problems that have left
behind by those schools, as well as a responsibility to act in a manner
consistent with reconciliation. Canadian sentencing has at least since
1996 developed distinctive principles of sentencing that try to account
for the specific circumstances of Indigenous Peoples, but there remain
concerns even there.

INDIGENOUS-SPECIFIC SENTENCING

As discussed, there is some recognition in Canadian law that Indigenous
Peoples face a unique set of social circumstances that has contributed to
Indigenous over-incarceration. Section 718.2(e) of the *Criminal Code*,
enacted in 1996, reads in part:

> A court that imposes a sentence shall also take into considera-
> tion the following principles: ... (e) all available sanctions other
> than imprisonment that are reasonable in the circumstances
> should be considered for all offenders, with particular attention
> to the circumstances of Aboriginal offenders.

The Supreme Court of Canada interpreted the provision in its landmark
decision, *R. v. Gladue*, stating that section 718.2(e) was enacted in response to alarming evidence that Indigenous Peoples were incarcerated disproportionately to non-Indigenous people in Canada.[68] Section
718.2(e) is thus a remedial provision, enacted specifically to oblige the
judiciary to reduce incarceration of Indigenous offenders and seek reasonable alternatives for them.[69] Justice Cory adds:

> It is often the case that neither Aboriginal offenders nor their
> communities are well served by incarcerating offenders, par-
> ticularly for less serious or non-violent offences. Where these
> sanctions are reasonable in the circumstances, they should be
> implemented. In all instances, it is appropriate to attempt to
> craft the sentencing process and the sanctions imposed in ac-
> cordance with the Aboriginal perspective.[70]

A judge must take into account the background and systemic factors that bring Indigenous people into contact with the justice system, such as poverty, substance abuse, and "community fragmentation," when sentencing.[71] A judge must also consider the role of these factors in bringing a particular Indigenous accused before the court,[72] and the judge is obligated to obtain that information with the assistance of counsel, through probation officer reports, or through other means. A judge must also obtain information on community resources and treatment options that may provide alternatives to incarceration.[73]

Gladue does provide a potential vehicle by which the Canadian criminal justice system can address the legacy of residential schools in arriving at a fit sentence and ameliorating the problem of Indigenous over-incarceration. It must be recognized, however, that there are very significant limitations involved with *Gladue* itself. The call for restraint in the use of imprisonment in section 718.2(e) is frequently at odds with other principles of Canadian law that stress deterrence and retribution. And indeed, certain offences, and offences committed under certain circumstances, could render an Indigenous accused ineligible for a community-based sentence. *Gladue* itself holds that the more serious an offence, the more likely the sentence will involve incarceration and be comparable to that received by a non-Indigenous offender.[74] Deterrence and retribution are prioritized in those cases. The inevitable result is that *Gladue's* applicability has been limited for the most part to less serious offences. One can also note that in many of the cases described in Chapter 2, judges did recognize that *Gladue* factors stemming from residential schools were part of the accused backgrounds. Yet the judges felt themselves constrained to apply Canadian sentencing principles that emphasized deterrence and retribution, with the result that many, if not most, of the cases used terms of incarceration.[75]

Whatever the Supreme Court's intentions in *Gladue* may have been, there is a real degree to which lower courts have demonstrated a clear preference for incarceration sentences in order to give effect to deterrence and retribution. Kent Roach, law professor with the University of Toronto, has noted that appellate courts in a variety of jurisdictions have prioritized the seriousness of the offence, thereby denuding *Gladue* of much of its potential promise.[76] Empirical analysis has validated these claims. Andrew Welsh and James Ogloff analyzed 691 reported sentencing decisions to determine the effects of section 718.2(e). They found that Indigenous status did not have any correlation with receiving either a custodial or non-custodial sentence. The strongest correlates instead were the presence of standard aggravating or mitigating factors recognized by sentencing law prior to the passing of s. 718.2(e).[77]

The paradoxical result is that many Indigenous persons who have been deeply damaged and traumatized by the legacy of residential schools, who are the most in need of *Gladue's* promise, end up being cut off from the remedial benefits intended by *Gladue*.[78] In fact, Judge Atwood, in a Nova Scotia Provincial Court decision, suggests that judges may in fact make themselves part of the problem by continuing to apply the usual sentencing principles to Indigenous accused. He acknowledged at some length that the residential schools have had devastating effects across generations and then stated: "Courts must resist any sort of self-congratulation or triumphalism in making these sorts of findings. This is because these injustices were readily obvious to all but the wilfully blind. And, in many cases, courts were implicated in them."[79]

Justice McEachern of the British Columbia Court of Appeal recognized the futility of calling upon incarceration in sentencing an Indigenous accused, but nonetheless felt constrained to do so by Canadian sentencing law:

> I have the view that in the fullness of time we will come to realize that we should go back well into the childhood of aboriginal persons who suffer the kind of misfortune this person suffered and determine whether it is appropriate to sentence them in a conventional way. I think that matter needs a great deal of attention. If I did not find myself constrained by authority, I would be seriously tempted to allow this appeal and to provide what I think would be a more enlightened sentence — a sentence that would return this person to his community under supervision where he would receive the kind of supervision and attention he deserves. In the present state of the law however, I do not think that I can say that the learned trial judge erred in failing to give proper consideration to the aboriginal status of the appellant.[80]

The Supreme Court of Canada recently attempted to provide a corrective to this trend through its decision in *R. v. Ipeelee*, stating that offence bifurcation limiting the applicability of *Gladue* to a small range of less serious offences amounted to "a fundamental misunderstanding and misapplication of both s. 718.2(e) and this Court's decision in *Gladue*."[81] *Ipeelee* reinforces that there is often justification for sentencing Indigenous offenders differently under s. 718.2(e), and that justification is tied to colonialism itself, of which residential schools were an integral part. Justice LeBel stated: "The overwhelming message emanating from the various reports and commissions on Aboriginal peoples' involvement in the criminal justice system is that current levels of criminality are intimately tied to the legacy of colonialism."[82] He continued:

> To the extent that *Gladue* will lead to different sanctions for Aboriginal offenders, those sanctions will be justified based on their unique circumstances.— circumstances which are rationally related to the sentencing process. Courts must ensure that a formalistic approach to parity in sentencing does not undermine the remedial purpose of s. 718.2(e).[83]

Debra Parkes, law professor with the University of British Columbia, and I have added: "The court also strongly endorsed the practice of producing *Gladue* reports, and affirmed that *Gladue* applies to all sentencing decisions involving Aboriginal people unless there is an explicit waiver. It is difficult to see the *Ipeelee* decision as anything other than a call to action for justice system participants across the country."[84]

Even so, one has to wonder if this "call to action" is being taken seriously by lower courts. An extensive review of 635 *Gladue* cases following *Ipeelee* has shown that the vast majority of cases resulted in incarceration (87.7%) with only a very small minority seeing a conditional sentence (5.8%) or probation (2.8%).[85] The sentencing of Indigenous accused continues to follow a definite trajectory even in the wake of fairly strong statements coming from the highest court in *Ipeelee*.

The fact remains that the overall framework for Canadian sentencing law remains heavily tilted in favour of deterrence and retribution. This tilt translates into a certain gravitas in sentencing decisions such that any statements the Supreme Court provides, whether in *Gladue* or *Ipeelee* or any case thereafter, may very well have minimal purchase with lower courts. In fact, part of the problem may be with *Ipeelee* itself, and in a way that reflects that fundamental tilt in Canadian sentencing law. The court emphasizes that section 718.2(e) does not amount to a "race-based discount on sentencing."[86] The court also asserts that proportionality — addressing factually similar cases with similar sentences — remains an important sentencing objective that can still justify incarceration.[87] The court also reaffirmed *Gladue*'s statement that the more serious the crime, the more likely that a sentence of incarceration will be appropriate.[88] And so in *Ipeelee*, we have a seemingly contradictory message — the need to consider non-custodial sentences for any Indigenous accused no matter how serious the offence alongside a demand for proportionality. It should therefore not be surprising that the trajectory that was observed with respect to *Gladue* continues after *Ipeelee*.

Many of the case excerpts indicated that Indigenous accused who were directly affected by the residential schools, or indirectly through intergenerational trauma, were sentenced for offences to which either the mandatory minimums[89] or the ineligibility for conditional sentences[90] under Bill C-10 would now be applicable. There were concerns about the scope or capacity of *Gladue* to provide remedial effect against Indigenous over-incarceration even prior to Bill C-10. Bill C-10 accentuates those concerns, either forcing mandatory minimums or denying a conditional sentence option for many offences with which Indigenous accused will get charged as a result of colonial legacies. Canadian judges, even those so inclined, thus cannot even begin to consider non-custodial alternatives pursuant to *Gladue*.[91] Elizabeth Sheehy, law professor with the University of Ottawa, adds that "Bill C-10 will effectively repudiate s. 718.2(e) and swell even further our jails with Aboriginal offenders."[92]

Perhaps some of the concerns about Bill C-10 may be alleviated by the stance the Supreme Court demonstrated in *R. v. Nur*, where it ruled that three- and five-year mandatory minimums for firearms offences were a violation of the s. 12 *Charter* against cruel and unusual punishment. The court's reasoning was that the mandatory minimums, and the resulting removal of judicial discretion, may in result in undeservedly severe punishments in individual cases where their facts could fall within reasonable hypothetical scenarios that would come to the courts with more than minimal frequency.[93] The court also applied this analysis to strike down a mandatory one-year minimum for trafficking in a Schedule I or II drug.[94] In *R. v. J.L.M.*, the Indigenous accused, who experienced poverty and racism as a youth, was sentenced to seven months for solicitation of the services of a minor where the mandatory minimum was six months. The British Columbia Court of Appeal found that the mandatory minimum was unconstitutional under s. 12 of the *Charter* and substituted a nine-month conditional sentence.[95]

It may be speculated at this point how far the reasoning in *Nur* will be taken against various components of Bill C-10. To completely dismantle the mandatory minimum scheme would require a lengthy process of multiple constitutional applications, and there is no assurance that such a process would be completed. That is especially the case when one views the results of other cases, some of them involving Indigenous accused.

In *R. v. Sharma*, the two-year mandatory minimum for trafficking in cocaine was struck down by the Ontario Superior Court of Justice. A sentence of seventeen months was imposed instead, in recognition that even without the mandatory minimum the trafficking of cocaine was still a very serious offence that often required some jail time. The issue was with sentence length.[96]

In *R. v. T.M.B.*, the accused was charged with sexual touching of a minor. He himself had been sexually abused as a child. The challenge to the six-month mandatory minimum was dismissed by Justice Code of the Ontario Superior Court of Justice.[97] Another such case also had its *Charter* challenge dismissed. In that case, numerous members of the accused's Anishinaabe community, as well as his family members and an Elder from the community, fully expressed support for a healing plan they considered more constructive than incarceration.[98]

Prime Minister Justin Trudeau made striking down mandatory minimums part of his 2015 electoral platform. That promise was part and parcel with a promise to implement every one of the TRC's Calls to Action, including Call to Action 32, which requires "the federal government to amend the *Criminal Code* to allow trial judges, upon giving reasons, to depart from mandatory minimum sentences and restrictions on the use of conditional sentences."[99] Trudeau's Liberal government spent several years after its election victory not delivering on that promise.[100] In fact, independent senator Kim Pate became so impatient with the government's lack of progress on that particular point that in 2019 she introduced her own Bill S-251 to the Senate, which would allow judges to waive application of mandatory minimums if it would be considered just to do so.[101] The Liberal government, in its second term after winning a minority government in 2019, finally acted. Bill C-22 repeals more than a dozen narcotics and firearms mandatory minimums from both the *Criminal Code* and the *Controlled Drugs and Substances Act*. The bill also covered approximately a sixth of the mandatory minimums and repealed the list of offences ineligible for conditional sentences brought in by Bill C-10.[102] It would seem that mandatory minimums remain here to stay to one degree or another, along with their disproportionate impacts on Indigenous Peoples.

Another problem with *Gladue* may be a lack of resource support, both for the production of *Gladue* reports, which can assist courts with cases involving Indigenous accused, and for the rehabilitation and reintegration of Indigenous accused so as to make non-custodial sentencing options meaningful.[103] Jonathan Rudin, director of Aboriginal Legal Services in Toronto, points out that another significant barrier to *Gladue* being able to affect any consequential change is government complacency: a lack of any meaningful support, inertia against providing services and infrastructure so that proper *Gladue* reports are available for sentencing judges.[104] A sociology thesis at the University of Manitoba explored why *Gladue* has thus far been underutilized in Manitoba. One of the key reasons was a lack of resources. At the time of the study, some rehabilitative services grounded in Indigenous cultures were available in Winnipeg — for example, the Métis Justice Strategy, the Interlake Peacemakers Project, and the Onashowewin diversion program — however, these programs had limited capacity and this often convinced the defence lawyers that they could not make meaningful submissions for non-custodial sentences.[105]

Even without these shortcomings associated with *Gladue*, there is an open question of how much difference the sentencing process can make. To try to make a positive difference through the sentencing process is very much in the spirit of *Gladue*.[106] However, some scholars have expressed concern that the social problems may be too large for section 718.2(e) to address, at least by itself.[107] Carol LaPrairie, a former Canadian criminologist, suggests that it is unrealistic to place too much emphasis on the justice system's ability to provide "real and long-lasting solutions to the over-representation problem."[108] Sanjeev Anand, law professor with the University of Saskatchewan, adds: "sentencing innovation cannot remove the causes of Aboriginal offending because it cannot address problems like inadequate housing, substance abuse, lack of education, and scarcity of employment opportunities for Aboriginal people."[109] Adam Vasey, now a social worker in Ontario, admits that the problem of Indigenous over-incarceration may be too large for sentencing reforms by themselves to tackle, but insists that this is not a reason to reject section 718.2(e) altogether. *Gladue* can still have a positive role, albeit limited, in addressing the social problems left behind by colonialism.[110]

NEED FOR MORE COMPREHENSIVE RESOLUTION

Fundamentally, the problems are so deep-seated and pervasive that it defies the capacity of any one isolated initiative to address. Perhaps Justice Perkins-McVey captures the aspiration of a lot of judges in *Gladue* cases with this quote: "This does not mean the accused's assaultive behaviour can be excused and she does not need to be held accountable but a fit and appropriate sentence must attempt to balance the need to denounce and deter the assault while at the same time appreciating the systemic factors that have led to her criminality."[111] Yet given that Canadian sentencing law itself remains so inherently tilted towards deterrence and retribution, one has to wonder whether the "balance" that is aspired to remains elusive.

A far more comprehensive set of resolutions is needed to address the problem and achieve true reconciliation, not just a patchwork of individual and minimalist "band-aid solutions." I also wish to be clear that a comprehensive resolution needs to be sustained for as long as it takes to fully address these problems, and this can mean years or even decades. We have this excerpt from a *Gladue* report in a British Columbia Court of Appeal case:

> Traditionally family has been at the very core of [the Cowichan] cultural structure. But that fundamentally important institution in all first nations communities was traumatised by 100 years of the government imposed residential school system. That system produced generations of young people, many of whom emerged with little knowledge of family life, or how to raise children of their own without using the same violent or abusive mechanisms that were inflicted upon them in those schools. The familial chaos stemming from that dark and savage experiment will take generations to overcome.[112]

Murray Sinclair was interviewed about his perceptions regarding progress in meeting the Calls to Action a year after the TRC ended. He stated: "Happy's not the right word. I'm feeling that the train is slowly moving.

But we still have a ways to go before we can get it up to any kind of speed. And we have a long distance to go once we get to that speed."[113]

A thorough set of resolutions is needed to intervene in every possible aspect that contributes to Indigenous over-incarceration. In searching for solutions, much has been made of Indigenous justice initiatives that resemble restorative justice. Indeed, this should be included in demands for a comprehensive resolution. But to focus solely on sentencing options is too narrow and incomplete — we need to go further in search for a comprehensive solution. Shereen Benzvy Miller, currently a federal deputy minister, and research consultant Mark Schacter argue that Canada needs to take matters further than reactive restorative justice and employ a wider paradigm called restorative governance. Restorative governance includes not just intervention after the fact for crimes, but also pursuing preventative policies that minimize the need for intervention.[114] Elizabeth Adjin-Tettey, law professor with the University of Victoria, adds:

> The complex nature of the problem of Aboriginal criminality and the cycle that perpetuates the problem requires concerted and long-term strategies to break the cycle of crime and violence. Given the correlation between marginality, crime, and victimization, sentencing reform will *likely* only play a limited role in remedying injustice against Aboriginal people and other marginalized groups in Canada. Even if contextual sentencing reduces recidivism, it might not necessarily result in crime prevention so long as others continue to be marginalized *by* systemic discrimination. To adequately redress the problem of over-incarceration, we must first remedy the underlying socioeconomic imbalance between Aboriginal and many non-Aboriginal Canadians and implement pro-active crime prevention measures. Social transformation will depend on strengthening social citizenship *by* improving the material conditions of marginalized people and *by* addressing racism and discrimination as part of crime prevention strategies.[115]

Of course, in order to pursue such a comprehensive set of initiatives, Indigenous Peoples need the legal and political space to do so. The transitory phase begins the process of acquiring and using that space. Revitalized Indigenous legal orders complete the acquisition of that space and can use restorative governance in ways that meet the needs of Indigenous communities and end Indigenous incarceration. Discussion must begin with preventative programming, with the intention of moulding healthier Indigenous communities so as to minimize even the need for responses to harmful behaviour by Indigenous persons.

Notes

1   *Baxter v. Canada*, 2005 ONSC 18717.

2   Residential Schools Settlement, Official Notice, "Agreement in Principle" <residentialschoolsettlement.ca/AIP.pdf>.

3   Carrie Menkel-Meadow, "Unsettling the Lawyers: Other Forms of Justice in Indigenous Claims of Expropriation, Abuse and Injustice," *University of Toronto Law Journal* 64, 4 (2014), 620; Kathleen Mahoney, "The Settlement Process: A Personal Reflection," *University of Toronto Law Journal* 64, 4 (2014), 505.

4   Andrew John Mallus, "Reparations for Cultural Loss to Survivors of Indian Residential Schools," LLM Thesis, University of Ottawa, 2010; Bruce Feldthusen, "Civil Liability for Sexual Assault in Aboriginal Residential Schools: The Baker Did It," *Canadian Journal of Law and Society* 22, 1 (2007), 61.

5   *R. v. Wasacase*, 2003 BCPC 2518, para. 4.

6   Indian Life, "Deaths Linked to Residential School Payouts" <indianz.com/News/2008/01/22/deaths_linked_t.asp>.

7   *R. v. Peters*, 2014 BCSC 1009.

8   Aboriginal Healing Foundation, "FAQs" <ahf.ca/faqs>.

9   Maya Rolbin-Ghanie, "Funding cuts a catastrophe for residential school survivors," *Rabble*, March 30, 2010 <rabble.ca/news/2010/03/funding-cuts-catastrophe-residential-school-survivors>.

10   Rolbin-Ghanie, "Funding cuts a catastrophe."

11   See, for example, *R. v. Kaiswatum*, 2015 SKQB 404.

12   *R. v. Kaiswatum*, 2015 SKQB, para. 29; *R. v. A.J.P.J.*, 2011 NWTCA 2, para. 9.

13   *R. v. Taniskishayinew*, 2018 BCSC 296.

14   *R. v. Taniskishayinew*, 2018 BCSC 296, para. 9–10.

15   Frank D. Williams and Marilyn P. McShane, *Criminological Theory*, 3rd ed. (New Jersey: Prentice Hall, 1999), 16–18.

16   Raymond Paternoster, "How Much Do We Really Know about Criminal Deterrence," *Journal of Criminal Law and Criminology* 100, 3 (2010), 765; Charles Tittle, Ekaterina Botchkovar, and Alena Antonaccio, "Criminal Contemplation, National Context and Deterrence," *Journal of Qualitative Criminology* 27, 2 (2011), 225.

17   Michael L. Radelet and Traci L. Lacock, "Do Executions Lower Homicide Rates? The Views of Leading Criminologists," *Journal of Criminal Law and Criminology* 99, 2 (2009), 489; Gary Kleck et al. "The Missing Link in General Deterrence Research," *Criminology* 43, 3: (2005), 623; Ellen Raiijmakers et al., "Why Longer Prison Terms Fail to Serve a Specific Deterrent Effect: An Empirical Assessment on the Remembered Severity of Imprisonment," *Psychology, Crime & Law* 23, 1 (2017), 32.

18   Avinashi Singh Bati and Alex R. Piquero, "Estimating the Impact of Incarcera-
tion on Subsequent Offending Trajectories: Deterrent, Criminogenic, or Null
Effect?" *Criminology* 98, 1 (2008), 207; George Bridges and James A. Stone,
"Effects of Criminal Punishment on Perceived Threat of Punishment: Toward
an Understanding of Specific Deterrence," *Journal of Research in Crime and
Delinquency* 23, 3 (1986), 207; David Weisburd, Elin Waring, and Ellen Chay-
et, "Specific Deterrence in a Sample of Offenders Convicted of White Collar
Crimes," *Criminology* 33, 4 (1995), 587.

19   Justice E.D. Bayda, "The Theory and Practice of Sentencing: Are They on the
Same Wavelength?" *Saskatchewan Law Review* 60 (1996), 317; Shawn D. Bush-
way and Peter Reuter, "Deterrence, Economics, and the Context of Drug Mar-
kets," *Criminology & Public Policy* 10, 1 (2011), 183; Thomas Baker and Alex
R. Piquero, "Assessing the Perceived Benefits — Criminal Offending Relationship," *Journal of Criminal Justice* 38, 5 (2010), 981.

20   Jo-Anne Fiske and Betty Patrick, *Cis Dideen Kat: The Way of the Lake Babine
Nation* (Vancouver: UBC Press, 2000); Bradley R.E. Wright et al. "Does the
Perceived Risk of Crime Deter Criminally Prone Individuals? Rational Choice,
Self-Control and Crime," *Journal of Research in Crime and Delinquency* 41, 2
(2004), 180; Stephen W. Baron and Leslie W. Kennedy, "Deterrence and Home-
less Male Youths," *Canadian Journal of Criminology* 40, 1 (1998), 27; Daniel S.
Nagin and Raymond Paternoster, "Personal Capital and Social Control: The
Deterrence Implications of a Theory of Individual Differences in Criminal Of-
fending," *Criminology* 32, 4 (1994), 581.

21   Kimberly N. Varna and Anthony Doob, "Deterring Economic Crimes: The
Case of Tax Evasion," *Canadian Journal of Criminology* 40, 2 (1998), 165; Sonja
Schulz, "Individual Differences in the Deterrence Process: Which Individu-
als Learn (Most) From Their Offending Experiences?" *Journal of Quantitative
Criminology* 30, 2 (2014), 215.

22   Thomas Baker and Alex Piquero, "Assessing the Perceived Benefits," 981.

23   Daniel O'Connel et al. "Decide Your Time: Testing Deterrence Theory's Cer-
tainty and Celerity Effects on Substance-Abusing Probationers," *Journal of
Criminal Justice* 39, 3 (2011) 261; John S. Goldkamp, "Optimistic Deterrence
Theorizing," *Criminology & Public Policy* 10, 1 (2011), 115; Cheryl Maxson,
Kristy Matsuda, and Karen Hennigan, "'Deterrability' Among Gang and Non-
Gang Juvenile Offenders: Are Gang Members More (or Less) Deterrable Than
Other Juvenile Offenders?" *Crime & Delinquency* 57, 4 (2011), 516; Jonathan
Shepherd, "Criminal Deterrence as a Public Health Strategy," *Lancet* 358, 9294
(2001), 1717; Daniel Nagin and Greg Pogarsky, "Integrating Celerity, Impulsiv-
ity, and Extralegal Sanction Threats Into a Model of Deterrence: Theory and
Evidence," *Criminology* 39, 4 (2001), 865.

24   Silvia Mendes, "Certainty, Severity, and Their Relative Deterrent Effects: Questioning the Role of Risk in Criminal Deterrence Theory," *Policy Studies Journal*
32, 1 (2004), 59.

25   Monica Barratt, "Cannabis Law Reform in Western Australia: An Opportunity
to Test Theories of Marginal Deterrence and Legitimacy," *Drug & Alcohol Review* 25, 4 (2005), 321.

26 Greg Pogarsky, Kim KiDeuk, and Ray Poternoster, "Perceptual Change in the National Youth Survey: Lessons for Deterrence Theory and Offender Decision-making," *Justice Quarterly* 22, 1 (2005), 1.

27 Douglas Marlowe et al. "Perceived Deterrence and Outcomes in Drug Courts," *Behavorial Sciences & the Law* 23, 2 (2005), 183.

28 Greg Pogarsky, Alex Piquero, and Ray Poternoster, "Modeling Change in Perceptions About Sanction Threats: The Neglected Linkage in Deterrence Theory," *Journal of Quantitative Criminology* 20, 4 (2004), 343; Shelly Keith Matthews and Robert Agnew, "Extending Deterrence Theory," *Journal of Research in Crime and Delinquency* 45, 2 (2008), 91; Stephen Baron, "When Formal Sanctions Encourage Violent Offending: How Violent Peers and Violent Codes Undermine Deterrence," *Justice Quarterly* 30, 5 (2013), 926.

29 D. Alex Heckert and Edward Gondolf, "The Effect of Perceptions of Sanctions on Batterer Program Outcomes," *Journal of Research in Crime and Delinquency* 37, 4 (2000), 369.

30 David Cayley, *The Expanding Prison: The Crisis in Crime and Punishment and the Search for Alternatives* (Toronto: House of Anansi Press, 1998), 101–22.

31 Jose Cid, "Is Imprisonment Criminogenic? A Comparative Study of Imprisonment Rates between Prison and Suspended Sentence Sanctions," *European Journal of Criminology* 6, 6 (2009), 459; Paul Hammel, "Nebraska Research Shows Probation Leads to Less Recidivism Than Probation," *Capitol Ideas* (2017), 1; David Harding, "Short- and Long-Term Effects of Imprisonment on Future Felony Convictions and Prison Admissions," *Proceedings of the National Academy of Sciences of the United States of America* 114, 42 (2017), 11103.

32 Cassia Spohn, "The Deterrent Effect of Imprisonment and Offenders' Stake in Conformity," *Criminal Justice Policy* 18, 1 (2007), 31.

33 Stuart A. Kinner and M.J. Milloy, "Collateral Consequences of an Ever Expanding Prison System" *Canadian Medical Association Journal* 183, 5 (2011), 632.

34 Rupert Ross, *Returning to the Teachings: Exploring Aboriginal Justice* (Toronto: Penguin Books Canada, 1996), 74.

35 *R. v. Gingell* (1996), 50 C.R. (4th) 326 (Y. Terr. Ct.), 342–43.

36 Mark Carter, "Of Fairness and Faulkner," *Saskatchewan Law Review*, Colloquy on "Empty Promises: Parliament, the Supreme Court, and the Sentencing of Aboriginal Offenders" 65 (2002), 65.

37 Robert DeFina and Lance Hannon, "For Incapacitation, There Is No Time Like the Present: The Lagged Effects of Prisoner Re-Entry on Property and Violent Crime Rates," *Social Science Research* 39, 6 (2010), 1004.

38 Fiske and Patrick, *Cis Dideen Kat*, 41.

39 George W. Knox, *The Problem of Gangs and Security Threat Groups (STGS) in American Prisons Today: Recent Research Findings from the 2004 Prison Gang Survey* (Peotone: National Gang Crime Research Center, 2004).

40 Dane Hautala, Kelly Sittner, and Les Whitbeck, "Prospective Childhood Risk Factors for Gang Involvement among North American Indigenous Adolescents," *Youth Violence and Juvenile Justice* 14, 4 (2016), 390; Analaise Goodwill, "A Critical Incident Technique Study of the Facilitation of Gang Entry: Perspectives of Indigenous Men Ex-Gang Members," *Journal of Aggression, Mal-*

treatment & Trauma 25, 5 (2016), 518.

41 Jana Grekul and Patti Laboucane-Benson, "Aboriginal Gangs and their (Dis) placement: Contexualizing Recruitment, Membership and Status," *Canadian Journal of Criminology* 50, 1 (2008), 59; Mark Totten, "Aboriginal Youth and Violent Gang Involvement in Canada: Quality Prevention Strategies," *Revue de l'IPC* 3 (2009), 135.

42 *2003 Annual Report on Organized Crime in Canada* (Ottawa: Criminal Intelligence Service Canada, 2003), 5.

43 Totten, "Aboriginal Youth and Violent Gang Involvement," 136.

44 Totten, "Aboriginal Youth and Violent Gang Involvement," 143.

45 *R. v. Lawrence*, 2010 NWTSC 102.

46 *R. v. Allan*, 2008 ONSC 35699, para. 76–77.

47 *R. v. Jerome*, 2002 NWTSC 101, para. 1.

48 *R. v. Charlie*, 2008 YKTC 17, para. 17.

49 *R. v. E.T.*, 2012 SKQB 169, para. 25.

50 *R. v. E.T.*, 2012 SKQB 169, para. 26–27.

51 *R. v. Baptiste*, 2009 BCSC 1626, para. 18–19.

52 *R. v. V.J.O.*, 2006 NWTTC 9, para. 15.

53 J. Andres Hannah-Suarez, "Moral Luck in Canadian Law: Socio-economic Deprivation, Retributive Punishment and the Judicial Interpretation of Section 718.2(e) of the Criminal Code," *Journal of Law & Equality* 2 (2003), 1.

54 *R. v. Elias*, 2009 YKTC 59, para. 55–56.

55 *R. v. Arcand*, (2013) 417 Sask. R. (C.A.).

56 *R. v. Arcand*, (2013) 417 Sask. R., para. 32.

57 *R. v. Arcand*, (2013) 417 Sask. R., para. 38.

58 *R. v. Moore*, 2016 MBQB 116, para. 32–33.

59 *R. v. Nasogaluak*, [2010] 2 S.C.R. 106, 2010 SCC 6.

60 *R. v. Nasogaluak*, [2010] 2 S.C.R. 106, para. 57.

61 For a quite similar argument, see Carmela Murdocca, "From Incarceration to Restoration: National Responsibility, Gender and the Production of Cultural Difference," *Social & Legal Studies* 18, 1 (2009), 23.

62 Clemens Kronenberg, Isolde Heintz, and Guido Mehlkp, "The Interplay of Moral Norms and Instrumental Incentives in Crime Causation," *Criminology* 48, 1 (2010), 259.

63 *R. v. Charlie*, 2016 YKTC 31, para. 51.

64 Willem De Hann and Jacob Vos, "A Crying Shame: The Over-Rationalized Conception of Man in the Rational Choice Perspective," *Theoretical Criminology* 7, 1 (2003), 29.

65 De Hann and Vos, "A Crying Shame," 43.

66 Federal Bureau of Investigation, *Crime in the United States: Uniform Crime Reports* (Washington, DC: US Government Printing Office, 1982–1996).

67 Mitchell Chamlin and John Cochran, "Unemployment, Economic Theory, and Property Crime: A Note on Measurement," *Journal of Quantitative Criminology* 16, 4 (2000), 443.

68 *R. v. Gladue* [1999] 1 S.C.R. 688, para. 58–65.

69 *R. v. Gladue*, para. 64.

70   *R. v. Gladue*, para. 74.

71   *R. v. Gladue*, para. 67.

72   *R. v. Gladue*, para. 69.

73   *R. v. Gladue*, para. 83–84. See also Alexandra Hebert, "Change in Paradigm or Change in Paradox? *Gladue* Report Practices and Access to Justice," *Queen's Law Journal* 17, 1 (2017), 149.

74   *R. v. Gladue*, para. 78 and 79.

75   See also Brian Pfefferle, "*Gladue* Sentencing: Uneasy Answers to the Hard Problem of Aboriginal Over-Incarceration," *Manitoba Law Journal* 32 (2008), 113.

76   Kent Roach, "One Step Forward, Two Steps Back: *Gladue* at Ten and in the Courts of Appeal," *Criminal Law Quarterly* 54 (2009), 503–4.

77   Andrew Welsh and James Ogloff, "Progressive Reforms or Maintaining the Status Quo? An Empirical Evaluation of the Judicial Consideration of Aboriginal Status in Sentencing Decisions," *Canadian Journal of Criminology* 50, 4 (2008), 479.

78   Renee Pelletier, "The Nullification of Section 718.2(e): Aggravating Aboriginal Over-Representation in Canadian Prisons," *Osgoode Hall Law Journal* 39 (2001), 479–80.

79   *R. v. Denny*, 2016 NSPC 83, para. 8–10.

80   *R. v. T.(L.)*, 2008 ONCA 2431, para. 4.

81   *R. v. Ipeelee*, 2012 SCC 13, para. 63.

82   *R. v. Ipeelee*, 2012 SCC 13, para. 77.

83   *R. v. Ipeelee*, 2012 SCC 13, para. 79.

84   Debra Parkes et al., *Gladue Handbook: A Resource for Justice System Participants in Manitoba* (Winnipeg: University of Manitoba Faculty of Law, 2012), 1.

85   Marie-Andree Denis-Boileau and Marie-Eve Sylvestre, "*Ipeelee* and the Duty to Resist," *University of British Columbia Law Review* 51, 2 (2018), 578.

86   *R. v. Ipeelee*, 2012 SCC 13, para. 75.

87   *R. v. Ipeelee*, 2012 SCC 13, para. 38.

88   *R. v. Ipeelee*, 2012 SCC 13, para. 84.

89   *R. v. Tootoosis*, 2010 ABQB 574; *R. v. J.O.*, 2007 QCCQ 716; *R. v. W.R.G.*, 2010 BCPC 330; *R. v. R.L.W.*, 2011 BCSC 1363; *R. v. Williams*, 2010 BCPC 436; *R. v. McLeod*, 2012 NWTSC 26; *R. v. T.B.M.*, 2012 BCSC 286; *R. v. G.C.*, 2011 NWTSC 57; *R. v. H.(T.D.J.)*, 2011 BCPC 3619.

90   *R. v. B.E.B.*, 2011 MBQB 255; *R. v. Knight*, 2012 MBPC 52; *R. v. Paulette*, 2010 NWTSC 31; *R. v. Addley*, 2012 ONSC 137; *R. v. Michel*, 2012 NWTSC 17; *R. v. Brien*, 2011 CQ 14350; *R. v. Carlick*, 2011 BCPC 1392; *R. v. Beardy and Maytwayashing*, 2011 MBQB 86432; *R. v. Patrick*, 2017 BCPC 223; *R. v. M.E.W.*, 2011 BCPC 267; *R. v. Lennie*, 2012 NWTC 21; *R. v. Caissey*, 2008 BCPC 716; *R. v. Alkenbrack*, 2011 BCPC 424; *R. v. M.(O.N.)*, 2011 BCPC 1097; *R. v. Sutherland*, 2010 ONCJ 103; *R. v. Knott*, 2012 MBQB 105; *R. v. Tourville*, 2011 ONSC 1897; *R. v. Killitkee*, 2011 ONSC 12404; *R. v. R.J.N.*, 2016 YKTC 55; *R. v. Berens*, 2011 MBQB 633; *R. v. Smith*, 2011 YKTC 62; *R. v. R.P.B.*, 2011 YKTC 12; *R. v. Bertrand*, 2011 NWTSC 38; *R. v. R.(N.R.)*, 2011 MBQB 190; *R. v. Wycotte*, 2010 BCPC 463; *R. v. Charlie*, 2012 YKSC 5; *R. v. Payou*, 2012 NWTSC 34; *R. v.*

J.E.R., 2012 BCPC 103; *R. v. Brien*, 2011 QCCQ 15643; *R. v. Audy*, 2010 MBQB 55; *R. v. N.R.R.*, 2011 MBQB 90.

91   For a similar critique, see Larry Chartrand, "Aboriginal Peoples and Manda-
     tory Minimums," *Osgoode Hall Law Journal* 39 (2001), 449.
92   Elizabeth Sheehy, "The Discriminatory Effects of Bill C-15's Mandatory Mini-
     mum Sentences," *Criminal Reports*, 6th series 70 (2010), 311.
93   *R. v. Nur*, 2015 SCC 15.
94   *R. v. Lloyd*, [2016] 1 S.C.R. 130.
95   *R. v. J.L.M.*, 353 C.C.C. (3d) 40 (B.C.C.A.).
96   *R. v. Sharma*, 2018 ONSC 1141.
97   *R. v. T.M.B.*, 299 C.C.C. (3d) (Ont. S.C.J.).
98   *R. v. S.A.*, 2016 ONSC 5355.
99   Truth and Reconciliation Commission of Canada, *Calls to Action* (Winnipeg:
     Truth and Reconciliation Commission of Canada, 2015), 3–4.
100 Amanda Carling et al., "Mandatory Minimum Sentencing Should Be Trudeau's
     First Resolution," *Globe & Mail*, January 2, 2018.
101 Senate of Canada, "'Cruel Consquences': Senator Pate's Public Bill Targets
     Mandatory Minimum Penalties" <sencanada.ca/en/sencaplus/opinion/cruel-
     consequences-senator-pates-public-bill-targets-mandatory-minimum-penal-
     ties/>.
102 Justin Ling, "A First Step in Repealing Mandatory Minimums: After Six Years
     and in its Second Mandate, the Trudeau Government Has Finally Acted on its
     Promise to Pursue Sentencing Reform," *National Magazine*, February 18, 2021
     <nationalmagazine.ca/en-ca/articles/law/hot-topics-in-law/2021/a-first-step-
     in-repealing-mandatory-minimums>.
103 See also Pfefferle, "*Gladue* Sentencing," 113.
104 Jonathan Rudin, "Addressing Aboriginal Over-Representation Post-*Gladue*: A
     Realistic Assessment of How Social Change Occurs," *Criminal Law Quarterly*
     54 (2009), 447; see also Hebert, "Change in Paradigm or Change in Paradox?"
     149.
105 Rana McDonald, "The Discord Between Policy and Practice: Defence Lawyers'
     Use of Section 718.2(e) and Gladue," MA thesis, University of Manitoba, 2008,
     114–20.
106 *R. v. Atkinson*, 2012 YKTC 62, para. 42.
107 Phillip Stenning and Julian V. Robert, "The Sentencing of Aboriginal Offend-
     ers in Canada: A Rejoinder," Colloquy on "Empty Promises: Parliament, the
     Supreme Court, and the Sentencing of Aboriginal Offenders" 65, 1 (2002), 88;
     Jonathan Rudin, "Aboriginal Over-Representation and *R. v. Gladue*: Where We
     Were, Where We Are and Where We Might Be Going," *Supreme Court Law
     Review* 40 (2008), 713.
108 Carol LaPrairie, "The Role of Sentencing in the Over-Representation of Ab-
     original People in Correctional Institutions," *Canadian Journal of Criminology*
     32 (1990), 436.
109 Sanjeev Anand, "The Sentencing of Aboriginal Offenders, Continued Confu-
     sion and Persisting Problems: A Comment on the Decision in *R. v. Gladue*,"
     Canadian Journal of Criminology 42 (2000), 416.

110 Adam Vasey, "Rethinking the Sentencing of Aboriginal Offenders: The Social Value of s. 718.2(d)," *Windsor Review of Legal and Social Issues* 15 (2003), 73.

111 *R. v. Killiktee*, 2017 ONCJ 966, para. 23.

112 *R. v. Jack*, 2008 BCCA 2315, para. 55–56. Appeal denied from sentence for second-degree murder.

113 Nancy McDonald, "Sen. Murray Sinclair on Truth and Reconciliation's Progress: One Year after the Truth and Reconciliation Commission's Report Was Released, its Leader Discusses Forgiveness, Inspirations, and Challenges Ahead," *National Post*, June 1, 2016.

114 Shereen Benzvy Miller and Mark Schacter, "From Restorative Justice to Restorative Governance," *Canadian Journal of Criminology* 42 (2000), 405.

115 Elizabeth Adjin-Tettey, "Sentencing Aboriginal Offenders: Balancing Offenders' Needs, the Interests of Victims and Society, and the Decolonization of Aboriginal Peoples," *Canadian Journal of Women & the Law* 19 (2007), 215.

7

PREVENTATIVE
PROGRAMMING

The next set of discussions raises fundamental questions about criminal justice policy. I argue for allocating more resources toward improving social conditions in Indigenous communities and away from incarceration. The idea is that by addressing the social conditions that encourage Indigenous persons to become prosecuted under Canadian law, the need to incarcerate Indigenous persons would be minimized. There are at least two justifications for such an approach: One relies on a pragmatic appeal to pursue long-term savings by lessening reliance on incarceration; the other is a substantive demand for social reparation.

JUSTICE REINVESTMENT AND LONG-TERM SAVINGS

There is no doubt that incarceration is an immensely expensive sanction to administer. As of 2010, it cost annually $150,808 to keep an inmate in a maximum security institution, $98,219 for medium security, and $95,038 for minimum security.[1] As of 2017, the average annual amount spent on one inmate in a federal penitentiary was $105,286 and $77,630 for one provincial jail inmate.[2] Howard Sapers, the former correctional investigator of Canada, indicated in his 2009–2010 annual report that the annual cost of keeping somebody on community supervision is one eighth the cost to keep the same person incarcerated.[3] As of 2017, provincial corrections systems expended 81 percent of their budgets on provincial jails even though provincial jail inmates accounted for only 22 percent of the provincial correctional services population. Administering community supervision sanctions such as conditional sentences or probation accounted for 15 percent of the budget.[4]

It is obvious that prison is far more expensive than non-custodial sentences. This reality has spurred the coining of the term "justice reinvestment": the idea that, first, it will be more cost-effective in the long term to invest in social programming that steers prospective offenders away from lives of crime before they even come into contact with the justice system and, second, we must invest in more robust correctional and supervisory services for those persons who do get charged.[5] Commissions in both Canada and the United Kingdom have urged the movement of resources from incarceration to community-based alternatives, with the idea that while it may mean greater short-term spending, the investment could see returns with interest over the long term.[6]

Can Canadian leaders be persuaded to embark on a fundamental change in course? The American experience provides at least limited evidence that it is possible. What is remarkable is that several American states have embraced justice reinvestment to varying degrees as they found themselves having to contend with mounting correctional budgets and increasing prison populations. Texas did a massive overhaul of their justice system, tilting heavily in favour of preventative programming where the previous emphasis was on "tough on crime." Senator John Whitmire explains:

> It reduces crime because you don't have the recidivism. If you treat people for their addictions and educate them, give them life-skill courses, have a re-entry program that works, you'll not have recidivism. If you cut down on recidivism, you cut down on crime. Also you save billions of dollars.... It all goes to trying to release a better person than the one you received.[7]

Numerous other states have jumped on, including Ohio and North Carolina.[8]

Some commentators argue that the concept of justice reinvestment is relatively underexplored and underdeveloped, and therefore caution is still needed.[9] However, if recent developments are any indication, cautious optimism is justified. The Council of State Governments Justice Center's report on justice reinvestment indicated tentatively positive results. Several states that had implemented justice reinvestment policies in recent years were examined for empirical results. Those states had experienced reduced recidivism for persons on community supervision as measured by decreased convictions for parole revocation and probation revocation. Parole revocations dropped by 29 percent for Texas, 34 percent for Kansas, and a projected 40 percent for New Hampshire. Probation revocations dropped by 3 percent for Texas, 16 percent for

Kansas, 28 to 31 percent for Arizona, and a projected 20 percent for Arizona. Decreases in prison population were 1,125 for Texas, a decrease from a projected influx of 700 new inmates for Kansas to a mere 10, and a projected decrease by 646 for New Hampshire. Decreased revocations also meant savings of $44.3 million by the 2008–2009 budget for Texas, and Arizona saved $36 million by 2010. New Hampshire saved from $7.8 to $10.8 million on account of revocations and an additional $179 million that would have gone to construction costs for accommodating the new influx of prisoners had they not initiated their reinvestment policy.[10]

Joanna Savage and Brian Vila, criminology professors from American University in Washington, DC, and Washington State University, respectively, advance what they call the lagged nurturance hypothesis: that it is better — vital, in fact — to allocate resources toward services that promote healthy child development and enhance nurturance conditions instead of toward incarceration. A key benefit of this is reduced crime rates, although this may not be observable until well after the nurturance conditions have been enhanced and the children who have benefited from them have advanced into adulthood (i.e., ten to fifteen years afterward). Their study examined the relationship in many countries between crime rates and several measures of child nurturance. Improvements in infant mortality rates, primary school enrolment, availability of hospital beds, and caloric intake were found to have significant and beneficial effects in terms of reducing crime rates.[11] They also argue that prioritizing incarceration and law enforcement at the expense of child programming is self-defeating. Neglecting child programming assures that more children will, instead of growing into healthy adult lives, end up in trouble and increase the demands for justice system resources. That in turn can encourage even more justice spending, to the even greater neglect of needed child programming. It becomes a negative and unproductive cycle.[12]

There are indications that justice reinvestment may be a sound approach in Canada as well. Brian Howe, former political science professor with Cape Breton University, performed a quite interesting study on the role of social policy in youth crime rates. Quebec had the lowest rates for overall youth crime: 1,882 incidents per 100,000 in 2001 and 1,539 in 2005, and for violent crime, 556 in 2001 and 522 in 2005. The Prairie provinces and the Northern Territories had the highest rates: The

Prairies averaged 8,047 incidents in 2001 and 5,963 in 2005 for aggregate youth crime, and 1,445 incidents in 2001 and 1,250 in 2005 for violent crime. The Northern Territories averaged 11,301 in 2001 and 9,180 in 2005 for aggregate crime, and 2,085 in 2001 and 1,674 in 2005 for violent crime.[13] Howe then considers a number of possible reasons for this variance. Differences in police charging practices may be a possible explanation. Howe downplays this as being a key reason behind such considerable variance, though, since police have less and less discretion for serious offences, violent offences in particular.[14] Rural versus urban demographics are not a sufficient explanation, since crime is higher in the more rural Northern Territories, but also lower in the more rural Atlantic provinces.[15] Socio-economic differences are also inadequate as an explanation, since Quebec has lower average incomes than the Prairies — or Ontario or British Columbia, both of which had crime rates in between Quebec and the Prairies.[16]

Howe also suggests that the Prairies and the Territories having higher crime rates also reflects having higher Indigenous populations, where the long-term consequences of colonialism are making themselves felt.[17] The Prairie provinces and the Territories have since made some efforts to expand health, education (e.g., the Head Start program), and violence prevention services for Indigenous children. They have also expanded child welfare services, showing greater respect for Indigenous traditions.[18] Howe adds:

> In comparison to the past, these policies and programmes have been progressive. But in relation to the scope of the problems facing Aboriginal communities, they have been grossly inadequate. In the territories, as well as across Canada, policies have had a very limited impact in significantly improving the social situation of Aboriginal children and their families.[19]

Howe argues that the strongest explanation is the greater relative emphasis that Quebec places on social policies that support families and child development. He describes the general trend in Canada as follows:

> Over time, with more pressures on government for the greater support of children and families, provincial and territorial governments have moved in the direction of the social responsibility model. Policies have been developed and expanded in such

areas as child care, parental leave, child benefits, domestic violence, and child protection. But reflecting the continuing influence of the individual responsibility model, the level of support for children and families has been relatively weak in comparison to much of Europe.[20]

Howe relates that it was a demographic crisis prior to the 1980s that prompted Quebec to overhaul its programs. The province had a birth rate that had declined to become the lowest in the developed world, alongside a rise in working mothers, single parents, and divorce and separation rates. Quebec's reply was a comprehensive program that included economic supports for families; family housing; a considerable range of services against family violence; health and social services for families and children; parental education and skills programs; and child care and parental leave systems.[21] He adds:

> Quebec also became a leader in the initiation of crime prevention projects under the National Crime Prevention Strategy. With the support of the federal government, a wide number of projects with substantial funding were launched in the province in the late 1990s and early 2000s, with a special focus on projects in support of at-risk children and youth.[22]

Another justification relies not so much on pragmatic appeal, but speaks to multiple substantive concerns.

PREVENTATIVE PROGRAMMING AS SOCIAL REPARATION

Reallocation of resources from the contemporary justice system to social programming as a more preventative approach is a key concept advanced by prison abolitionists. And the justifications for it go well beyond a pragmatic appeal to long-term savings. The war on drugs and the mass incarceration of Black people represents a newer form of racial segregation, warehousing Blacks as the undesirable Other away from mainstream society and thereby perpetuating white privilege and leaving Blacks in desperate social circumstances. Reallocation is seen as accomplishing numerous substantive objectives. It ends mass incarceration as an exercise in segregation. It also provides a social remedy for centuries of discrimination by shifting resources into fields such as education and health so as to improve conditions in Black communities.

It is also a form of restitution that has aspects of accountability, apology, and taking ownership of past wrongs against Blacks.[23]

Prison abolition advocates often stress the need for reparations to the point that the social purposes intended for reparations — moving resources away from prisons and toward socially revitalized communities — are held to be of far greater importance than any long-term savings enjoyed by broader society. And advocates insist that reparations must continue for however long it takes to accomplish its social objectives, even if broader society makes greater resource expenditures on the balance for years afterward.[24] Prison abolitionists often express concern that emphasizing long-term savings in the form of top-down policies that cut prison spending presents a danger without the accompanying and needed investment into communities themselves.[25]

Quite similar arguments have been made with respect to demands for reparations for Indigenous Peoples in various parts of the world, including North America, Latin America, and Australia. Indigenous demands for reparations stress the need to address the enduring social harms caused by colonialism, as well as the loss of past cultures.[26] Chris Cunneen, criminology professor with the University of Technology Sydney, views reparations as vital to reconciliation. Colonizing states such as Canada and the United States crafted their laws in ways that justified the subjugation of Indigenous Peoples, thereby denying Indigenous Peoples any avenue to pursue justice within the colonizers' legal systems. Cunneen sees reparations as a needed response to injustices against Indigenous Peoples by overcoming the limitations of state legal systems.[27]

The argument can certainly be made that reparations to Indigenous Peoples with reference to residential schools needs to go well beyond the Settlement Agreement. It is only by fully accepting responsibility for the schools — which includes acknowledging that they and other colonial processes underlie the horrid social conditions in which Indigenous Peoples find themselves — that Canada can reconcile with its Indigenous Peoples.[28] The AHF, by its very existence, amounted to an implicit admission of that responsibility. But the fact that the foundation was shuttered due to the withdrawal of funding also shows a lack of serious and sustained support by Canada for undoing the harms of residential schools.

The lack of funding for improving Indigenous social conditions has been seen in other fields as well. A 2000 report by the Assembly of First Nations found that federal child welfare expenditures per Indigenous child have generally been 22 percent less than provincial expenditures per non-Indigenous child.[29] A 2005 report by the First Nations Child and Family Caring Society (FNCFCS) found that discrepancy to be 30 percent.[30] Both organizations commenced an action in the Canadian Human Rights Tribunal with the intention of addressing that inequity. The tribunal ruled in favour of the Indigenous organizations in a 2016 decision that ordered the federal government to redress the funding inequities.[31] The federal government, however, continues to refuse to remedy the inequitable funding. Cindy Blackstock, the executive director of the FNCFCS, has at the time of writing filed at least nine non-compliance motions against the federal government following the tribunal's decision.[32] A report produced in 2016 by former Toronto-Dominion economics analyst Don Drummond likewise found that First Nations schools receive 30 percent less federal funding per student compared to provincial funding per non-Indigenous student.[33]

It could be said that Canadian governments have given relatively little consideration to addressing social programs in Indigenous communities. For example, Harper's Conservative government made its priorities clear. The Kelowna Accord had been negotiated over eighteen months between the federal government of Paul Martin and Indigenous leaders. It was finalized in November of 2005 and promised $5.1 billion over ten years to address Indigenous social problems in areas such as health, education, and poverty.[34] Martin's minority Liberal government was subsequently defeated and replaced by a Harper's minority Tory government. Under the original accord, $600 million would have been spent during the 2006 fiscal year on meeting the agreement's objectives. Harper's government, upon assuming power, replaced the accord with a budgetary allocation of $150 million during 2006 and $300 million during 2007 to address similar objectives.[35] Indigenous Peoples and their leaders have many times since decried this development as bad faith and neglect on the part of the federal government.[36]

During Harper's tenure, one initiative that naturally fell by the wayside along with the Kelowna Accord was the AHF. Richard Wagamese wrote in an open letter to Harper published in the *Globe & Mail*:

> You said "sorry" and you were not. In aboriginal context, an apology means that you recognize the flaw within yourself that made the offence possible and you offer reconciliation based on understanding the nature of that flaw. That reconciliation takes

the form of living and behaving in the opposite manner. You have not done this. In fact, you have continued in the same vein that made the original apology necessary.

Residential schools effectively separated aboriginal children from the influence of everything that could sustain, perpetuate and define them. When you cut funding for the National Aboriginal Health Organization and the Native Women's Association of Canada's health program and ended the mandate of the Aboriginal Healing Foundation, you did the same thing.[37]

By comparison, the Tory government made it obvious that investing in mass incarceration was a much higher priority for them than investing in social programming. The annual budget for the federal prison system went from $1.6 billion in the 2005–2006 fiscal year to $2.98 billion for 2011–2012. Much of that can be attributed to the Tory government's measures, including revoking the two-for-one credit for interim custody and amendments to section 752 of the *Criminal Code* that restricted the availability of conditional sentences for serious personal injury offences.[38] Funding for incarceration increased even more with the passing of the omnibus crime bill, which made extensive use of mandatory minimum prison terms for many offences. The Parliamentary Budget Officer estimated that come the 2016 fiscal year, annual spending for both federal and provincial prison systems would increase by $9.5 billion, with the federal government's share of costs amounting to 44 percent and the provincial share at 56 percent.[39] Ontario estimated its yearly costs for corrections would increase by $1 billion in order to accommodate the additional influx of inmates. Quebec estimated that its yearly costs would increase by $600 million. Ministers of both provinces publicly indicated that they were not willing to pick up the whole tab.[40]

Sufficient reparations require a significant overhaul, reassigning resources away from incarceration and into Indigenous social programming that minimizes the need for incarceration. But it was obvious that the Tory government had a preference for spending massive amounts of money on imprisonment to deal with crimes after the fact and comparatively minimal interest in investing in social programming that can address the root causes of many crimes. To call such an approach "cost-ineffective" is being generous from the pragmatic lens of justice reinvestment. And Wagamese's open letter makes it clear that such policy priorities are void of any element of apology, acceptance of responsibility, or any real effort to redress the harm done to Indigenous Peoples. Prioritizing incarceration over Indigenous programming also amounts to a form of victim-blaming. It blames Indigenous Peoples for being disproportionately incarcerated while absolving the Canadian state of any responsibility for creating the social conditions that have led to Indigenous over-incarceration.

It remains to be seen whether Justin Trudeau's Liberals will mark any kind of improvement. Trudeau promised to implement all the TRC Calls to Action as part of his election platform in 2015. He has come under criticism for dragging his feet in delivering on his promises for Indigenous reconciliation.[41] As noted, his government did delay repealing mandatory minimums for several years before repealing only a fraction of them. His Liberal government has, however, as of 2021, pledged $18 billion over the next five years to try to improve the living conditions of Indigenous Peoples.[42]

Recall that prison abolition envisions a fundamental overhaul in policy priorities to the point that human civilization at large will have little if any need for prisons as a sanction. It would be difficult to connect the Liberal government's recent actions with that kind of dramatic step toward a fundamentally different paradigm. Federal expenditures on the federal penitentiary system totalled $2.68 billion during the 2017/2018 fiscal year. Provincial and territorial expenditures on provincial jails totalled $2.55 billion during the same fiscal year.[43] I would not necessarily insist that mainstream Canadian society has to embark on a fundamental paradigm change for itself at the same time. What is demanded is that Canada do enough to end Indigenous over-incarceration, and the conditions in Indigenous communities that fuel over-incarceration, in recognition of its own responsibility for creating those problems. Even so, it may still be beneficial to Canadians and their leaders to ponder in earnest the questions raised here and by abolitionists.

The allocated $18 billion may be a step in the right direction. But some, of course, may question whether it is enough and whether it marks the kind of long-term and sustained commitment that is needed to address these issues. The prior discussions clearly indicate that policy objectives can change alongside governments as a result of elections. There is a danger that the priority given to Indigenous concerns can oscillate along with the vagaries of shifting government priorities. And that can result in a lack of long-term and sustained commitment to effect the fundamental changes that are needed. National Chief Perry Bellegarde of the AFN noted, with reference to the $18 billion allocation, that sustained investment in Indigenous programming lasting at least ten to fifteen years is needed to address the problems.[44]

I acknowledge that the prison abolitionists have valid concerns about limiting justice reinvestment to just a pragmatic appeal to monetary savings. But I also do not necessarily see the pragmatic appeal to long-term savings as incompatible with community reparations, at least for the purposes of moving forward for Indigenous Peoples in Canada. Both justifications can inform an overhaul of resources away from incarcerating Indigenous Peoples and reallocating them to investing in healthier Indigenous communities. This overhaul can signify Canada truly accepting responsibility, remedying the social conditions it has created through colonialism, and apologizing through concrete action and not just words. Reconciliation still requires both sides to buy into it in order for it to work. The pragmatic orientation of justice reinvestment theory can offer the incentive for Canada to buy in and commit to the reparations that are needed, that it would be in Canada's long-term self-interest to buy in. But there is a need for Canada to fully embrace all the objectives of justice reinvestment with respect to Indigenous Peoples. I agree that cutting back on incarceration spending without an accompanying investment in remedying Indigenous social conditions would indeed justify the critiques that prison abolitionists have raised with respect to justice reinvestment. The question remains whether Indigenous preventative programming can deliver on the promise.

INDIGENOUS-SPECIFIC PREVENTATIVE PROGRAMMING

Resource reallocations by themselves are not enough, and more than generic programming is necessary to tackle the problems in Indigenous communities. What is needed is sustained and comprehensive programming that integrates Indigenous cultures so as to best meet the needs of communities as well as individuals who may be at risk of falling into criminal lifestyles.[45] Todd Clear, criminology professor with Rutgers University, adds:

> Yet something is left wanting about the movement of correctional funds to social service budgets. The people who work for social services are not necessarily the citizens who live in high-

incarceration communities. Although the services they provide might result in improving the social-adjustment prospects for those who live in high incarceration communities, the salaries spent employing those service providers end up being spent outside of those troubled places.[46]

Lisa Monchalin, criminology professor with Kwanten Polytechnic University, argues that merely Indigenizing conventional Canadian institutions, police, courts, and correctional systems is inadequate to address Indigenous over-incarceration. She argues instead for preventative initiatives to address risk factors and which are operated for and by Indigenous communities themselves. One example she provides is the Nemi'simk ("Seeing Oneself") program for Mi'kmaw youth in Nova Scotia. She found that for a sample of twenty-nine Mi'kmaw youth in the program, alcohol abuse (a risk factor for youth offending) was substantially reduced. She also found a positive side benefit: reduced marijuana use among the youth, even though that had not been an explicit program objective.[47] Likewise, Dane Hautala, professor with the Johns Hopkins Bloomberg School of Public Health, argues that in order for preventative initiatives to succeed in decreasing Indigenous youth gang entry, they must address the multiplicity of social factors that encourage Indigenous youth to join gangs.[48]

This is an argument that has been strenuously made with respect to mental health services for Indigenous Peoples. The idea is that Western medicine is too narrow in its approach by focusing on physical and mental symptoms; Indigenous medicine also addresses the crucial aspects of emotional and spiritual health. Indigenous medicine may also be more likely to reach Indigenous individuals on a personal level.[49] Peter Menzies, an Anishinaabe social worker and psychotherapist, suggests that developing a comprehensive Indigenous healing model that integrates traditional cultures addresses not just individual therapeutic needs but also community and family structures, and this is key to undoing the harm of intergenerational trauma.[50] A survey of seventy-three Indigenous persons from various communities, mostly women, revealed that almost all of them believed that healthy parenting from birth was crucial in reversing the legacy of residential schools. They also believed that program development in communities, grounded in Indigenous cultures, to assist with prenatal care and early child-rearing was crucial to support this.[51] Evidence-based studies verifying the efficacy of this approach have been slow to come, but they have started to arrive.[52]

A study of the Knaw Chi Ge Win program in northern Ontario found that integrating Indigenous culture with mental health services resulted in lowering acute care admissions from three to four annually to one or even no admissions. This reflected clients becoming healthier and no longer prone to recidivism.[53] An evaluative study of the Mibbinbah Project in Australia, a mental health program that drew on Indigenous spirituality, observed that Indigenous men who regularly attended the program showed decreases in both domestic violence and dependency on substance abuse.[54]

Success stories come not just from Indigenous-oriented mental health services, but also family services, therapeutic services for survivors of trauma, and harm reduction programs. In a qualitative study based on interviews with eighty Indigenous fathers, several of the fathers expressed the hope that greater involvement of the extended family in contemporary child-rearing, with parallels to past kinship networks in pre-contact societies, could go a long way toward undoing the intergenerational disruption of colonialism.[55] The Nimkee NupiGawagan Healing Centre in Ontario has also provided anecdotal evidence of having successfully treated solvent abuse in youth.[56] As another example, a study conducted in northern Saskatchewan showed that Cree and Dene Elders' approaches to counselling and healing were effective in both reducing beatings of domestic violence victims and in mitigating the trauma and symptoms experienced by victims after abuse.[57]

Sometimes results can establish a direct link with reduced crime rates and recidivism. A study showed that the Sexual Abuse Intervention Program in British Columbia, which combines therapy with Indigenous culture and spirituality, was preliminarily effective in preventing sexually abused children from developing later problems. Program participants showed a reduction in developing mental health disorders (20%) in comparison to a sample group who did not go through the program (48.2%). Improvements were also shown when it came to becoming sexually aggressive later in life (10% to 25%) and developing a behaviour disorder (20% to 58.9%).[58]

An evaluative study was done of the Aboriginal Community Alcohol Harm Reduction Policy Project in Ontario. The program's premise was to provide an Indigenous community space in which alcohol could be used but not anywhere else in the community. The study surveyed key stake-holders (e.g., chiefs, counsellors) from the participant Indigenous com-munities on whether the project had reduced social problems. Responses were rated on a scale from zero (a problem never occurs) to four (a prob-lem is very likely to occur). Assaults went from an average rating of al-most three prior to the project to approximately 1.5 after the project had been in operation for two years. Vandalism went from almost three to a little under one. Sexual assaults went from almost one to zero.[59]

A government evaluation of the AHF found that it was successful in its mandate, with program clients experiencing improvements in famil-ial relationships, self-esteem, education, and employment. Indigenous communities also experienced strengthened volunteerism, community assistance networks, and cultural revitalization.[60] The problem is that the AHF, from the outset, was designed by the federal government as only a brief initiative, and this is simply inadequate to undo the ongoing harm suffered by Indigenous communities. The evaluation's respondents noted that over half of their community members were still in need of healing and that the complexity and intensity of their needs meant that there was an ongoing need for AHF-funded programs.[61]

There is considerable evidence, as outlined here, that Indigenous-specific preventative programming can go a long way toward address-ing community problems — but it is imperative that Canada makes a sustained commitment to reallocating resources in such a fashion. There are, as discussed, normative reasons that Canada should make that com-mitment: It would amount to Canada accepting responsibility for creat-ing Indigenous community issues through its colonial processes, with the residential schools representing an especially harmful process. It would mean reparations to rectify the problems and also be consistent with the official apology provided in 2008. It would, at the same time, be in Canada's own interest to embark on such a course. The social fallouts in Indigenous communities, and the resultant problem of Indigenous over-incarceration, has meant enormous resource expenditures. Fully addressing the problems may be mean greater resource demands in the short term but it can realize immense savings in the long term. But brief projects are not enough. It is imperative that this commitment last years, maybe even decades, until the problems are fully addressed. The next three chapters consider the role of Indigenous justice processes in ad-dressing these problems.

Notes

1   *Corrections and Conditional Release Statistical Overview: Annual Report 2011* (Ottawa: Correctional Service of Canada, 2011), 26.

2   Jamil Malakieh, *Adult and Youth Correctional Statistics in Canada, 2016/2017* (Ottawa: Canadian Centre for Justice Statistics, 2018), 5.

3   Howard Sapers, *Annual Report of the Office of the Correctional Investigator, 2010* (Ottawa: Office of the Correctional Investigator, 2010), 6.

4   Malakieh, *Adult and Youth Correctional Statistics in Canada, 2016/2017*, 5.

5   Rob Allen, "Justice Reinvestment and the Use of Imprisonment," *Criminology & Public Policy* 10, 3 (2011), 617.

6   *Aboriginal Peoples and Criminal Justice: Equality, Respect and the Search for Justice*, Report no. 34 (Ottawa: Law Reform Commission of Canada, 1991); *Cutting Crime: The Case for Justice Re-Investment* (London: House of Commons Justice Committee — First Report, 2009). For academic discussions that suggest that the concept of justice reinvestment is relatively underexplored and underdeveloped, and therefore caution is still needed, see Chris Fox, Kevin Alberton, and Frank Wharburton, "Justice Reinvestment: Can It Deliver More for Less?" *Howard Journal of Criminal Justice* 50, 2 (2011), 119; Shadd Maruna, "Lessons for Justice Reinvestment from Restorative Justice and the Justice Model Experience," *Criminology & Public Policy* 10, 3 (2011), 661.

7   Mary Branham, "Deal with Juvenile Offenses Early to Avoid Bigger Problems Later" *Capitol Ideas* 54, 5 (2011), 19.

8   Robert Coombs, "Justice Reinvestment Approach Increases Public Safety, Cuts Millions in Spending," *Capitol Ideas* 54, 6 (2011), 38.

9   Fox, Alberton, and Wharburton, "Justice Reinvestment," 119; Maruna, "Lessons for Justice Reinvestment," 661.

10 Council of State Governments Justice Center, *The National Summit on Justice Reinvestment and Public Safety: Addressing Recidivism, Crime, and Corrections Spending* (New York: Council of State Governments Justice Center, 2011), 56–67.

11 Joanna Savage and Brian Vila, "Changes in Child Welfare and Subsequent Crime Rate Trends: A Cross-National Test of the Lagged Nurturance Hypothesis," *Applied Developmental Psychology* 23 (2002), 51.

12 Savage and Vila, "Changes in Child Welfare and Subsequent Crime Rate Trends," 74–75.

13 R. Brian Howe, "Children's Rights as Crime Prevention," *International Journal of Children's Rights* 16, 4 (2008), 463.

14 Howe, "Children's Rights as Crime Prevention," 464–66.

15 Howe, "Children's Rights as Crime Prevention," 467.

16 Howe, "Children's Rights as Crime Prevention," 467.

17 Howe, "Children's Rights as Crime Prevention," 470.

18 Howe, "Children's Rights as Crime Prevention," 472.

19 Howe, "Children's Rights as Crime Prevention," 472.

20 Howe, "Children's Rights as Crime Prevention," 468.

21 Howe, "Children's Rights as Crime Prevention," 468–69.

22 Howe, "Children's Rights as Crime Prevention," 469. The source Howe refers to

is *Over $6.3 Million for Projects in Quebec under the National Crime Prevention Strategy* (Ottawa: Public Safety and Emergency Preparedness Canada, 2005).

23   William A. Darity Jr. and A. Kirsten Mullen, *From Here to Equality: Reparations for Black Americans in the Twenty-First Century* (Chapel Hill: University of North Carolina Press, 2020); Angela Davis, *Are Prisons Obsolete?* (New York: Seven Stories Press, 2003).

24   Allegra McLeod, "Prison Abolition and Grounded Justice," ucla *Law Review* 62 (2015), 1225–26; Colleen Hacket and Ben Turk, "Shifting Carceral Landscapes: Decarceration and the Reconfiguration of White Supremacy," *Abolition: A Journal of Insurgent Politics* 1 (2018); Angela Davis, *Are Prisons Obsolete?*

25   Hackett and Turk, "Shifting Carceral Landscapes"; *The Intercept*, "Ruth Wilson Gilmore Makes The Case For Abolition," June 10, 2020 <theintercept. com/2020/06/10/ruth-wilson-gilmore-makes-the-case-for-abolition/>.

26   Federico Lenzerini, ed., *Reparations for Indigenous Peoples: International and Comparative Perspectives* (Oxford: Oxford University Press, 2008).

27   Chris Cunneen, "Colonialism and Historical Injustice: Reparations for Indigenous Peoples," *Social Semiotics* 15, 1 (2010), 59.

28   Maegan Hough, "Taking Responsibility for Intergenerational Harms: Indian Residential School Reparations in Canada," *Northern Review* 50 (2020), 137.

29   Rose Alma J. MacDonald, *First Nations Child and Family Services Joint National Policy Review, Final Report June, 2000* (Ottawa: Assembly of First Nations, 2000), 14.

30   John Loxley et al., *Wen:de, The Journey Continues: The National Policy Review on First Nations Child and Family Services Research Project: Phase Three* (Ottawa: First Nations Child and Family Services Caring Society, 2005), 133 and 189.

31   Cindy Blackstock, "The Complainant: The Canadian Human Rights Case on First Nations Child Welfare," *McGill Law Journal* 62, 2 (2016), 285.

32   Anna MacMillan, "Canada Accused of Continued Short-Changing of First Nations Kids, Despite Order to Stop," *Global News*, February 5, 2021.

33   Jody Porter, "First Nations Students Get 30 Percent Less Funding than Other Students, Economist Says," *cbc News*, March 14, 2016.

34   John Ibbitson, "In Praise of a Flawed Native Accord," *Globe & Mail*, November 26, 2005, A4.

35   Sue Bailey, "Tories Gut Liberal Brokered $5.1 billion in Native Funding," *Toronto Star*, May 3, 2006, A6.

36   See, for example, Colin Perkel, "Fontaine Calls on Ottawa to Fulfill its Responsibility to Aboriginals," *Globe and Mail*, October 13, 2007, A7; Alison Auld and Keith Doucette, "Aboriginal Leaders Call for More Protests, Days of Action," *Globe and Mail*, July 11, 2007, A8; "Ottawa's Neglect Invites Indian Anger," *Toronto Star*, May 20, 2007, A16.

37   Richard Wagamese, "Aboriginal Reconciliation: An Open Letter to Stephen Harper," *Globe & Mail*, April 30, 2012.

38   Jeff Davis, "Prison Cost Soar 86% in Past Five Years: Report," *National Post*, July 18, 2011.

39   Ashutosh Rajekar and Ramnarayanan Mathilakath, *The Funding Requirement*

and Impact of the "Truth in Sentencing Act" on the Correctional System in Canada (Ottawa: Office of the Parliamentary Budget Officer, 2010), 13.

40   Tobi Cohen, "Tories Use Majority to Pass Omnibus Crime Bill," *National Post*, March 12, 2012.

41   John Paul Tasker, "'We Are All Impatient': Trudeau Promises First Nations Leaders Fundamental Change," CBC *News*, May 2, 2018.

42   "Liberals Pledge $18B for Indigenous Communities in 2021 Federal Budget," *Global News*, April 19, 2021.

43   Public Safety Canada, *Corrections and Conditional Release Statistical Overview 2019* (Ottawa: Public Safety Canada, 2019), 25.

44   "Liberals Pledge $18B for Indigenous Communities," *Global News*.

45   For an example of this argument made with reference to Australian Aboriginals, see Ross Homel, Robyn Lincoln, and Bruce Herd, "Risk and Resilience: Crime and Violence Prevention in Aboriginal Communities," *Australian and New Zealand Journal of Criminology* 32, 2 (1999), 182.

46   Todd Clear, "A Private-Sector, Incentives-Based Model for Justice Reinvestment," *Criminology & Public Policy* 10, 3 (2011), 593.

47   Lisa Monchalin, "Canadian Aboriginal Peoples' Victimization, Offending and its Prevention: Gathering the Evidence," *Crime Prevention and Community Safety* 12 (2010), 119.

48   Dane Hautala, Kelly Sittner, and Les Whitbeck, "Prospective Childhood Risk Factors for Gang Involvement among North American Indigenous Adolescents," *Youth Violence and Juvenile Justice* 14, 4 (2016), 390.

49   Lewis Mehl-Madrona and Gordon Pennycook, "Construction of an Aboriginal Theory of Mind and Mental Health," *Anthropology of Consciousness* 20, 2 (2009), 85; Robin Jones and Andrew Day, "Mental Health, Criminal Justice and Culture: Some Ways Forward?" *Australian Psychiatry* 19, 4 (2011), 325; Glen McCabe, "Mind, Body, Emotions and Spirit: Reaching to the Ancestors for Healing," *Counselling Psychology Quarterly* 21, 2 (2008) 143; Laurence Kirmayer, Gregory Brass, and Caroline Tait, "The Mental Health of Aboriginal Peoples: Transformations of Identity & Community," *Canadian Journal of Psychiatry* 45 (2000), 607; Rod McCormick, *Mentally Healthy Communities: Aboriginal Perspectives* (Ottawa: Canadian Institute for Health Information, 2009).

50   Peter Menzies, "Developing an Aboriginal Healing Model for Intergenerational Trauma," *International Journal of Health Promotion and Education* 46, 2 (2014), 41; Terry Mitchell and Dawn Maracle, "Healing the Generations: Post-Traumatic Stress and the Health Status of Aboriginal Populations in Canada," *Journal of Aboriginal Health* (March 2005), 14; Paul Memmott, "On Regional and Cultural Approaches to Australian Indigenous Violence," *Australian and New Zealand Journal of Criminology* 43, 2 (2010), 333; Phillip Lane Jr. et al., *Mapping the Healing Journey: The Final Report of a First Nation Research Project on Healing in Canadian Aboriginal Communities* (Ottawa: Solicitor General of Canada and Aboriginal Healing Foundation, 2002).

51   Dawn Smith, Colleen Varcoe, and Nancy Edwards, "Turning around the Intergenerational Impact of Residential Schools: Implications for Health Policy and Practice," *Canadian Journal of Nursing Research* 37, 4 (2005), 38.

52   Andrew Day et al., "Indigenous Family Violence: An Attempt to Understand the Problems and Inform Appropriate and Effective Responses to Criminal Justice System Intervention," *Psychiatry, Psychology and Law* 19, 1 (2012): 104.

53   Marion A. Maar et al., "Innovations on a Shoestring: A Study of a Collaborative Community-based Aboriginal Mental Health Service Model in Rural Canada," *International Journal of Mental Health Systems* 3, 1 (2009), 27.

54   Jack Bulman and Rick Hayes, "Mibbinbah and Spirit Healing: Fostering Safe, Friendly Spaces for Indigenous Males in Australia," *International Journal of Men's Health* 10, 1 (2011), 6.

55   Jessica Ball, "Indigenous Fathers' Involvement in Reconstituting 'Circles of Care,'" *American Journal of Psychology* 45 (2010), 133.

56   Colleen Dell et al., "From Benzos to Berries: Treatment Offered at an Aboriginal Youth Solvent Abuse Treatment Centre Relays the Importance of Culture," *Canadian Journal of Psychiatry* 56, 2 (2011), 75.

57   Chassidy Pachula et al., "Using Traditional Spirituality to Reduce Domestic Violence within Aboriginal Communities," *Journal of Alternative and Complementary Medicine* 16, 1 (2010), 89.

58   Patrick Holland, Kevin Gorey, and Anne Lindsay, "Prevention of Mental Health and Behavior Problems Among Sexually Abused Aboriginal Children in Care," *Child and Adolescent Social Work Journal* 21, 2 (2004), 113.

59   Louis Gliksman, Margaret Rylett, and Ronald Douglas, "Aboriginal Community Alcohol Harm Reduction (acahrp) Project: A Vision for the Future," *Substance Use & Misuse* 42 (2007), 1851.

60   *Evaluation of Community-Based Healing Initiatives Supported Through the Aboriginal Healing Foundation* (Ottawa: Indian and Northern Affairs Canada, 2009), 4.

61   *Evaluation of Community-Based Healing Initiatives*, 5.

8

ARGUMENTS FOR INDIGENOUS CRIMINAL JUSTICE

This chapter explores how Indigenous communities are making fuller use of contemporary adaptations of their past justice practices that parallel restorative justice. As of yet, there is not a universally accepted definition of restorative justice, but it can be thought of as a justice process that includes the participation of anyone who may have been affected by the crime (and not necessarily limited to lawyers and judges), with the goal of searching for alternatives to imprisonment.

At this point I wish to clarify my frequent use of both *prison abolition* and *restorative justice*. It is easy to conflate prison abolition and restorative justice, as their objectives align with each other to some degree. But there are differences. Restorative justice is consistent with prison abolition in that both try to minimize the need for incarceration. But restorative justice focuses on designing justice processes that are more inclusive and accessible, while prison abolition strives to fundamentally reorganize society to minimize the need for incarceration. Restorative justice may be one means to arrive at that reorganization, but it would certainly not be the only one. And if prison abolitionists accomplish the fundamental reorganization they envision, the need for any justice process, restorative justice included, would be minimized.

What I advance is similar. I myself want to minimize Indigenous incarceration, and my prior emphasis on preventative programming is consistent with prison abolition to that degree. I want to mitigate harmful behaviour by Indigenous people and in turn minimize the need for justice processes to the greatest extent possible. But I recognize that even with the best intentions and should optimal conditions in Indigenous communities ever become reality, there will inevitably be those few who make bad choices at times. The justice processes of Indigenous legal orders, which invite comparisons to restorative justice, are a means to ending Indigenous incarceration to the greatest extent possible. But those processes will need to remain available even after we reach optimal conditions for Indigenous Peoples, for those few who will still deviate away from community standards.

This chapter canvasses numerous arguments in favour of restorative justice, along with examples of success, particularly among Indigenous communities.[1] Controversies and criticisms have emerged over at least the past two decades with respect to both restorative justice and Indigenous justice initiatives. Those concerns will be considered in Chapter 9.

COMPARING INDIGENOUS JUSTICE TO RESTORATIVE JUSTICE

Essentially, restorative justice envisions a horizontal process where persons with a stake in a conflict negotiate a resolution, unlike the adversarial system where a judge imposes the resolution (also known as vertical decision making). "Persons with a stake in a conflict" is not restricted to the parties to a legal matter should the dispute proceed in an adversarial court. It can include a wider circle of persons who have been affected, even indirectly, by the conflict.[2]

In the adversarial justice system, the interests of the victim are collapsed into the state's interests in prosecuting crime. The prosecutor speaks to the harm done to the victim before an adversarial court. This has been criticized as deflecting attention away from the fact that in many crimes it is the individual victim, and not so much the state or society at large, that has suffered tangible harm and has a legitimate interest in obtaining redress from the offender.[3] The horizontal emphasis of restorative justice provides the victim with an opportunity to participate directly in the process. A restorative resolution will ideally have the victim's agreement and satisfactorily address the victim's interests, such as personal safety and healing the victim from any traumas.[4]

One reason Indigenous justice is often likened to restorative justice is that many Indigenous societies in the past held councils to negotiate resolutions to conflicts. These councils typically involved the presentation of material gifts to the victim, or the victim's kin, as reparation for the offence. These gifts were often accompanied by apologies or acknowledgements of responsibility. The acceptance of the gifts signified the resolution of the conflict and the restoration of community harmony. This practice is known to have occurred among the Cree, the Anishinaabe,[5] the Haudenosaunee,[6] the Dene,[7] the Twanas, Clallams, the Puyallups, the Nisquallys,[8] the Mi'kmaq in New Brunswick,[9] and the Coast Salish in British Columbia.[10]

A key goal of restorative justice is the repairing of relationships and furthering harmony between those affected by the conflict.[11] An integral part of this emphasis on relationship reparation is the reintegration of the offender back into the community as they correct their behaviour and strengthen relationships with those around them and those affected by their behaviour. Criminology professors John Braithwaite and Stephen Mugford hold that there is more than one facet to this reintegration, though. While one aspect emphasizes the role of community members who provide support and encouragement to the offender as they reform, another aspect — one that is not necessarily incompatible with the first — is that those who have been adversely affected confront the offender so that they understand the gravity of their actions and develop motivation to change.[12] Restorative justice pursues a resolution that aims to facilitate this reintegration. Restorative resolutions therefore often emphasize alternatives to incarceration, such as requiring the offender to perform community service, make restitution to the victim, and participate in counselling programs to address problems such as substance abuse or anger management.[13]

The ceremonial feasts of the Lake Babine people, called Balhats, combined several themes that parallel restorative justice. First, the aggrieved party had to present gifts to the offending party along with a declaration of what the offender did wrong. The challenge was for the offending party to provide reparation to the aggrieved party in the form of material wealth with interest. The reparation would be accompanied by a public affirmation of proper and expected behaviour, as well as a final recounting of the infraction, after which it was never to be mentioned again. These elements blended together to mark reconciliation and an end to the conflict. The ultimate goal was the strengthening of social relationships within the community.[14]

There are parallels between Indigenous conflict resolution and restorative justice. Both emphasize reparation to the aggrieved party and improving relationships in the community. Both restorative justice and Indigenous justice are presented as more constructive alternatives to dealing with crime, and this in turn has fuelled a number of criticisms against traditional Western approaches to crime. We will now examine in detail those criticisms, along with considerations, where appropriate, of their relevance to Indigenous Peoples.

WHY WE NEED ALTERNATIVES TO INCARCERATION

Restorative justice proponents frequently claim that faith in the threat of imprisonment to deter crime is misguided, and indeed we have previously discussed the significant drawbacks involved with deterrence through imprisonment.[15] There is also, of course, the aforementioned concern that prisons often expose more people to recruitment into gangs, thus entrenching them further into lives of crime.

Another argument is that reliance on imprisonment does not involve any rational consideration of whether it actually works, but rather an effort to score political points with a public that fears the spread of crime and wants the assurance of safety.[16] Cayley also views American "get tough on crime" and "war on drugs" policies in a similar light.[17] He asserts that such policies represent efforts to score political points with the public by showing that "something has been done," but without a rational consideration of whether such a policy effectively reduces crime.[18] Edward Bayda, a former chief justice of the Saskatchewan Court of Appeal, also condemns such policies as "politicians pandering to public fears and stereotypes in order to get re-elected."[19]

Such policies, however, do not get to the bottom of why crime occurs in the first place — a reliance on imprisonment fails to address the underlying causes of criminal behaviour. The ability to deter, either the specific offender or society at large, through more severe sentences is questionable to say the least. The certainty and swiftness of punishment may have deterrent value, but even then not in certain circumstances. Many Indigenous Peoples find themselves in social circumstances where deterrence, whether it is dependent on certainty or swiftness or severity, has little value. These include crimes fuelled by poverty, substance abuse, intergenerational trauma, negative peer association (e.g., gangs), and domestic violence. Prison will not only provide no deterrent to many Indigenous Peoples who come into the system, but it also makes matters worse by entrenching many of them further into lives of crime. Mass incarceration offers nothing constructive when it comes to addressing the social problems that have been left by residential schools and that fuel Indigenous crime generation after generation. This speaks to why restorative justice is held out as a better alternative to incarceration. Restorative justice discussions aim to flush out those underlying causes and then explore more constructive solutions to them.[20] Daniel Kwochka, a practising lawyer in Regina, Saskatchewan, states: "Aboriginal traditions suggest that the acts are no more than signals of disharmonies in relationships, and it is the disharmonies that should be focused upon."[21] Once the causes are discovered, then healing can begin for the offender, the victim, and others affected by the crime.[22]

GREATER VICTIM INCLUSION

Western justice systems often collapse the harm done to the victim into the state's interest in prosecuting crime. The victim does not tend to have direct involvement in the proceedings, while the prosecutor speaks to the public interest as a surrogate victim before the court. Restorative justice, on the other hand, provides a better alternative by providing a crime victim with a direct opportunity to speak to his or her fears, concerns, and interests in the course of the process, in an atmosphere of safety and honesty. By incorporating the victim's dialogue into the proceedings, their interests and concerns will be addressed in the resolution.[23] Through victim participation, and reaching a resolution that directly accounts for the individual victim's interests, restorative justice claims to better serve the victim better than state-administered punishment. The victim also benefits if the process effectively addresses the offender's behaviour. A key potential benefit is the victim's safety, which is particularly important after the victim has suffered serious violence.[24]

An evaluation of the RESTORE program in Arizona, which used victim-offender conferencing for sexual assaults, found that victims experienced a significant reduction in post-traumatic stress disorder symptoms by the end of the process.[25] An Australian quantitative study involving 245 Australian students and 314 American residents had the Australian participants either recall previous transgressions in their lives or a constructed academic infraction by another student, and they were asked to compare punitive responses versus restorative responses based on dialogue with the transgressing party. The American participants were asked to compare direct apologies from the transgressor, a third-party apology on behalf of the transgressor, a retributive response, and inaction. The study concluded that restorative responses were more likely to result in feelings of genuine forgiveness toward the transgressor.[26]

ENCOURAGING THE OFFENDER TO BE RESPONSIBLE

The standard sentencing process is thought to be problematic when it comes to encouraging offender responsibility. The sentence is given by a judge, which is often accompanied by a lecture. But chances are the offender will never see that judge again. Neither the punishment nor the lecture is likely to deliver any meaningful message to the accused.[27] If the standard justice system does not enhance the victim's concerns or further an offender's acceptance of responsibility, then community relationships remain fractured. Restorative justice is also held to be better at promoting offender responsibility — it does not aspire to punish for its own sake, but rather to heal the offender and correct behaviour. This leads to offender reintegration, which in turn is part of the broader agenda of restoring relationships and harmony in the community.[28]

The victim, and perhaps other members of the community, have the opportunity to describe how the offender's actions have affected them and the offender is forced to face up to the consequences of their behaviour. This in turn can lead to contrition, remorse, and an acceptance of responsibility. It can instill a genuine desire on the part of the offender to change his or her ways and make right by those who have been affected. This in turn provides stronger assurance that the accused will complete any agreed-upon rehabilitative measures, such as counselling and community service.[29] Restorative justice does not necessarily present a softer option than jail. The meeting with the victim (and perhaps others affected by the crime) and the rehabilitative measures that are employed can make a restorative justice resolution just as or even more onerous than a prison term.[30] In fact, an empirical study involving 101 psychology students participating in a deceptive restorative justice simulation found that the presence of the victim increased remorse, a sense of responsibility, and the sincerity of apology compared to when the victim was not present.[31] This forms the basis of the next criticism.

REPAIRING RELATIONSHIPS

Adversarial justice processes, such as the right to cross-examine witnesses or to present submissions that contradict the other party, are also critiqued by restorative justice proponents because of their competitive emphasis, which is held to be counterproductive to repairing and strengthening relationships in the community. This represents one of the key aspirations behind Indigenous demands for self-determination over justice. Canadian criminal procedure is often seen as culturally inappropriate and incompatible with Indigenous processes. The imposition of adversarial procedures has had the effect of suppressing Indigenous legal orders along with processes that nurtured community relationships. Indigenous control over justice, in theory, aspires to reinvigorate traditional processes that emphasize harmony and relationship reparation in place of imposed adversarial processes that do not have cultural legitimacy with Indigenous Peoples.[32]

MORE EFFECTIVE THAN INCARCERATION

Restorative justice proponents have garnered some pretty impressive statistical evidence to support their frequently made claim that by successfully changing the offender's behaviour and addressing its underlying causes, restorative justice can effectively address criminal recidivism. One study found that youth who participated in selected victim-offender mediation programs in California and Tennessee reoffended at a rate 32 percent less than those who did not participate.[33] A study of community justice committees in Arizona likewise found that youth who completed the program were 0.64 times less likely to reoffend.[34] A study of a program in Australia found a 38 percent reduction in driving while intoxicated and violent offences by juveniles.[35] And success with restorative justice has not just been found in lower juvenile crime rates. Meta-analyses of such programs, both juvenile and adult, in Australia, Canada, and the United States have consistently found a substantial aggregate reduction in recidivism relative to non-restorative approaches.[36]

Restorative justice has also been successfully applied to serious crimes that would normally warrant incarceration. In Ottawa, the Collaborative Justice Project applies restorative approaches to offences regardless of seriousness, such as robbery, intoxicated driving causing bodily harm or death, and sexual offences. Of those who completed the program in the years 2002 to 2005, 15.4 percent reoffended within a year of completion and 32.3 percent within three years. A comparison group of offenders reoffended at rates of 28 percent within the first year and 54 percent within three years.[37] A evaluation of a program in South Australia dealing with youth sexual offences found that those who completed the program reoffended at a lower rate (48%) than those who were dealt with through the standard court process (66%).[38]

Remarkable successes have occurred in Indigenous contexts as well. A juvenile justice program in the Northern Territory of Australia, for example, was able to report an 89 percent successful completion rate, and only one out of thirty-two participants from 2003 to 2006 reoffended.[39] Rupert Ross describes the success of the Hollow Water Holistic Circle Healing Program, which dealt with pervasive sexual abuse in a Manitoba Indigenous community, as follows: "Out of the forty-eight offenders in Hollow Water over the last nine years, only five have gone to jail, primarily because they failed to participate adequately in the healing program. Of the forty-three who did, only two have repeated their crimes, an enviable record by anyone's standards."[40] A follow-up evaluation found that the number of recidivists remained at two even after another sixty-four had gone through the program.[41]

The Aboriginal Justice Strategy provides federal funding to Indigenous justice initiatives. A 2016 evaluation of the strategy found that the programs it funded consistently achieved lower recidivism rates throughout an eight-year period following program completion, as per the following table:[42]

Recidivism Rates				
Time after Program Completion	Cumulative % of Offenders Who Have Re-offended		Likelihood of Participant Group to Re-offend Over Comparison Group (%)	
	Participant	Comparison	Likelihood Each Year (%)	% Difference Year 1 Versus Year 8
1 year	11.9	20.7	-42.51	-43
2 years	17.6	29.8	-40.94	
3 years	20.4	34.1	-40.18	
4 years	23.0	38.0	-39.47	
5 years	24.7	40.5	-39.01	
6 years	26.7	43.2	-38.19	
7 years	28.1	45.3	-37.97	
8 years	29.6	47.3	-37.42	-37

Note: Recidivism rates are fitted from Cox Proportional Hazards Model and are based on the average characteristics of the national sample: number of prior drug convictions (mean=0.2), number of prior violent convictions (mean=1.2), number of prior nonviolent convictions (mean=2.1), and age (mean=30).

This relates to another criticism that was previously described: that the high costs of incarceration are just not worth it.

Consider this in light of the success of the family group conferencing program in New Zealand, which drew upon traditional Maori principles of mediation. Judge F.M.W. McElrea reported that admissions to youth custody facilities dropped from 2,712 in 1988 to 923 in 1992/93. Half of those facilities closed as a result. Youth prosecutions also dropped by 27 percent from 1987 to 1992.[43] Mandeep K. Dhami and Penny Joy note that in a diversionary program in Chilliwack, British Columbia, an average of 12.45 hours was spent for each participant in comparison to an average of 34.5 hours for an offender in the standard justice system.[44] They then add:

> The insufficient funding of RJ initiatives in Canada is particular-ly difficult to accept in light of the large amount of money that the federal and provincial governments save through diversion cases from the traditional system into RJ programs. Volunteer-run, community-based programs are both efficient and cost-effective.[45]

The 2016 evaluation of the Aboriginal Justice Strategy estimated that $24,591,255 was spent on approximately two hundred Indigenous jus-tice programs in the 2014 fiscal year. That meant an average of $2,831 was spent on 9,039 clients. An average of $4,435 was spent on a compari-son group that went through the mainstream justice system, with the av-erage factoring in court room resources, prosecutorial services and legal aid costs but not policing costs. That meant savings of $1,604 per client, and aggregate savings of $14,498,556 over the course of the fiscal year.[46] And that is before you consider that expenditures made by the strategy pale in comparison to the federal budgetary allocations for correctional facilities. The argument is that restorative approaches represent the bet-ter demand on resources.

Proponents for restorative justice can certainly make a compelling case. There is more to the picture, however.

Notes

1   Larry Chartrand and Kanatese Horn, *A Report on the Relationships between Restorative Justice and Indigenous Legal Traditions in Canada* (Ottawa: Depart-ment of Justice, 2016).

2   Nils Christie, "Conflicts as a Property," *British Journal of Criminology* 17, 1

(1977), 1; Meredith Gibbs, "Using Restorative Justice to Resolve Historical Injustices of Indigenous Peoples," *Contemporary Justice Review* 12, 1 (2009), 45; Patrick Gerkin, "Who Owns This Conflict? The Challenge of Community Involvement in Restorative Justice," *Contemporary Justice Review* 15, 3 (2012), 277.

3   Randy Barnett, "Restitution: A New Paradigm of Criminal Justice," *Ethics* 87 (1977) 279; Ralph Henman and Grazia Mannozzi, "Victim Participation and Sentencing in England and Italy: A Legal and Policy Analysis," *European Journal of Crime, Criminal Law and Criminal Justice* 11, 3 (2003), 278; Albert Dzur and Susan Olson, "The Value of Community Participation in Restorative Justice," *Journal of Social Philosophy* 35, 1 (2004), 91; Stephanos Bibas, "Transparency and Participation in Criminal Procedure" *New York University Law Review* 81, 3 (2006), 911; Jonathan Doak, "Victims' Rights in Criminal Trials: Prospects for Rehabiliation," *Journal of Law and Society* 32, 2 (2005), 294.

4   Margarita Zernova, *Restorative Justice: Ideals and Realities* (Hampshire: Ashgate Publishing, 2007), 42–43; Marian Liebmann, *Restorative Justice: How It Works* (London: Jessica Kingsley Publishers, 2007), 26; Dzur and Olson, "The Value of Community Participation in Restorative Justice"; Susan Sarnoff, "Restoring Justice to the Community: A Realistic Goal?" *Federal Probation* 65, 1 (2001), 3.

5   Michael Coyle, "Traditional Indian Justice in Ontario: A Role for the Present?" *Osgoode Hall Law Journal* 24 (1986), 621–24.

6   Michael Coyle, "Traditional Indian Justice in Ontario," 615–21.

7   Joan Ryan, *Doing Things the Right Way* (Calgary: University of Calgary Press, Arctic Institute of North America, 1995), 33.

8   These societies lived in what is now Washington state. Brad Asher, *Beyond the Reservation: Indians, Settlers, and the Law in Washington Territory, 1853–1889* (Norman: University of Oklahoma Press, 1999), 25–26.

9   Leslie Jane McMillan, "Koqqwaja'ltimk: Mi'kmaq Legal Consciousness," PhD diss., University of British Columbia, 2002, 74.

10   Bruce Miller, *The Problem of Justice: Tradition and Law in the Coast Salish World* (Lincoln and London: University of Nebraska Press, 2001), 63–64.

11   Zenon Szablowinski, "Punitive Justice and Restorative Justice as Social Reconciliation," *Heythrop Journal* 49, 3 (2008), 18; Gordon Bazemore, "Young People, Trouble and Crime: Restorative Justice as a Normative Theory of Informal Social Control and Social Support," *Youth & Society* 33, 2 (2001), 199.

12   John Braithwaite and Stephen Mugford, "Conditions of Successful Reintegration Ceremonies: Dealing with Juvenile Offenders," *British Journal of Criminology* 34 (1994), 139. See also Nathan Harris, "Reintegrative Shame, Shaming, and Criminal Justice," *Journal of Social Issues* 62, 2 (2006), 327; Nathan Harris, Lode Walgrave, and John Braithwaite, "Emotional Dynamics in Restorative Conferences," *Theoretical Criminology* 8, 2 (2004), 191.

13   Zernova, *Restorative Justice*, 65–70; Liebmann, *Restorative Justice*, 27; Loren Walker and Leslie A. Hayashi, "Pono Kaulike: A Hawaii Criminal Court Provides Restorative Justice Practices for Healing Relationships," *Federal Probation* 71, 3 (2007), 18. Note that Tony Ward and Robyn Langland emphasize that

restorative justice and offender rehabilitation are distinct concepts. There are some common goals and overlap, but restorative justice has objectives above and beyond those concerning an individual offender. See Tony Ward and Robyn Langlands, "Repairing the Rupture: Restorative Justice and the Rehabilitation of Offenders," *Aggression and Violent Behavior* 14, 3 (2009), 205.

14   Jo-Anne Fiske and Betty Patrick, *Cis Dideen Kat: The Way of the Lake Babine Nation* (Vancouver: ubc Press, 2000), 97–101.

15   David Cornwell, *Criminal Punishment and Restorative Justice: Past, Present and Future* (Winchester: Waterside Press, 2006), 61.

16   Franklin E. Zimring and David T. Johnson, "Public Opinion and the Governance of Punishment in Democratic Political Systems," *The Annals of the American Academy of Political and Social Science* 605, 1 (2006), 265; Julian V. Roberts and Loretta J. Stalans, *Public Opinion, Crime, and Criminal Justice* (Boulder: Westview Press, 2006).

17   Cayley, *The Expanding Prison*, 23–26; See also Marie Gottschalk, "The World's Warden: Crime, Politics and Punishment in the United States," *Dissent* 55, 4 (2008), 58; Kevin B. Smith, "The Politics of Punishment: Evaluating Political Explanations of Incarceration Rates," *Journal of Politics* 66, 3 (2004), 925.

18   Cayley, *The Expanding Prison*, 3 and 98; see also David Garland, *The Culture of Control: Crime and Social Order in Contemporary Society* (Oxford: Oxford University Press, 2001).

19   Justice E.D. Bayda, "The Theory and Practice of Sentencing: Are They on the Same Wavelength?" *Saskatchewan Law Review* 60 (1996), 326.

20   Barry Stuart, *Building Community Justice Partnerships: Community Peacemaking Circles* (Ottawa: Department of Justice, 1997), 8 and 13; Rupert Ross, *Returning to the Teachings: Exploring Aboriginal Justice* (Toronto: Penguin Books Canada, 1996), 44–51; Melanie Randall and Lori Haskell, "Trauma-Informed Approaches to Law: Why Restorative Justice Must Understand Law and Psychological Coping," *Dalhousie Law Journal* 36, 2 (2013), 501.

21   Daniel Kwochka, "Aboriginal Injustice: Making Room for a Restorative Paradigm," *Saskatchewan Law Review* 60 (1996), 159. See also Moana Jackson, *The Maori and the Criminal Justice System, He Whaipaanga Hou — A New Perspective*, Part 2 (Auckland: New Zealand Department of Justice, 1988), 36–44; Juan Tauri and Allison Morris, "Re-forming Justice: The Potential of Maori Processes," *Australian and New Zealand Journal of Criminology* 30, 2 (1997): 149.

22   There is significant literature, both in Indigenous and non-Indigenous contexts, that stresses the healing function of restorative justice for offenders, victims, and other participants. See, for example, Jarem Sawatsky, *The Ethic of Traditional Communities and the Spirit of Healing Justice: Studies from Hollow Water, the Iona Community, and Plum Village* (Philadelphia: Jessica Kingsley Publishers, 2009); Douglas E. Knoll and Linda Harvey, "Restorative Mediation: The Application of Restorative Justice Practice and Philosophy to Clergy Sexual Abuse Cases," *Journal of Child Sexual Abuse* 17, 3–4 (2008), 377; Barbara Gray and Pat Lauderdale, "The Great Circle of Justice: North American Indigenous and Contemporary Justice Programs," *Contemporary Justice Review* 10, 2 (2007), 215; Philip Lane, "Mapping the Healing Journey: First Nations

Research Project on Healing in Canadian Aboriginal Communities," in Wanda D. McCaslin (ed.), *Justice as Healing: Indigenous Ways* (St. Paul: Living Justice Press, 2005), 369; Suzanne Goren, "Healing the Victim, the Young Offender, and the Community via Restorative Justice: An International Perspective," *Issues in Mental Health* 22 (2001), 137.

23   Mark S. Umbreit, Robert B. Coates, and Betty Vos, "Restorative Justice Dialogue: A Multi-Dimensional, Evidence-Based Practice Theory," *Contemporary Justice Review* 10, 1 (2007), 23; John S. Ryals Jr., "Restorative Justice: New Horizons in Juvenile Offender Counseling," *Journal of Addictions & Offender Counseling* 25, 1 (2004), 18.

24   Heather Strang, *Repair or Revenge? Victims and Restorative Justice* (Oxford: Clarendon Press, 2002); Katherine van Wormer, "Restorative Justice: A Model for Personal and Societal Empowerment," *Journal of Religion & Spirituality in Social Work* 23, 4 (2004), 103; Susan Miller and M. Kristen Hefner, "Procedural Justice for Victims and Offenders?: Exploring Restorative Justice Processes in Australia and the US," *Justice Quarterly* 32, 1 (2015), 142.

25   Mary Koss, "The RESTORE Program of Restorative Justice for Sex Crimes: Vision, Process and Outcomes," *Journal of Interpersonal Violence* 29, 9 (2014), 1623.

26   Michael Wenzel and Tyler Okimoto, "On the Relationship between Justice and Forgiveness: Are All Forms of Justice Made Equal?" *British Journal of Social Psychology* 53, 3 (2014), 463.

27   Cayley, *The Expanding Prison*, 219.

28   Ross, *Returning to the Teachings*, 20.

29   Cayley, *The Expanding Prison*, 219–20 and 290; Jennifer Kitty, "Gendering Violence, Remorse, and the Role of Restorative Justice: Deconstructing Public Perceptions of Kelly Ellard and Warren Glotawski," *Contemporary Justice Review* 13, 2 (2010), 155; Leonard Dagny, "When Offenders and Victims Sit Down and Talk," *CQ Researcher* 20, 9 (2010), 206; Daniel Johnson, "From Destruction to Reconciliation: The Potential of Restorative Justice," *Journal of Religion & Spirituality in Social Work* 23, 1/2 (2004), 83; Mark S. Umbreit, Robert B. Coates, and Betty Vos, "Restorative Justice Circles: An Exploratory Study," *Contemporary Justice Review* 6, 3 (2003), 265; Tara Ney, "Contesting Policy that Undermines Restorative Justice for Victims of Crime," *Contemporary Justice Review* 15, 3 (2012), 297.

30   Ross, *Returning to the Teachings*, 263 and 265–66.

31   Alana Saulnier and Diane Sivasubramaniam, "Effects of Victim Presence and Coercion in Restorative Justice: An Experimental Paradigm," *Law and Human Behavior* 39, 4 (2015), 378.

32   Barbara Grey-Kanatiiosh and Pat Lauderdale, "The Web of Justice: Restorative Justice Has Presented Only Part of the Story," *Wicazo Sa Review* 21, 1 (2006), 32; Richard Gosse, "Charting the Course for Aboriginal Justice Reform Through Aboriginal Self-Government," in Richard Gosse, James Youngblood Henderson, and Roger Carter (eds.), *Continuing Poundmaker and Riel's Quest: Presentations Made at a Conference on Aboriginal Peoples and Justice* (Saskatoon: Purich Publishing, 1994), 1; Alvin Hamilton and Murray Sinclair, *The*

Justice System and Aboriginal People: The Report of the Aboriginal Justice Inquiry (Winnipeg: Indigenous Justice Inquiry, 1991), 22. See also Robert Porter, "Strengthening Tribal Sovereignty Through Peacemaking: How the Anglo-American Legal Tradition Destroys Indigenous Societies" *Columbia Human Rights Law Review* 28 (1996–1997), 278–80.

33   William Nugent et al., "Participation in Victim-Offender Mediation and Reoffense: Successful Replication?" *Research on Social Work Practice* 11, 1 (2001), 5.

34   Kimberly de Beus and Nancy Rodriguez, "Restorative Justice Practice: An Examination of Program Completion and Recidivism," *Journal of Criminal Justice* 35, 3 (2007), 337.

35   Lawrence Sherman, Heather Strang, and Daniel Woods, "Recidivism Patterns in the Canberra Reintegrative Shaming Experiments (rise)" [unpublished, 2000].

36   Jeff Latimer, Craig Dowden, and Danielle Muise, *The Effectiveness of Restorative Justice Programs: A Meta-Analysis* (Ottawa: Department of Justice, Research and Statistics Division, 2001); Lawrence Sherman and Heather Strang, *Restorative Justice: The Evidence* (London: The Smith Institute, 2009); William Bradshaw, David Roseborough, and Mark S. Umbreit, "The Effect of Victim-Offender Mediation on Juvenile Offender Recidivism: A Meta-Analysis," *Conflict Resolution Quarterly* 24, 1 (2006), 87.

37   Tanya Rugge, James Bonta, and Suzanne Wallace-Capretta, *Evaluation of the Collaborative Justice Project: a Restorative Justice Program for Serious Crime 2002–2005* (Ottawa: Public Safety and Emergency Preparedness Canada, 2005).

38   Kathleen Daly, "Restorative Justice and Sexual Offences: An Archival Study of Court and Conference Cases," *British Journal of Criminology* 46 (2006), 334.

39   Alan R. Clough, Kylie Kim San Lee, and Katherine M. Conigrave, "Promising Performance of a Juvenile Justice Diversion Programme in Remote Aboriginal Communities, Northern Territories, Australia," *Drug and Alcohol Review* 27 (2008), 433.

40   Ross, *Returning to the Teachings*, 36.

41   J. Couture et al., *A Cost-Benefit Analysis of Hollow Water's Community Holistic Circle Healing Process* (Ottawa: Ministry of the Solicitor General, 2001).

42   Department of Justice, *Evaluation of the Aboriginal Justice Strategy December 2016* (Ottawa: Department of Justice, 2016), 48.

43   Judge F.M.W. McElrea, "Restorative Justice: The New Zealand Youth Court — A Model for Development in Other Courts?" *Journal of Judicial Administration* 4 (1994), 53.

44   Mandeep K. Dhami and Penny Joy, "Challenges to Establishing Volunteer-Run, Community-Based Restorative Justice Programs," *Contemporary Justice Review* 10, 1 (2007), 19.

45   Dhami and Joy, "Challenges to Establishing Volunteer-Run, Community-Based Restorative Justice Programs," 19.

46   Department of Justice, *Evaluation of the Aboriginal Justice Strategy December 2016*, 55–57.

9

ARGUMENTS AGAINST RESTORATIVE JUSTICE

Restorative justice, and Indigenous justice practices that resemble restorative justice, have come under increasing criticism in recent years. These criticisms will now be canvassed, along with examples that illustrate their relevance to Indigenous efforts to use restorative alternatives.

POWER IMBALANCES

Restorative justice idealizes a process with less adversarial competition and less emphasis on formal rules. However, a restorative process can become corrupted if there is a power differential between the participants. Without formal rules to impose consistency and fairness, and without lawyers as advocates, the party with greater power has a free hand to leverage for a favourable resolution by using its advantage in order to coerce, intimidate, or manipulate the weaker party.[1]

Some commentators have pointed out that the fairness of consensus-based processes is especially crucial in Indigenous communities. In Indigenous communities, some of which are very small, where everybody may know everybody else and where some will enjoy greater power and influence than others, can it be taken for granted that an accused will be treated fairly? Will a victim be treated fairly in a small community? Mary Crnkovich, a former lawyer who frequently represented Inuit clients, makes this comment regarding the assumption

> that "the community" is a relatively homogeneous unit. This assumption overlooks the fact that even relatively small settlements are segmented by such considerations as wealth, gender, family connections, inherited or acquired authority, and so on. Unless these inequalities are acknowledged and attended to, they can easily undermine the equality with which the pursuit of a common good is assumed to endow the sentencing circle.[2]

David Cayley further adds:

> A place is not always a community. For many native groups, a settled way of life is no more than two or three generations old. Old family rivalries persist in the new circumstances and are complicated when the new political structure created by elected band councils is overlaid on older patterns of influence and authority. The assumption that there is an identity of interest in these circumstances is questionable.[3]

If an Indigenous offender lacks support in the community, he or she may be vulnerable to the exploitation of a power differential enjoyed by community factions who are hostile to the offender. This can result in a chorus of disapproval against an offender that results in especially harsh sanctions.[4] Joyce Dalmyn, a Crown prosecutor in Manitoba, observes that such realities have tainted sentencing circles:

> If the feather gets passed around and no-one makes any comment whatsoever, I have heard a judge state, right on the record, "Well it's clear that because nothing has been said, obviously they're not willing to say anything good about this person therefore I can only draw the conclusion that there's no sympathy for this person and I have to use the harshest penalties available to me."[5]

These concerns are not exclusive to marginalized offenders, either. The prosecution, supported by the power of the state, would not normally be susceptible to coercive tactics on the part of the accused. The prosecution participates fairly in the process on behalf of the victim and can pursue measures to protect the victim, either in the final resolution (e.g., peace bond, jail term) or in the interim (e.g., a no contact condition as a part of bail release). Restorative justice idealizes the direct participation of the victim in the process itself. This, however, has the effect of removing the state from the process as the surrogate participant.

By explicitly incorporating the victim's dialogue into the process, the victim's interests and concerns should be addressed by the resolution, providing them with the opportunity to speak to their fears, concerns, and interests in a safe atmosphere and in complete honesty. One advantage that restorative justice claims over traditional sentencing practices is an increased capacity to inspire contrition and responsibility in the offender. This is seen as integrally bound up with the victim's participation in the restorative process. By including victim participation and reaching a resolution that accounts for the victim's concerns and interests, restorative justice claims to provide a result that serves the victim better than state-administered punishment. By effectively addressing the offender's behaviour, the victim also stands to benefit. The benefits can include the victim's safety, even after they have suffered serious harm (e.g., domestic violence).[6]

There are critiques, however, that suggest that this ideal can prove flawed and unrealistic in practice. There are some crimes that, by their very nature, involve a considerable power imbalance between offender and victim. Sexual assault and domestic assault are obvious examples that often occur in some Indigenous communities. There is the frequently expressed fear that trying to apply restorative justice or Indigenous peacekeeping to these kinds of offences will only replicate and reinforce the pre-existing power dynamic between the offender and the victim.[7] Annalise Acorn, law professor with the University of Alberta, points out that domestic abuse often follows patterns of apology (by the abuser) and forgiveness (by the victim) that sustain a relationship of power over the victim. Restorative justice replicates that pattern with its expectations of apology and forgiveness. Without having to face retribution or a permanent severance of the relationship, the restorative process can end up reinforcing that relationship of power whereby the abuser continues the pattern of abuse against the victim.[8] Even without restorative processes implicitly replicating the imbalanced dynamics of an abusive relationship, there are concerns that applying restorative justice to Indigenous domestic violence leaves open the potential for the abuser to overtly intimidate the victim, especially when the restorative meeting itself is adjourned or concluded.[9] Donna Coker, law professor with the University of Miami, in particular notes that applying Navajo Peacemaking in their tribal courts has seen domestic abusers use physical violence against victims even in the parking lot following peacemaking sessions.[10]

Acorn also argues that the very nature of the restorative process itself is intrinsically tipped in favour of the offender. If the process brings out the offender's life circumstances, and reasons why the crime was committed, it can generate a certain emotional momentum favouring the offender. It can encourage a feeling of fellowship towards the offender, a desire to welcome the offender back in as the prodigal son, that ends up prioritizing the offender's suffering over that of the victim.[11] This in turn generates pressure on the victim. The victim will be expected to extend understanding and forgiveness to the offender on the road to repairing relationships. The process may frown upon the victim for not meeting this expectation. If the victim will not comply, they are seen as acting against their own interests, against the interests of the broader community, imposing isolation upon both themselves and the community, and sabotaging a legitimate effort to promote harmony.[12] These standardized expectations of restorative processes thus favour the offender over the victim. This point has also been reinforced by Emma Cunliffe and Angela Cameron, law professors with the University of British Columbia and University of Ottawa, respectively, who performed a textual analysis of several written decisions involving judicially convened sentencing circles in Canada. Their analysis found that the text of the judgments placed (in their view) inordinate emphasis on the needs and situation of the offender, with at best scant or peripheral mention of the victims' dialogue or interests, and at worst none at all.[13]

As mentioned, Indigenous communities are often infused with power relationships that can corrupt restorative processes. This can compound the difficulties involved with applying restorative justice to offences that involve a significant power differential between the offender and the victim. The vulnerability faced by victims of crime during such processes can then be multilayered and especially intense.[14] Sherene Razack, professor of gender studies with the University of California Los Angeles, cautions that using community-based sentencing in Indigenous communities may reflect any gender imbalance in those communities. Indigenous communities are typically suffused with patriarchal power structures that replicate Canadian forms of governance. It is male Indigenous leaders who pursue community-based sentencing initiatives to the benefit of male Indigenous offenders who commit crimes against Indigenous women and children.[15] She adds:

> In the Northwest Territories, the Status of women Council has also been clear that women's relationship to community is fraught with contradictions. The Council's report on violence identifies as problematic community denial of abuse, alcohol used as an excuse for violent behaviour, and the fact that 'some of our worst abusers may be community leaders.'[16]

Anne McGillivray, former law professor with the University of Manitoba, and Brenda Comaskey, former research associate with the University of Manitoba's College of Nursing, note that this phenomenon is particularly worrisome where it concerns domestic violence. Indigenous women often find themselves victims of domestic violence where their concerns are not taken seriously in community power structures that support lighter resolutions for abusers. Indigenous women are often between a rock and a hard place — staying in an Indigenous community where violence against women is normalized or moving to an urbanized environment where they face racism and marginalization.[17]

Indigenous Elders have often been presented as idealized participants on whom communities can depend in realizing their visions of justice.[18] Certainly there are times when Indigenous Elders use their knowledge, wisdom, and status with sincere intentions to make a positive difference. The Saskatchewan Cree and Dene Elders' approaches to counselling both perpetrators and victims of domestic violence is one example.[19] Experience has unfortunately borne out, though, that there are times when individual Elders have fallen short of conducting themselves in accordance with expectations, with serious repercussions for justice processes. Bruce Miller, anthropology professor with the University of British Columbia, relates that abuses of power plagued the South Vancouver Island Justice Education Project. Elders, often from powerful families, would try to convince female victims to acquiesce to lighter sanctions for offenders under the project rather than using the justice system. Their tactics included attempts to lay guilt, persuade in favour of dropping the allegations, threaten use of witchcraft to inflict harm, or threaten to send the abuser or use physical intimidation. Some women felt that the problem was exacerbated by the fact that some of the Elders were themselves convicted sex offenders, which left victims wondering how seriously their safety and concerns would be addressed. The ultimate result was the end of the project in 1993.[20] In another example, an Elder named Neil Hall was convicted of sexual assault because he abused his position as a spiritual counsellor at the Winnipeg Remand Centre to coerce a female inmate into giving him oral sex on several occasions.[21]

GETTING OFF EASY

Another one of Acorn's key criticisms concerns an assumption latent in restorative justice theory as to the sincerity of an offender's display of contrition and accepting responsibility. That assumption may be unduly optimistic. Her argument is that the restorative process has devolved into a set of standardized expectations, a constantly repeated and rehearsed a script of displaying remorse, contrition, apologizing to the victim and others affected by the crime, and the offender's promise to mend their ways. As such, it is open to the offender to manipulate the process to their benefit by effectively playing the expected role, knowing that, in doing so, they can escape a harsher sanction. In the end, restorative justice does not necessarily promote a genuine acceptance of responsibility.[22]

The objective of playing to the script, of course, is to escape from the heavier sanction that the standard justice system would assess. Thus, so goes the criticism, restorative justice is truly softer justice. Mary Crnkovich related that Inuk accused in the Canadian north often saw sentencing circles as "a quick way out of jail."[23] Another example may be seen in an American case involving two Tlingit men named Adrian Guthrie and Simon Roberts. They assaulted a pizza delivery man named Tim Whittesley with a baseball bat. He suffered a fractured skull and was left deaf and partially blind. Under Washington state law, they would each have faced three to five and a half years. Tlingit tribal officials and a Tlingit Elder named Rudy James persuaded Judge Allendoerfer of the Snohomish Superior Court to release the two offenders. The conditions were banishment into a remote wilderness for at least a year and restitution to Whittesley. They would appear before Judge Allendoerfer again after eighteen months to determine whether further punishment would be needed. This resolution instead turned into a part-time camping trip whereby the offenders continued to live in town at leisure, while little to no progress had been made with respect to restitution. Judge Allendoerfer, when he found out what was going on, sentenced them to fifty-five and thirty-one months' imprisonment, respectively, and held them liable for $35,000 restitution to the victim.[24] These are not examples of restorative justice placing onerous obligations, and promoting accountability and responsibility, but instead reflect attempts to abuse restorative idealism to get off easy.

The incentive to use peacemaking or restorative process to secure lighter sanctions can then present troubling repercussions for crime victims. Lighter sanctions can trivialize harms done to victims, and this in turn can lead to a sense in a community that causing harm will not lead to any meaningful sanction. Potential offenders know that there is little risk involved. Potential victims, particularly vulnerable people such as women or children, end up in an unsafe environment.[25] This concern comes back to Silvia Mendes's point, that the severity of the sanction cannot be neglected altogether. The sanction still has to be at least significant in order for the other aspects of deterrence, certainty and swiftness, to have any real force. If the sanctions provided for by Indigenous justice systems are not taken seriously by offenders as signalling the need to reform behaviour and make right by the victim and the community, if they are viewed as getting off easy and devolve to the point that they become insignificant or meaningless for the offender, there may very well be serious concerns for community safety.[26]

DOUBTS ABOUT GREATER EFFICACY

There are also criticisms that question the capacity of restorative justice, and Indigenous initiatives that resemble restorative justice, to deliver any substantial or measurable improvements over the standard justice system. Restorative justice proponents have been able to marshal statistical evidence in support of their positions. As it turns out, for nearly any study that indicates success, detractors can point to another study that indicates failure. Some studies have suggested that some restorative justice programs have made little to no progress in addressing juvenile criminal recidivism.[27] Jane Dickson-Gilmore, law professor with Carleton University, and Carol LaPrairie found that among Indigenous offenders who participated in a sentencing circle in Saskatchewan from 1993 to 2000, 54 percent reoffended.[28] A study by Jacqueline Fitzgerald found that circle sentencing had little to no impact at all on Aboriginal criminal recidivism in Australia.[29] LaPrairie and Dickson-Gilmore also emphasize that Aboriginal justice projects have not made a significant impact over the years on Aboriginal over-incarceration.[30] Annalise Acorn assesses Sherman's study as follows:

> However, the evidence about the effectiveness of restorative justice in reducing repeat offending is equivocal. Empirical research on restorative justice and recidivism has found that re-

peat offending was lower for violent offenders, higher for drunk drivers, and the same for property offenders who participated in restorative processes in comparison to those who went through the court.[31]

Concerns about the efficacy of restorative approaches are particularly pertinent in the context of family violence, an issue that is especially troublesome for Indigenous communities. The latest statistical estimates are that at least 25 percent of Indigenous women in Canada have been victims of spousal abuse, a rate that is at least three and a half times greater than the rate experienced by non-Indigenous women. Indigenous men are also at greater relative risk for spousal abuse, at a rate of 18 percent.[32] Restorative justice has often lauded in theory as a more constructive alternative for addressing intimate and family violence crimes.[33] There are indications, however, that family violence is a crime that is especially intractable and difficult to deal with, either for the standard justice system or for restorative approaches. Other studies have concluded that restorative justice initiatives in the United States have failed to address family violence offences with any degree of improvement over standard justice.[34] Angela Cameron notes that sentencing circles have failed, both on a statistical level and in documented individual cases, to demonstrate improvement in domestic violence cases when it comes to either offender recidivism or realizing safety for abused victims.[35]

Recidivism may be thought of as a crucial challenge for restorative justice, since the ability to address crime more effectively relative to the standard justice system is one of its key claims. Nonetheless, other criticisms against restorative justice abound. Leena Kurki and Kay Pranis, who worked together as restorative justice researchers in Minnesota, contend that effects on victims and communities should be emphasized as more important measures of success rather than offender recidivism.[36] Dickson-Gilmore and LaPrairie question the success of the New Zealand family group conferences in this manner:

First, if victims were present in only about 50 percent of the family group conferences held, and 60 per cent of those victims felt positively about the process, this means that only about one-third of all victims obtained benefits from the conference process. While this is not to be scoffed at, it certainly suggests a much more modest degree of success than popular discourse around the FGC's would tend to associate with these processes.[37]

An evaluation study of the Hollow Water program discovered that only 28 percent of victims found participation to be a satisfactory experience in contrast to 72 percent of offenders. Only 33 percent of victims felt that they had the support of the broader community. The study also concluded that while the community was supportive of the general principles of the program, very few had either participated in it or had knowledge of its specific operations.[38] Dickson-Gilmore and LaPrairie also point out that there is gap in our research, as there is no empirical demonstration that restorative justice succeeds in one of its key claims, that it can improve relationships and harmony in the broader community.[39]

DIVERGENCE OF INTERESTS BETWEEN THE PARTICIPANTS

Restorative justice idealizes an agreement that harmonizes the interests of the participants, including the victim and the offender. As it turns out, though, there are plenty of questions surrounding that whether such a harmonization can truly occur. At the heart of those questions is that many times, the interests of the victim and the offender, and possibly other participants as well, may be so divergent that reaching an agreement may untenable. Acorn argues that not every victim may have an interest in the conciliatory aspects of restorative justice, particularly when applied to domestic violence. A contrived continuation of the relationship between victim and offender, where the offence reflects strained circumstances, may lead only to further hostility, resentment, and even offenders' repeating of the crime. This is particularly so in the context of domestic abuse. Sometimes the victim, for the sake of their own sense of security and peace of mind, may want the relationship to end permanently.[40] Acorn also argues that the denunciatory and retributive aspects of punishment may in themselves be something of value to the victim. She elaborates:

> Retributive justice aspires to bracket the desire for vengeance, to interpose the state between the victim and offender, and even handily to deal out proportionate allotments of punishment commensurate with the nature of the offence. Thus, retribution

confines the extent of comeuppance for the offender *by* claiming a monopoly on violence and insisting that the offender's suffering not extend beyond the token of punishment authorized and delivered by the state. At the same time, punishment stands for vengeance and gives official, though circumscribed. acknowledgment and legitimacy to the victim's and community's sense of indignation.[41]

Some programs have indeed been undermined by low victim participation rates, although the particular reasons for this are not clearly documented.[42] But it reveals, at the very least, that not every victim may take an interest in what restorative processes strive for.

The same could be said for offenders. Perhaps not every offender has an interest in accepting responsibility or reforming. As it turns out, available empirical evidence on whether reintegrative shaming can facilitate offender improvement and acceptance of responsibility relative to the standard justice system is equivocal. Some studies have found improvement,[43] while others have found little or no improvement at all.[44] A recent study of a sample of victim-offender conferencing sessions in Canada revealed that offender responses to victim input regarding harm and effects were often defensive and/or minimized responsibility and the harm caused.[45] An evaluation of the South Australia Juvenile Justice Project found that most young offenders apologized to the victim and that 61 percent were truly sorry for what they did. The picture was more complex than that, though. A minority of 43 percent found that the victims' story had an effect on them, while the majority said it had little to no effect on them. The same breakdown occurred when they were asked what was important about participating in the conference. A minority of 43 percent stated that repairing the harm caused was important, while the majority were more concerned about avoiding a downfall in reputation and being seen in a more positive light. This included 27 percent who did not feel sorry about what happened but participated in order to get off easier, 39 percent who said they participated in order to make their families feel better, and a nearly identical percentage who felt pushed into participating.[46]

Natalia Blecher, an Australian lawyer, argues that apology is a gesture that can be fragile, complex, or insincere and not readily accepted by the victim. There is a certain degree to which it runs against human nature for offenders to genuinely apologize and for victims to truly forgive past harms. She reinforces this point with an empirical overview of family group conferences in Australia. She noted that approximately 60 percent of offenders were sincere in apologizing and wanting to accept responsibility. This was not an overwhelming majority, though, as a third were observed to be defiant, non-responsive, or sullen during their participation. Compare this with only 27 percent of victims believing that the offender apology was sincere. Many of the victims viewed the offenders' apologies as motivated by other concerns, such as offenders trying to please their family members or trying to get off easy. Blecher thus notes that while the family group conferences did very well on measures such as recidivism and compliance with conditions, there was a gap between restorative justice theory and empirical results on other measures.[47]

NOT TAKING HARM SERIOUSLY

Another criticism is that when offenders commit the same crime, and with a similar degree of moral culpability, there should be at least some degree of parity with the sentences received by the offenders. Of course, restorative justice proponents emphasize broader societal contexts and mitigating circumstances in offenders' lives to argue for greater flexibility and individualization in sentencing. A point stressed by those who emphasize parity in sentencing is that for the same crimes with a similar degree of moral culpability, individualization in sentencing should only go so far.[48]

Another criticism suggests that restorative efforts to lessen formal state control may yield an ironic result. Restorative justice often imposes some pretty onerous obligations upon the offender. These can include community service, substance abuse counselling, and making restitution to the victim. These obligations can also endure for lengthy periods of time. There is plenty of room for an offender to slip. A typical inducement to comply with the demands of a restorative sanction is the threat of incarceration should the offender fall short in discharging his obligations. Kent Roach points out that determining what is criminal conduct is a highly subjective and normative exercise.[49] Expanding the reach of restorative justice initiatives, especially when extended to minor offences, can lead not to a more effective method of dealing with crime but to a frightening expansion of social control over citizens. Roach describes some of the mechanics of how this net widening can operate. A conditional sentence under Canadian law involves serving incarceration within the offender's own home under strict curfew conditions as an alternative to going to prison. A conditional sentence can include many other conditions, such as community service, counselling, and appearing before a court or probation officer as required. If an offender breaches a sentence condition, the consequences can be grave. There is a presumption, subject to a hearing before a judge, that the offender will serve the remainder of the sentence in jail. There is also a presumption that the offender will be subject to interim detention after a breach charge. The Crown only needs to prove the breach on the balance of probabilities.[50]

ECONOMIC CONCERNS

Another objection is that restorative justice processes can make immense demands on resources, often requiring additional funding for treatment programs, facilities, and human resources, either as volunteers or as paid staff.[51] Acorn includes resource demands as another reason we should not embrace restorative justice uncritically.[52] Roach also states that if restorative justice programs do not receive adequate funding, the initial enthusiasm may soon wane.[53]

There is a specifically documented example of this. The Mi'kmaq Justice Institute had apparently made some progress dealing with crime in Mi'kmaq communities and received the Canadian Law Award in 1998. However, maintaining minimum operating staff and a volunteer base was challenging enough within a small community. With shrinking financial resources, volunteer participation declined as well. The decreasing financial and human resources meant the institute was unable to meet the growing demand for justice programs in the communities. The staff were laid off in 1999 due to insufficient resources.[54]

A lack of adequate programs and resources can spell trouble for the success of the restorative process itself. Julian Roberts, former Oxford law professor, and Philip Stenning, criminology professor with Griffith University, warn that giving lenient sentences to Indigenous accused, but without the resources and programs to make a supervisory sentence effective, is a recipe for failure, as Indigenous accused will end up incarcerated following breaches of conditions.[55] Simon Owen, a member of the University of Victoria's Indigenous Law Research Unit, observed many sentencing cases resolved by guilty plea in Provincial Court #102 and the Downtown Community Court, both in Vancouver, as well as the First Nations Court in New Westminster. He found that these courts often engaged in discussions or used practices that shared similarities with restorative justice. For example, the courts often tried to ascertain the reasons behind criminal behaviour (e.g., drug addiction) with a view toward a forward-looking rehabilitation plan. He nonetheless found that many of these practices fell well short of what restorative justice idealizes. For example, plea bargains worked out between lawyers, brief submissions to the judge, and short, stilted comments by some offenders come nowhere close to the broader and fuller discussions that restorative justice promotes. Victim impact statements also fell well short of the goal of empowering direct victim participation in restorative justice.[56] Owen argues that part of this reality is that court systems themselves face heavy caseloads. This induces common law court systems to reduce the sentencing process to assembly-line justice.[57]

The troubling implication from this is that if restorative justice, with its emphasis on much fuller (and therefore lengthier) discussion, is implemented for a far greater breadth of criminal cases, it would make even greater demands on time and resources, at least to begin. And indeed, William Wood, criminology professor with Griffith University, questions the capacity of restorative justice to make any significant progress with incarceration rates. Some individual offenders might exhibit small-scale changes in their individual lifestyles and behaviour after participating in a restorative processes. But the benefits of those instances, even considered altogether, are so modest that it cannot alter the fundamental penal structures of Western justice systems.[58]

Certainly, there are concerns with an uncritical expansion of restorative justice or Indigenous justice programs without any heed for what can go wrong. Can the concerns be addressed, or are they fatal to the very concept of restorative justice? The next chapter will engage with that question.

Notes

1   Michel G. Herman, "The Dangers of adr: A Three-Tiered System of Justice," *Journal of Contemporary Legal Issues* 3 (1989–1990), 117; Michael Coyle, "Defending the Weak and Fighting Unfairness: Can Mediators Respond to the Challenge?" *Osgoode Hall Law Journal* 36 (1998), 625; Ilan G. Gewurz, "(Re) Designing Mediation to Address the Nuances of Power Imbalance," *Conflict Resolution Quarterly* 19, 2 (2001), 135; Terenia Urban Gill, "A Framework for Understanding and Using adr," *Tuledo Law Review* 71 (1996–1997), 1313.

2   Cayley, *The Expanding Prison*, 206. The quote is Cayley's description of Crnkovich's views in his words.

3   Cayley, *The Expanding Prison*, 207.

4   Ross Gordon Green, "Aboriginal Community Sentencing and Mediation: Within and Without the Circle," *Manitoba Law Journal* 24 (1997), 114.

5   Quote is in Green, "Aboriginal Community Sentencing and Mediation," 113.

6   Allison Morris and Loraine Gelsthorpe, "Re-visioning Men's Violence against Female Partners," *Howard Law Journal* 39, 4 (2000), 412; Jonathan Rudin and Kent Roach, "Broken Promises: A Response to Stenning and Robert's' 'Empty Promises,' Colloquy on 'Empty Promises: Parliament, the Supreme Court, and the Sentencing of Aboriginal Offenders," *Saskatchewan Law Review* 65, 1 (2002), 30–31.

7   Julie Stubbs, "Domestic Violence and Women's Safety: Feminist Challenges to Restorative Justice," in Heather Strang and John Braithwaite (eds.), *Restorative Justice and Family Violence* (Cambridge: Cambridge University Press, 2002); Quince C. Hopkins, Mary Koss, and Karen Bachar, "Applying Restorative Justice to Ongoing Intimate Violence: Problems and Possibilities," *St. Louis University Public Law Review* 23, 1 (2004), 289; Angela Cameron, "Stopping the Violence: Canadian Feminist Debates on Restorative Justice and Intimate Violence," *Theoretical Criminology* 10, 1 (2006), 49.

8   Annalise Acorn, *Compulsory Compassion: A Critique of Restorative Justice* (Vancouver: ubc Press, 2004), 74.

9   Jane Dickson-Gilmore, "Whither Restorativeness? Restorative Justice and the Challenge of Intimate Violence in Aboriginal Communities," *Canadian Journal of Criminology and Criminal Justice* 56, 4 (2014), 417.

10 Donna Coker, "Restorative Justice, Navajo Peacemaking and Domestic Violence," *Theoretical Criminology* 10, 1 (2006), 67.

11 Coker, "Restorative Justice, Navajo Peacemaking and Domestic Violence," 150–58.

12 Coker, "Restorative Justice, Navajo Peacemaking and Domestic Violence," 75–76.

13 Emma Cunliffe and Angela Cameron, "Writing the Circle: Judicially Convened Sentencing Circles and the Textual Organization of Criminal Justice," *Canadian Journal of Women & the Law* 19, 1 (2007), 1.

14 Anne McGillivray and Brenda Comaskey, *Black Eyes All of the Time: Intimate Violence, Aboriginal Women, and the Justice System* (Toronto: University of Toronto Press, 1999), 116.

15 Sherene Razack, *Looking White People in the Eye: Gender, Race, and Culture in Courtrooms and Classrooms* (Toronto: University of Toronto Press, 1998), 77–78.

16 Razack, *Looking White People in the Eye*, 66.

17 McGillivray and Comaskey, *Black Eyes all the Time*.

18 Mary Ellen Turpel-Lafond and Patricia Monture-Angus, "Aboriginal Peoples and Canadian Criminal Law: Rethinking Justice," Special Edition on Aboriginal Justice, *University of British Columbia Law Review* (1992), 246.

19 Pachula et al., "Using Traditional Spirituality," 89.

20 Miller, *The Problem of Justice*, 198–99.

21 Dean Pritchard, "Perv Elder Spared Jail," *Winnipeg Sun*, July 28, 2010, 3.

22   Acorn, *Compulsory Compassion*, 56–60.

23   Quoted in Cayley, *The Expanding Prison*, 206.

24   William C. Bradford, "Reclaiming Indigenous Autonomy on the Path to Peaceful Coexistence: The Theory, Practice, and Limitations of Tribal Peacemaking in Indian Dispute Resolution," *Notre Dame Law Review* 76 (2000), 590–96.

25   Razack, *Looking White People in the Eye*; Pauktuutit Inuit Women's Association, *Setting Standards First: Community-Based Justice and Corrections in Inuit Canada* (Ottawa: Pauktuutit, 1995); Kelly MacDonald, *Literature Review: Implications of Restorative Justice in Cases of Violence against Aboriginal Women and Children* (Vancouver: Aboriginal Women's Network, 2001).

26   Royal Commission on Aboriginal Peoples, *Bridging the Cultural Divide: A Report on Aboriginal People and Criminal Justice in Canada* (Ottawa: Minister of Supply and Services Canada, 1996), 269.

27   Hennessey Hayes, "Assessing Reoffending in Restorative Justice Conferences," *Australian and New Zealand Journal of Criminology* 38, 1 (2005), 77; Mike Niemeyer and David Schicor, "A Preliminary Study of a Large Victim/Offender Reconciliation Program," *Federal Probation* 60 (1996), 30; Mark S. Umbreit, *Victim Meets Offender: The Impact of Restorative Justice and Mediation* (Monsey: Willow Tree Press, 1994); Sudipto Roy, "Two Types of Juvenile Restitution Programs in Two Midwestern Counties: A Comparative Study," *Federal Probation* 57 (1993), 48.

28   Carol LaPrairie and E. Jane Dickson-Gilmore, *Will the Circle Be Unbroken? Aboriginal Communities, Restorative Justice, and the Challenges of Conflict and Change* (Toronto: University of Toronto Press, 2005), 218.

29   Jacqueline Fitzgerald, "Does Circle Sentencing Reduce Aboriginal Offending?" *Contemporary Issues in Crime and Justice* 115 (2008), 1.

30   LaPrairie and Dickson-Gilmore, *Will the Circle Be Unbroken?*, 208–12.

31   Acorn, *Compulsory Compassion*, 61.

32   Jodi-Anne Brzozowski, Andrea Taylor Butts, and Sara Johnson, *Victimization and Offending among the Aboriginal Population in Canada* (Ottawa: Canadian Centre for Justice Statistics, 2006), 6.

33   Peggy Grauwiler and Linda G. Mills, "Moving Beyond the Criminal Justice Paradigm: A Radical Restorative Justice Approach to Intimate Abuse," *Journal of Sociology and Social Welfare* 31, 1 (2004), 49; Robert J. Hampton et al., "Evaluating Domestic Violence Interventions for Black Women," *Journal of Aggression, Maltreatment, & Trauma* 16, 3 (2008), 330; Van Wormer, "Restorative Justice as Social Justice," 107.

34   Andrew Fulkerson, "The Use of Victim Impact Panels in Domestic Violence Cases: A Restorative Justice Approach," *Contemporary Justice Review* 4, 3–4 (2001), 355; Robert C. Davis, "Brooklyn Mediation Field Test," *Journal of Experimental Criminology* 5, 1 (2009), 25.

35   Angela Cameron, "Sentencing Circles and Intimate Violence: A Feminist Perspective," *Canadian Journal of Woman & the Law* 18, 2 (2006), 479.

36   Leena Kurki and Kay Pranis, *Restorative Justice as Direct Democracy and Community Building* (St. Paul: Minnesota Department of Corrections, Community and Juvenile Services Division, 2000).

37 LaPrairie and Dickson-Gilmore, *Will the Circle Be Unbroken?*, 195.

38 Therese Lajeunesse, *Evaluation of the Hollow Water Community Holistic Circle Healing Project* (Ottawa: Solicitor General Canada, 1996).

39 LaPrairie and Dickson-Gilmore, *Will the Circle Be Unbroken?*, 209–10.

40 Acorn, *Compulsory Compassion*, 99–119.

41 Acorn, *Compulsory Compassion*, 53.

42 Ros Burnett and Catherine Appleton, *Joined-up Youth Justice: Tackling Youth Crime in Partnership* (Lyme Regis: Russell Publishing, 2004); Adam Crawford and Tim Newburn, *Youth Offending and Restorative Justice: Implementing Reform in Youth Justice* (Devon: Willan Publishing, 2003); David Karp, Gordon Bazemore, and J.D. Chesire, "The Role and Attitudes of Restorative Board Members: A Case Study of Volunteers in Community Justice," *Crime & Delinquency* 50, 4 (2004), 487; Christina Stahlkopf, "Restorative Justice, Rhetoric or Reality?: Conferencing with Young Offenders," *Contemporary Justice Review* 12, 3 (2006), 231; Gerkin, "Who Owns This Conflict?," 277.

43 Avery Calhoun and William Pelech, "Responding to Young People Responsible for Harm: A Comparative Study of Restorative and Conventional Approaches," *Contemporary Justice Review* 13, 3 (2010), 287; Barton Poulson, "A Third Voice: A Review of Empirical Research on the Psychological Outcomes of Restorative Justice," *Utah Law Review* (2003), 167; Hee Joo Kim and Jurg Gerber, "The Effectiveness of Reintegrative Shaming and Restorative Justice Conferences: Focusing on Juvenile Offenders' Perceptions in Australian Reintegrative Shaming Experiments," *International Journal of Offender Therapy and Comparative Criminology* 56, 7 (2012), 1063.

44 Ibolya Losoncz and Graham Tyson, "Parental Shaming and Adolescent Delinquency," *Australian and New Zealand Journal of Criminology* 40, 2 (2007), 161; Kimberly J. Cook, "Doing Difference and Accountability in Restorative Justice Conferences," *Theoretical Criminology* 10, 1 (2006), 107; Hee and Gerber, "The Effectiveness of Reintegrative Shaming and Restorative Justice Conferences," 1063.

45 Scott J. Kenney and Don Clairmont, "Using the Victim as Both Sword and Shield," *Journal of Contemporary Ethnography* 38, 3 (2009), 279.

46 Kathleen Daly, "Mind the Gap: Restorative Justice in Theory and Practice," in Andrew Von Hirsch, Julian V. Roberts, and Anthony Bottoms (eds.), *Restorative Justice and Criminal Justice: Competing or Reconcilable Paradigms?* (Oxford: Hart Publishing, 2003), 224.

47 Natalia Blecher, "Sorry Justice: Apology in Australian Family Group Conferencing," *Psychiatry, Psychology and Law* 18, 1 (2011), 95.

48 Phillip Stenning and Julian V. Robert, "The Sentencing of Aboriginal Offenders in Canada: A Rejoinder," Colloquy on "Empty Promises: Parliament, the Supreme Court, and the Sentencing of Aboriginal Offenders" 65, 1 (2002), 85.

49 Kent Roach, "Changing Punishment at the Turn of the Century: Restorative Justice on the Rise," *Canadian Journal of Criminology* 42 (2000), 259–60.

50 Roach, "Changing Punishment at the Turn of the Century," 261.

51 Hughes and Mossman, "Re-Thinking Access to Criminal Justice in Canada," *Windsor Review of Legal and Social Issues* 13 (2002), 117–19.

52 Acorn, *Compulsory Compassion*, 11–12.
53 Roach, "Changing Punishment at the Turn of the Century," 269.
54 Leslie Jane McMillan, "Koqqwaja'ltimk: Mi'kmaq Legal Consciousness," PhD diss., University of British Columbia, 2002, 258–60.
55 Stenning and Robert, "The Sentencing of Aboriginal Offenders in Canada," 88.
56 Simon Owen, "A Crack in Everything: Restorative Possibilities of Plea-Based Sentencing Courts," *Alberta Law Review* 48 (2011), 871–86.
57 Simon Owen, "A Crack in Everything," 860–61 and 888.
58 William Wood, "Why Restorative Justice Will Not Reduce Incarceration," *British Journal of Criminology* 55, 5 (2015), 883.

10

WAYS FORWARD FOR INDIGENOUS JUSTICE

There is no doubt that Acorn and others have made some fairly powerful and persuasive critiques against restorative justice. The issue that needs to be addressed, though, is whether the problems they have identified are fatal to restorative justice endeavours. I would argue that they provide valuable insights into what can go wrong and what needs to be avoided. The criticisms do not ultimately reveal fatal flaws for contemporary adaptations of Indigenous justice that resemble restorative justice.

PROCEDURAL PROTECTIONS

Many of the problems may in fact stem from parties being left to their own devices, without any form of oversight. It is precisely when there is this lack of oversight that the stronger party can exploit a power differential.

There is the possibility that these concerns can be addressed so that Indigenous justice is fair to all of its constituents and is not abused. Chief Justice Robert Yazzie of the Navajo Supreme Court states: "What, you might say, if the victim is being coerced? That is why we have the victim's relatives attend."[1] How about if restorative discussions occur outside the courtroom? It is then obviously more difficult for formal judicial supervision to ensure fairness. Ross Gordon Green, a former defence lawyer in Manitoba, suggests that mediators provide an "outside of court" alternative as follows: "trained and experienced community members could eventually perform the facilitation function currently performed by judges during circle sentencing."[2] This is indeed a feature of the Navajo Peacemaker Court, whereby Peacemakers, who are trained in mediation and Navajo culture, oversee the out-of-court discussions between disputants. As mentioned, Hollow Water generated considerable success in the context of pervasive sexual abuse. Green ascribes this in part to the program ensuring that support teams were assigned to work with both the offender and the victim. The victim and offender would not be brought together into the restorative process until they were both ready to face each other. As such, it is apparently possible to address even serious power imbalances with intervention prior to the restorative process itself.[3]

And indeed, a British case study may offer tentative support in favour of Green's conclusions and contrary to the critiques against restorative justice. Their study involved a woman named Lucy, who was sexually abused as a child by an older member of the family. The conference included a senior police officer involved with Lucy's case, Lucy's rape crisis counsellor, and the conference facilitator. The abuser had the option to have a support person present with him during the conference but chose not to. The conference facilitator and the counsellor were there at least in part to manage and minimize the risks with holding a restorative justice conference for an offence like sexual assault that involves an inherent power imbalance between the offender and the victim. Lucy, benefiting from the measures that were in place to ensure equitable participation, felt that she had a real opportunity to speak to her feelings over what had happened and that she came away from the conference with a sense of closure and being able to move forward. She also felt it was a considerable improvement over the standard justice system, where she felt revictimized by the investigative police officer deciding not to investigative her complaint fully on the basis that it was a stale matter.[4]

There is still a need for further research on the subject of how the criticisms against restorative justice, and Indigenous justice, can be addressed.[5] I would go a little further and suggest that what is needed is research into how these concerns can be addressed in ways that are sensitive to the cultures, and particular needs, of Indigenous communities.

For example, I have previously suggested that the *Canadian Charter of Rights and Freedoms* can have a role to play in ensuring the fairness of contemporary adaptations of Indigenous justice. The concept is one of culturally sensitive interpretation of legal rights applicable to criminal justice. One of my proposals is the idea that Indigenous communities can administer their own community courts. These courts would have an important role in ensuring that the participants in the process behave fairly towards each other, without intimidation or coercion. This concept, however, is not necessarily a poor imitation of the Canadian justice system, or Indigenization as it were. The customary law of Indigenous communities would govern the disputes and the resolutions that are used irrespective of which offences they are dealing with, without reference to Canadian sentencing law that sustains offence bifurcation. So long as the participants act fairly toward each other, without coercion or intimidation, the parties' resolution becomes binding on a community court judge such that he or she must adopt it as a court order. The caveat to this idea is that community court judges intervene only when one party has tried to exploit a power differential or coerce the other party. The community court judge could, for example, suspend matters *sine die* (indefinitely) if an accused is being marginalized by the process. If it is the victim who is being coerced or harassed, the community court judge could then impose a resolution that prioritizes the victim's safety, even over the objections of the other party. A community court judge thus becomes not so much a full-fledged judge but more of an arbitrator and mediator with some judicial powers.[6] But as previously indicated, more research to address the concerns associated with restorative justice and contemporary adaptations of Indigenous justice is recommended.

MAKING INDIGENOUS JUSTICE MORE EFFECTIVE

There are also, of course, concerns about the efficacy of the restorative process. This debate over whether restorative justice is truly capable of fulfilling its stated goals suggests an entrenched war of statistics and theoretical arguments that cannot be resolved. I would propose, however, that there is still the potential, although many of the studies we have mentioned suggest we clearly have a long way to go before realizing it fully. There is, nonetheless, some encouraging evidence not just with respect to recidivism, but also for victim satisfaction and safety as well. An Australian study that surveyed victim satisfaction with participating in restorative programs found overwhelmingly positive responses to questions such having been pleased with the outcome (85 to 91%), having experienced any negative consequences afterward (3 to 10%), whether they were willing to do it again (87 to 92%), and whether they would recommend it to anyone else (84 to 92%).[7] The evaluation of the South Australia Juvenile Justice Project found that 60 percent of victim participants in 1999 indicated that they were fully recovered and that the offence was truly behind them. Fear of the offender dropped from

40 percent prior to participating in a conference to 25 percent after the conference, and even further to 18 percent a year after the conference.[8] The issue of addressing victim safety and interests is, however, still unresolved, as is the issue of recidivism. It must again be asserted, though, notwithstanding Kurki and Pranis's argument, that reducing offender recidivism and addressing victim safety can be intertwined within a community. If crime drops, the community is relatively safer than beforehand, if I may indulge in simple logic. A study that interviewed participants in a conferencing program in Honolulu, Hawaii, found both overwhelming evidence of victim satisfaction (fifty-nine out of sixty-two interviewees) and half the recidivism rate of offender participants in comparison to the non-participant control group.[9] A meta-analysis of previous research spanning four decades found that offenders and victims alike were more satisfied with restorative processes and that offenders were less likely to reoffend compared to standard court processes.[10]

How, then, is the question to be resolved when the empirical evidence is equivocal on every front? Why does it work in some instances but not others? One explanation that readily comes to mind is the issue of financial support and resources. Restorative justice initiatives will be empty shells unless certain programs are available to the community to enable meaningful resolutions. These can include treatment programs, educational programs, job training initiatives, life skills training, and counselling services.[11] Initiatives will require monetary resources for treatment programming and facilities, for operational costs, and for volunteers or paid staff. Restorative justice also places significant demands for human resources.[12] In small Indigenous communities, finding enough committed individuals to provide qualified staff or a sustained volunteer base can be a challenge. Personnel are needed to run the project itself, and this can include monitoring offender progress. In small communities, there may not be as stringent a need for justice staff to monitor the offender, since the offender may be ever under the watchful eye of his or her peers. The concept of community control may not be as meaningful in urban areas, however, where an offender would enjoy a greater degree of mobility and a less intimate sense of membership in a community than would be the case in a small, isolated locale. This raises the possibility that an urban Indigenous community is less able to conduct local offender follow-up and monitoring to ensure that the offender is complying with the agreed conditions.[13] This may mean a greater number of justice project staff or probation officers assuming that role, and it may mean that location may not rule out the possibility of restorative justice, but this affects the specifics of its implementation. If the staff, facilities, and programs are there, a restorative justice program has every chance of success. Of the first 214 offenders dealt with by the Community Council Project in Toronto, only 13.9 percent had failed to perform their requirements.[14]

On the other hand, a lack of adequate resources to meaningfully support restorative-type initiatives can portend failure.[15] The Royal Commission noted that funding for Indigenous justice initiatives has been dominated by a pilot-project mentality, whereby justice initiatives are accorded modest sums and have very short time commitments (e.g., one to three years). Once the initial time commitment expires, support for the initiative evaporates as budgetary resources are allocated elsewhere, leaving communities unable to pursue any long-term goals with respect to Indigenous crime and recidivism.[16] Dickson-Gilmore and LaPrairie also argue that lack of stable funding presents risks such as fewer staff to make a project run smoothly and burnout for those staff and volunteers a project can employ. This in turn endangers the long-term success of any restorative justice initiative.[17]

A consultation report concerning the development of the Canadian Restorative Justice Consortium indicated that a lack of sustained funding is a top concern for many restorative justice practitioners.[18]

How do we know that the varied results from Indigenous justice projects and their failure to make an appreciable dent in over-incarceration thus far cannot be attributed to Canadian governments' emphasis on piecemeal support and a political culture that sustains offence bifurcation? Until we see real financial, legal, and political commitments to community-based alternatives to incarceration, whether from Canada or driven by Indigenous communities themselves, the question of whether restorative processes can deliver on their promise remains unresolved.

If you have all the resources in place to fully develop programs, and safeguards to ensure fair processes, what then? Will the process just take care of itself and churn out the desired results? Not likely. More is needed than to simply throw more money at these issues. More research is needed into what empirical factors and conditions can contribute to the success or failure of restorative-based projects.[19]

So, what can identified as crucial to the empirical success of restorative justice at present, leaving aside for a moment the need for further research? I suggest that the ability of any restorative or Indigenous peace-making process to produce empirical success is integrally tied to its ability to facilitate genuine agreement between participants. Katherine Doolin, law professor with the University of Auckland, relates that much of the literature thus far has sought to define and conceptualize restorative justice by emphasizing its procedural frameworks. Doolin argues that the desired outcomes of restorative justice should have just as much, if not more, importance as process in its definition and valuation. Restoration as an outcome is what is important, with process providing the means to get there. What we mean by genuine agreement, and what Doolin emphasizes as integral to restoration, is when the offender is truly committed and motivated to make reparation and reform behaviour, where the victim's interests are genuinely accounted for and looked after, and where community members are committed to both offender reintegration and looking out for the victim's interests at the same time.[20] I would suggest that if a process cannot facilitate such genuine agreement, things like lowered recidivism and victim satisfaction will not easily follow. The evaluation of the South Australia Juvenile Justice Project concedes that some of the study data was equivocal but nonetheless notes that "when YPs were remorseful and when outcomes were achieved by genuine consensus, they were less likely to re-offend."[21]

A critical issue is, therefore, when participants' interests diverge from each other, at least to begin with. If their viewpoints are so widely different, or if they are unwilling to budge from what they perceive to be their own interests, then the harmonization of their interests into a workable agreement is problematic to say the least. Does this mean the endeavour is, on a practical level, futile or miniscule, no matter what we do to try to assure legal fairness in restorative processes? Perhaps not. Jennifer Langdon, criminology professor with Towson University, argues that an improved way to understand restorative justice is through positioning theory. The victim is likely to assume an initial position of anger toward the offender and view the offender as evil. The offender is in turn likely to assume an initial position of being defensive and minimize their personal responsibility. The key to bringing the process to fruition is for the participants to negotiate a relative repositioning with each other. The victim can move to a new position of admitting vulnerability in the wake of having been harmed, as well as a willingness to see the offender as a fellow human being with frailties and needs. The offender, in turn, can move to a new position of appreciating the harm done to the victim and seeing him- or herself as worthy of forgiveness (to which defensiveness and minimizing had been barriers). This repositioning can thereby lay the groundwork for a workable agreement that will succeed.[22]

Can such repositioning occur? In Australian lawyer Declan Roche's book focused on accountability in restorative justice, he found that, aside from power differentials arising from certain kinds of offences or community power dynamics, the presence of a few strong and assertive individuals in a restorative justice meeting with relatively few participants can dominate the meeting and prove detrimental to the prospect of a genuine and voluntary agreement.[23] Roche argues that there are possible measures to counteract this, such as including a wider circle of participants so that assertive individuals will have a much harder time imposing their will,[24] allowing the attendance of a professional advocate who can represent a party who is identified as vulnerable,[25] extensive preparatory work prior to the meeting,[26] and allowing breakout sessions so that participants may voice concerns that they were hesitant to in front of the larger group.[27] Measures like these can improve the prospect of a genuine and workable agreement.[28]

A study by Meredith Rossner, criminology professor with Australian National University, indicates other possibilities as well. The study was based on a videotaped conference that was recorded in London in 2004. The subject matter was a mugging suffered by the victim. Rossner argues that it is possible to gauge whether a restorative meeting is progressing from a situation marked by hostility and anxiety toward one of agreement and solidarity by closely observing the interactions among the participants. Various indicators such as facial expressions, eye contact, and verbal and non-verbal cues can signal the participants' emotions (e.g., anger, understanding, empathy), their degree of engagement with the process and with the other participants, and the degree to which they are, at a given moment, open to agreement with the other participants.[29] Rossner theorizes that building a positive and progressive rhythm is crucial for restorative justice being able to progress from a negative and hostile situation to a positive solidarity. That in turn means reaching the desired goal of a restorative resolution. She lists some of the crucial elements of the rhythm as follows:

1. Shared focus through conversational rhythm. Although initially

disjointed, over time, participants settle into a turn-taking dynamic marked by a lessening of stutters and silences. They begin to share a common focus and communicate with each other directly.

2. Conversational and power balance. All participants feel empowered to contribute, and no one is dominated. In this conference above, Christy talks more than anyone else, but this does not alter the balance of the conference. All participants continue to engage with each other and do not withdraw from the conversation.

3. Turning point. Strong expression of emotions acts as a high point for participants, providing a common focus and drawing them all into the rhythm and the flow of the interaction.

4. Public displays of solidarity. After a rhythm has developed and the interaction has reached a crescendo, participants engage in high-solidarity interactions, such as touching or sustained eye contact.[30]

A possibly fruitful avenue of research is to explore how to build rhythm in the setting of an Indigenous restorative meeting. I suggest this specifically because the cues that Rossner observed in the London conference may not necessarily have the same meaning among Indigenous persons. A lack of eye contact on the part of an Indigenous participant, for example, may be explained by a cultural standard that views direct eye contact with other persons as rude and disrespectful rather than signalling a lack of engagement with the process. If subsequent research does reveal how to build interactional rhythm in Indigenous restorative meetings, this can become part of the training of justice personnel who work with Indigenous justice systems and help facilitate genuine agreements among the parties. The development of such knowledge, by the way, may potentially also address Acorn's suggestion about how the process can be manipulated by playing to the script. A trained facilitator may be able to observe whether an offender is earnestly moving toward consensus by observing the offender's cues, apart from their spoken words.

Another study argues that a further crucial ingredient for program success is thorough and proper training for restorative justice practitioners, which includes how to help participants understand the principles of restorative justice, increase participant sensitivity toward victims, and the ability to guide discussions in a manner consistent with restorative justice ideals. Another key element is extensive participant preparation prior to the restorative justice session itself. This preparation can include being instructed on proper boundaries during discussions, what realistic expectations are, what the potential benefits and risks are, and understanding participants' roles. The study also suggests that restorative justice needs to be dialogue driven instead of outcome driven. In other words, allowing restorative justice meetings to proceed according to a tired script may produce more "surface agreements," but those agreements may prove to be empty if the dialogues leading to them have not resulted in a genuine consensus. If open and honest dialogue is encouraged (i.e., gauging how the participants really feel), it may result in fewer points of agreement but the agreements that are reached will be more genuine and productive in the long run.[31]

It is not my intention at this point to engage in exhaustive discussions of the issues raised by Roche, Rossner, and others. What I am trying to convey is that there are practical and logistical possibilities for Indigenous justice processes to produce genuine consensus. It well behooves Indigenous communities to explore such practical and logistical methods and, as I have said, more research in this direction is needed. If safeguards, resource support, and effective program design are in place, then perhaps a genuine alignment of interests can occur. There can then be progress with recidivism, victim safety, and community harmony.

Of course, there is also the possibility that despite the presence of legal safeguards, preparatory work, effective program design, resource support, and anything else that can be tried, the participants just cannot come to a genuine agreement. An individual victim may not want to forgive, may want more compensation than the offender is willing to provide, or may even want retributive vindication. The offender may not be willing to step up and accept genuine responsibility. Supporters for either sides may feel intractably antagonistic towards each other. The nature of restorative justice, with its emphasis on voluntary participation, is such that there will always be this possibility. Sometimes, no matter how hard you try, no matter the abundance of good intentions beforehand, a given case may just not attain consensus. Such cases may, in some instances, be better left to more formal adjudicatory sentencing processes. I would even then caution that sentencing processes, if administered by Indigenous communities during the transitory phase or as part of Indigenous legal orders, should still exercise restraint in the use of incarceration whenever it is possible to do so without compromising public safety.

INDIGENOUS JUSTICE AND OFFENDER RESPONSIBILITY

There are, as previously noted, criticisms of restorative justice that question its capacity to truly motivate offenders to accept responsibility and change. Other criticisms question whether restorative justice takes seriously enough the harm done by offenders. Those critiques may in fact inform a state policy of limiting restorative justice initiatives to a narrow range of offences deemed to be less serious. A policy that restricts restorative justice to relatively minor offences implies that offender responsibility becomes less likely for more serious offences and that applying restorative justice for more serious offences will compromise public safety. Members of the voting public may not be particularly alarmed at applying a restorative process for simple shoplifting, but they could become anxious at the thought of restorative processes applying to acts of significant bodily violence.

Much of what has been discussed during the previous two chapters describes what Indigenous restorative programming in partnership with the mainstream justice system can look like during the transitory phase. And even mainstream restorative programming does try to provide for offender responsibility and furthering public safety. Arguments have been made that it is erroneous to think of punishment and restorative justice in purely oppositional terms. Christopher Bennett, professor of philosophy with the University of Sheffield, stresses that while a criminal justice system can accommodate restorative ideals such as apology and victim restitution, it should not compromise other important functions such as retribution and public denunciation.[32] Some scholars argue that restorative justice is really about alternative approaches to punishment. A restorative resolution can impose onerous burdens and restrictions on an offender. It is punishment, but with a greater emphasis on rehabilitation and reintegration. Restorative resolutions are often backed by the prospect of punitive sanctions in the regular justice system, in order to encourage compliance with their conditions. They also provide a backup when an offender fails to comply with the terms of a restorative resolution.[33] Restorative and standard punitive approaches should be seen as complementary instead of oppositional. Each can fill in the gaps of the other to provide a comprehensive system of responding to crime.[34]

Offender responsibility may be accounted for through conventional restorative justice programming during the transitory phase. How about beyond that? The argument here is that Indigenous legal orders, if they become reality after the transitory phase, can take matters further and provide for accountability, responsibility, and safety in ways that do not rely on incarceration. And that means Indigenous-based alternatives to incarceration can be applied to a much wider range of offences than the narrow range of offences typically seen in state-administered restorative justice programs. Hadley Friedland, law professor with the University of Alberta, explains that Cree law could call upon various remedies for misbehaviour. These include healing ceremonies, verbal reprimands, offender apology, compensation to aggrieved parties, and temporary or even permanent banishment.[35] There is, of course, the question that while these approaches may have worked well enough in precolonial times, can they be meaningfully adapted for contemporary use?

The potential for Indigenous legal orders to operate effectively is at least hinted at through the tragic story of Christopher Pauchay, a member of the Yellow Quill Cree nation in Saskatchewan, and his two young daughters. Pauchay was home alone with Kaydance, aged three, and Santana, aged one, in January 2008. The temperatures during the night in question were close to minus 50 degrees Celsius. Pauchay was drunk that night and refused the offer of his brother-in-law to take care of the girls, asserting that he could look after them himself. One of the girls was apparently hurt. Christopher, while intoxicated, decided to try and bring them to his sister's house in order to get help. At some point, he became separated from the girls and only managed to arrive at a neighbour's house during the early hours of the next morning. He was overcome with frostbite and hypothermia. Eight hours later, he recovered enough to remember the night before and asked about his daughters. This realization set off a frantic search. Both girls were found frozen to death beneath snowdrifts, wearing only T-shirts and diapers.[36]

Some of the reactions to the tragedy within the Yellow Quill community itself reflect Indigenous philosophies on how to deal with harmful behaviour. The girls' grandmother, Irene Nippi, said in an interview: "I was worried about my grandchildren. I did not want them to leave this world in vain. I hope there's change now that happens — a lot of changes like no alcohol and counselling and stuff to be brought in here. Our old teachings should be brought back."[37] Community members' responses provide examples of how an individual tragedy can signal the pressing need to address issues affecting the community at large. Pauchay's step-mother, Jo Anne Machiskinic, said she felt angered that a tragedy such as this one had to happen before the community was alerted to the need to address problems of alcohol abuse. Elder Howard Walker called the tragedy a "wake-up call to society."[38]

Efforts to have Pauchay's case resolved through a sentencing circle and non-custodial alternatives inspired a significant number of scathing newspaper editorials across the country. Mindelle Jacobs, for example, writes:

> Nothing will bring back his children, Kaydance and Santana. At the same time, nothing will be accomplished by concluding such a horrific crime merits a mere community sentence. In this case, accepting responsibility and expressing remorse isn't enough. There has to be some expression of societal contempt for such behaviour and a non-custodial group hug just doesn't cut it.[39]

John Mohan, chief executive officer of the Siloam Mission in Winnipeg, emphasized the viewpoint that harm to the victims demands retribution:

> A just society should consider circumstances and intent when determining sentencing. But what is too often overlooked in cases like these is justice for the victims. To deem someone not criminally responsible or absolve them of consequences because they were drunk or not treating their mental illness devalues both their crime and the people wronged. Valuing and ensuring justice for victims may do far more to restore sanity to our communities than deflected responsibility or a lenient sentence could.[40]

Such opinions have not just come from newspaper columnists, either. This rather strongly worded opinion letter was sent to the *Winnipeg Sun*:

> I read that the defence team for Christopher Pauchay (the fa-

ther that killed his two children by blindly stumbling about the freezing prairies with them both dressed in nothing but diapers and a light shirt) is asking for him to be sentenced by a native sentencing circle. I truly hope the judge sees what bull this is and puts him away for the prescribed time in a real jail. It stated that he has accepted his responsibility — big deal. If I go out and rob a bank and not kill anyone I'm still going away to jail. Maybe being Scottish I should ask for the ancient punishment of banishment. I'm sure that this would teach me a lesson. Let's get real.[41]

A sentencing circle was nonetheless held, with the result that the Yellow Quill Elders as well as the chief of the reserve, Larry Cachane, wanted Pauchay to undergo spiritual healing and rehabilitation instead of going to prison.[42] Tim Quigley, law professor at the University of Saskatchewan, emphasized during a CBC interview that a sentencing circle would actually be a much more difficult ordeal for Pauchay than a standard sentencing hearing because he will have to listen to community members describe to him how his actions have effected their lives.[43] That is a theme that has been touched on during previous discussions about restorative justice.

But what the Yellow Quill community had in mind did not end at Pauchay verbally accepting responsibility or community members speaking to him directly. An Elder who attended the circle recommended that Pauchay should serve as an assistant, an *oskapew*, to three Cree Elders who were recognized as pipe carriers. His responsibilities would have included providing transportation for the Elders, helping the Elders construct sweat lodges, helping to move the rocks for sweat ceremonies, filling and lighting pipes for pipe ceremonies, and other tasks. The recommendation was that Pauchay carry on these responsibilities for life.[44]

No one should ever downplay the tragedy of two infant girls dying in freezing temperatures. However, the dismissive comments seen in the newspapers betray a lack of cognitive appreciation for what the Yellow Quill community had in mind. The work of putting together a sweat lodge can be physically intense. The same is true of moving the frequently heavy rocks for a sweat lodge ceremony. And as an Elder ages and becomes less physically capable, the *oskapew* can be expected to carry more and more of the physical burdens of the Elders' tasks.[45] The commitment was also for life. It was not temporary. Compare that to the maximum three-year limit on terms of probation and two years for conditional sentences under the *Criminal Code*.[46] And recall that the commitment would have been made to three Elders, not just one. It would not have been an exaggeration to call it a life sentence, but a life sentence that reflected principles of a particular Indigenous legal order. And it was a sentence that was meant to hold Pauchay accountable and responsible for the rest of his life, but in ways that were unfamiliar to Western democracies that uncritically equate criminal responsibility with incarceration.

The presiding judge, Barry Morgan, rejected the sentencing circle recommendations and gave Pauchay a sentence of three years imprisonment, in part because he was not convinced that Pauchay fully understood his role in the girls' deaths.[47] It must be kept in mind that Judge Morgan, as a judge sworn to apply Canadian law, was not allowed to craft the sentence according to the dictates of public outrage or passions. His job was to apply Canadian law on the appropriate sentence for criminal negligence causing death, which carries a maximum term of life imprisonment under section 220(b) of the *Criminal Code* and very often requires at a minimum a term of incarceration.[48]

The case therefore represents an instance where the state legal system marginalized an Indigenous legal order in an act of colonialism. It also provides an example of why any transitory phase where Indigenous programming operates as an appendage to the state system must at some point give way to revitalized Indigenous legal orders. Indigenous programming as a part of the state system can have positive outcomes and address the problems to some degree during the transitory phase. But the hope is that Indigenous legal orders can eventually call on Indigenous legal principles that share parallels with restorative justice to even greater effect. And Indigenous legal orders can apply those principles to a greater range of conduct than the state system's typical application of restorative justice programming to less serious offences. Indigenous legal orders can further responsibility and safety, but in ways that are different from what Western state justice systems rely on (i.e., incarceration). Such a direction would also align with the objectives of prison abolition, but in ways that are distinct to the needs of Indigenous Peoples. Of course, there is no assurance that we can get to the point where Indigenous legal orders are allowed to operate without colonial interference.

WILL NO PROGRESS BE MADE?

It is obviously open to question whether a transitory phase of programming in partnership with the state system can give way to revitalized Indigenous legal orders. It may seem far more likely that state-sponsored programming will entrench itself as an enduring status quo where little progress is made. George Pavlich, professor of sociology with the University of Alberta, describes what he calls an imitator paradox that is inherent in restorative justice itself. Restorative justice, on the one hand, depicts itself as a fundamentally different alternative to the state system, to appeal to those who are dissatisfied with the punitive emphasis of the status quo. And yet restorative justice functions through state support. Restorative justice programs garner that state support by presenting themselves as complementary, rather than adverse, to state justice objectives. Restorative justice programming thus remains an appendage to the state system without any fundamental change to the state's justice policies, which prioritize mass incarceration.[49]

Juan Tauri, Maori professor of criminology, relates that long-held assumptions about the family group conferences as a positive example of Indigenous empowerment may not hold up to reality. His studies indicate that Maori participants frequently felt marginalized during conference proceedings and that real decision-making power has been monopolized by state professionals. Likewise, participants felt that state professionals would exercise their powers in ways that did not prioritize the long-term good of Maori communities.[50]

There is certainly a risk that Indigenous Peoples will remain stuck in the status quo and that any aspirations of entering a transitory phase leading to Indigenous legal orders are an illusory hope. That would be an example of the politics of recognition, as described by Coulthard. And there are plenty of reasons to believe that societal dynamics will remain that way.

The reason Canada accords only limited accommodations of Indigenous visions of justice is that extensive support for Indigenous community-based alternatives may be politically controversial. Tough-on-crime policies are intended to win political support from the public. To be fair, Western democracies have often recognized the merits of restorative justice and have not infrequently implemented restorative justice programs to reflect such recognition.[51] This only goes so far, though. Western justice systems have a stake in the use of imprisonment for offences deemed more serious to avoid losing public support by appearing soft on crime, and this can translate into a hesitancy to implement alternatives, even if they may prove more effective.[52] And again, that theme plays into the politics of recognition.

Public demands on the Canadian state to respond to crime with incarceration, and lengthier terms of incarceration, present a powerful obstacle to any realization of Indigenous control over justice. Past Indigenous justice practices did not always have a restorative emphasis. Nonetheless, those that do resemble restorative practices retain an important contemporary significance in the effort to deal with the problem of Indigenous over-incarceration. A reasonable conclusion is that Canadian politicians are reluctant to extend greater accommodations for fear of losing public support if they give the appearance of being "soft on crime." A study by Julian Roberts and Loretta Stalans has verified that public opinion surveys have consistently demonstrated strong support for applying restorative approaches to less serious crimes (e.g., minor property offences), but that support falls dramatically when it comes to applying restorative approaches to more serious offences, like violent or sexual crimes.[53] This reverberates in the level of accommodation toward Indigenous approaches as well. Even as Indigenous Peoples are subject to over-incarceration, and all the social ills of which over-incarceration is a symptom, they are powerless to pursue their own solutions to these problems beyond the parameters set by the Canadian state. This reflects their relative powerlessness as a political minority.[54]

Section 718.2(e) has apparently sparked some public controversy in Canada. There were certainly plenty of scathing newspaper editorials directed at the provision in the years following its enactment.[55] Rachel Dioso and Anthony Doob studied Canadian public opinion on section 718.2(e). They admitted that their sample of survey participants was not necessarily representative of Canada as a whole. Survey participants who viewed the justice system as too lenient were significantly more likely to view section 718.2(e) negatively in comparison to those who viewed current sentences as about right and those who viewed sentences as too harsh.[56] One has to wonder how the Canadian public at large would view section 718.2(e) given that such opinion surveys still indicate that a substantial majority in Canada consider the justice system too lenient.

Policies that rely extensively on imprisonment, if applied to everybody, end up having a very adverse impact on Indigenous people, who are powerless to challenge such policies as a political minority. For the politicians, addressing harsh penal policies as applied to Indigenous Peoples in any truly meaningful fashion would give the especially unpalatable appearance of leniency toward offenders from an Indigenous minority that offenders from the non-Indigenous majority do not enjoy.

Public pressure may also act as a barrier to a more extensive realization of justice reinvestment. Jamie Fellows, law professor with James Cook University, and an Australian lawyer named Tamara Hage note that Australian states, Queensland in particular, have been willing to try more preventative initiatives with Indigenous youth that focus on education, health, and community services. These initiatives are frequently a response when an Indigenous community is experiencing issues like substance abuse and school truancy among youth. Fellows and Hage note that certain factors impede a more robust realization of justice reinvestment as a solution to Australian Indigenous over-incarceration. A key factor is prevailing tough-on-crime attitudes in Australia, and those in turn preclude the multi-jurisdictional and government support that enlarged justice reinvestment would need in Australia. Another factor is that proving efficacy requires data monitoring. That increases resource demands and in turn makes such strategies unappealing to governments.[57]

Kirsten Anker, law professor at McGill University, argues that in order for there to be true reconciliation in the sphere of criminal justice, settler Canadians have to be willing to accept a profound unsettling of what they take for granted as the standard or usual objectives of the criminal justice system even as it enlarges the space for Indigenous legal traditions that often contradict those mainstream objectives.[58] The question is whether that acceptance is possible.

I will suggest that it is. Scandinavian countries, for example, use incarceration for a very narrow range of serious violent offences, while preferring diversion and community service programs for the rest. They have experienced either minimal increases, or even mild decreases, in incarceration rates through the 1990s and 2000s.[59] Michael Tonry, however, cautions us against finding optimism in the Scandinavian setting. He holds that arguments based on cost-effectiveness will not sway those who, in Western democracies, normatively believe in the rightness of prison as punishment.[60]

Nonetheless, evidence is mounting that it is indeed possible to mould public opinion so that it can become more supportive of alternative approaches to justice. A study by Anthony Doob suggests it is not necessarily a given that the Canadian public will insist on longer and tougher punishments no matter what.[61] Doob acknowledges that public opinion surveys often indicate the attitude that sentences are not harsh enough. He contends, however, that a more complex picture emerges if people are asked more specific and nuanced questions about justice objectives and methods. When asked if they thought that increasing sentence terms was the best way of reducing a crime, less than a third of his survey respondents answered in the affirmative, while the majority preferred alternatives such as reducing unemployment and developing social programs.[62] When confronted with a hypothetical that involved the prisons being full, almost two thirds preferred reliance on sentencing alternatives to building more prisons.[63] Over 80 percent indicated that when a sum of money to spend on justice was available it was better to invest it in preventative measures rather than prisons.[64] Doob then presented the respondents with a hypothetical scenario involving a first-time break and enter. When confronted with a reminder that the monthly cost for imprisoning an offender ranged from $3,700 to $6,000, 84 to 86 percent preferred a conditional sentence and fine to jail.[65] Perhaps if the Canadian public was made aware that the alternatives are not only effective but also cost-effective in the long run, then the federal government may be able to secure a political mandate to implement the suggestions for reform that have been made here.

In fact, recent moves toward justice reinvestment in the United States occurred precisely because some state governments made this kind of effort. An example of the ability of policymakers to mould public opinion to become more supportive of community-based alternatives comes from Kansas. Kansas policymakers in 2006 were faced with the prospect of their prison population increasing by 26 percent by 2016, with the costs of building and operating additional prisons increasing by at least $500 million. In 2007, the policymakers solicited public opinion through the "Kansas Criminal Justice Public Opinion Survey." The results indicated overwhelming support for increasing the availability of rehabilitation programs to inmates and splitting the corrections budget between the programs and new prisons as opposed to just spending it on more prisons. Kansas policymakers, interpreting the survey as a confident mandate, reinvested $7 million into treatment programs and community supervision services that otherwise would have been spent building more prisons.[66]

In 2000, California voters showed overwhelming support for Proposition 36, a mandate to end mandatory sentencing for drug offences and instead emphasize probation plus treatment for drug offenders. In the background of this development was an awareness of the high costs for California taxpayers. The prisons were overcrowded and operating at 172 percent capacity. The annual costs of maintaining a prisoner ranged from $42,000 to $55,000 each year.[67]

A 2016 evaluation of state justice reinvestment initiatives by the Urban Institute in Washington, DC, found that states projected saving $7.7 million over five years and $875 million over ten years. Total savings was estimated at $1.1 billion.[68] The institute did not measure state recidivism rates, asserting that effectively measuring the efficacy of justice reinvestment in combating recidivism would take at least several years.[69] The Council of State Governments Justice Center's 2018 evaluation found that participating states had reduced both prison expenditures and prison populations. Texas claimed to have shut down three prisons and experienced historic lows in crime rates. North Carolina claimed a 19 percent reduction in crime rates since embarking on justice reinvestment.[70] The news was not all good, though. The centre had done a separate 2016 evaluation of Ohio and referred to University of Cincinnati research that revealed that "some programs were actually increasing recidivism rates because they did not filter out those participants who would not benefit from the intensive programming."[71]

Another thing to keep in mind is that successful rehabilitative efforts address a long-standing and legitimate concern of the voting public: their safety. James Le Blanc, secretary of the Louisiana Department of Public Safety and Corrections, writes:

> Indeed, we should not underestimate the role offender reprogramming plays in overall safety and security in our communities. Reentry initiatives play a crucial role in changing the behavior of the population we serve. For most of us, the focus on reentry is a culture of change — for management, staff, offenders and communities. It is also difficult for most law-abiding citizens to swallow because they believe prison should be punitive, not an opportunity for advancement. What we should keep reminding everyone is that people currently behind bars will

> eventually return to their communities. It is in everyone's best interests that they return with the education, skills and access to services that will ensure success. There will be some people that we can never change, no matter how hard we try, because they will not allow change to happen. But there are many individuals who haven't had the opportunity for change, and strong reentry programming, whether it be educational, vocational, faithbased or a combination thereof, provides that opportunity for change.[72]

This potentially represents another selling point to Canadian voters. Alternatives are not only more effective, but they may also enhance public safety. As Northwestern University law professor Robin Walker Sterling notes: "Certainly justice reinvestment requires a reallocation of money, but it also requires reinvestment of the emotional capital that undergirds the money flow."[73]

Public attitudes concerning punishment and sentencing are not ironclad constraints on the Canadian government's policy options, though. To the contrary, evidence suggests that governments can take an active hand in moulding public opinion to be more favourable toward constructive alternatives.[74] Canada as a colonial state can channel public opinion to be more supportive of restorative justice programming as part of its own mainstream system. And that in turn can lay the foundation for expanding the space for Indigenous approaches to justice. Such a pursuit is an example of being a Word Warrior in Canadian legal and political spaces, as described by Turner. And it admittedly relies in no small degree on appealing to Canadian self-interest as well as trying to align that self-interest with Indigenous aspirations.

It must be conceded that such an approach could play into the politics of recognition. But the limits of direct action have previously been explained, at least when it comes to trying to enlarge the space for Indigenous perspectives on justice. And on the contrary, there is solid evidence that the Word Warrior approach can possibly make headway for expanding the room for Indigenous justice. There is no guarantee this will occur, of course. But the evidence is there to warrant a cautious optimism.

It is interesting to note that the federal minister of justice, David Lametti, has pledged $10 million over five years as part of the 2019 federal budget to support the revitalization of Indigenous legal orders.[75]

The amount is small for a government budgetary allocation. But does it signal a willingness to begin acting in true partnership with Indigenous Peoples as a part of reconciliation? Or will it prove to be the kind of minimalist and token gesture that Coulthard would expect as an example of the politics of recognition? Only time will tell. Now it is time to explore another approach, also with a view toward minimizing the need to incarcerate Indigenous Peoples.

Notes

1   Robert Yazzie, "The Navajo Response to Crime," in Wanda D. McCaslin (ed.), *Justice as Healing: Indigenous Ways* (St. Paul: Living Justice Press, 2005), 121, 131.

2   Green, "Aboriginal Community Sentencing and Mediation," 112.

3   Green, "Aboriginal Community Sentencing and Mediation," 94–95. See also Barry Stuart, *Building Community Justice Partnerships*, 45–47.

4   Clare McGlynn, Nicole Westmarland, and Nikki Godden, "'I Just Wanted Him to Hear Me': Sexual Violence and the Possibilities of Restorative Justice," *Journal of Law and Society* 39, 2 (2012), 213.

5   Barbara Tomporowski et al., "Reflections on the Past, Present, and Future of Restorative Justice in Canada," *Alberta Law Review* 48, 4 (2011), 826.

6   David Milward, *Aboriginal Justice and the Charter: Realizing a Culturally Sensitive Interpretation of Legal Rights* (Vancouver: ubc Press, 2012).

7   Heather Strang et al. "Victim Evaluations of Face-to-Face Restorative Justice Conferences: A Quasi-Experimental Analysis," *Journal of Social Issues* 62, 2 (2006), 301.

8   Daly, "Mind the Gap," 230.

9   Loren Walker and Leslie A. Hayashi, "Pono Kaulike: A Hawaii Criminal Court Provides Restorative Justice Practices for Healing Relationships," *Federal Probation* 71, 3 (2007), 18.

10 Toran Hansen and Mark Umbreit, "State of Knowledge: Four Decades of Victim-Offender Mediation Research and Practice, the Evidence," *Conflict Resolution Quarterly* 36, 2 (2018), 99.

11 Carol LaPrairie, "Community Justice or Just Communities? Aboriginal Communities in Search of Justice," *Canadian Journal of Criminology* 37, 4 (1995), 521; Stuart, *Building Community Justice Partnerships*, 117–19; see also Karen A. Souza and Mandeep K. Dhami, "A Study of Volunteers in Community-Based Restorative Justice Programs," *Canadian Journal of Criminology* 50, 1 (2008), 31.

12 Hughes and Mossman, "Re-Thinking Access to Criminal Justice in Canada," 118.

13 Green, "Aboriginal Community Sentencing and Mediation," 116–17.

14 Royal Commission on Aboriginal Peoples, *Bridging the Cultural Divide*, 153.

15 Stenning and Robert, "The Sentencing of Aboriginal Offenders in Canada," 88.

16 Royal Commission on Aboriginal Peoples, *Bridging the Cultural Divide*, 294–302. See also Barbara Tomporowski, *Exploring Restorative Justice in Sas-*

katchewan, MA Thesis, University of Regina, 2004; Evelyn Zellerer and Chris Cunneen, "Restorative Justice, Indigenous Justice, and Human Rights," in Gordon Bazemore and Mara Schiff (eds), *Restorative Community Justice: Repairing Harm and Transforming Communities* (Lexington: Anderson Publishing, 2001), 245, 255.

17   LaPrairie and Dickson-Gilmore, *Will the Circle Be Unbroken?*, 198.

18   Steering Committee for the Canadian Restorative Justice Consortium, "Final Report on a Consultation Regarding the Potential Development of the Canadian Restorative Justice Consortium" (October 2009, unpublished), 15.

19   Carol LaPrairie, "The Impact of Aborigina Justice Research on Policy: A Marginal Past and an Even More Uncertain Future," *Canadian Journal of Criminology* 41, 2 (1999), 256–57; Barbara Tomporowski et al., "Reflections on the Past, Present, and Future of Restorative Justice in Canada," 826.

20   Katherine Doolin, "But What Does It Mean? Seeking Definitional Clarity in Restorative Justice," *Journal of Criminal Law* 71, 5 (2007), 513.

21   Daly, "Mind the Gap," 231.

22   Jennifer Langdon, "Talk It Out: Toward a Narrative Theory of Community Conferencing," *Contemporary Justice Review* 19, 1 (2016), 19.

23   Declan Roche, *Accountability in Restorative Justice* (Oxford: Oxford University Press, 2003), 83–84.

24   Roche, *Accountability in Restorative Justice*, 87–88.

25   Roche, *Accountability in Restorative Justice*, 91–92.

26   Roche, *Accountability in Restorative Justice*, 92–93, 169–70.

27   Roche, *Accountability in Restorative Justice*, 93–94.

28   Roche, *Accountability in Restorative Justice*, 93–94.

29   Meredith Rossner, "Emotions and Interaction Ritual: A Micro Analysis of Restorative Justice," *British Journal of Criminology* 51 (2011), 95.

30   Rossner, "Emotions and Interaction Ritual, 116.

31   Jun Jin Choi, Gordon Bazemore, and Michael Gilbert, "Review of Research on Victims' Experiences in Restorative Justice: Implications for Youth Justice," *Children and Youth Services Review* 34, 1 (2012), 35.

32   Christopher Bennett, *The Apology Ritual* (Cambridge: Cambridge University Press, 2008).

33   Kathleen Daly, "Revisiting the Relationship between Retributive and Restorative Justice," in Heather Strang and John Braithwaite (eds.), *Restorative Justice: Philosophy to Practice* (Dartmouth: Ashgate, 2000), 33; Roche, *Accountability in Restorative Justice*, 174–77; Mark Lokanan, "An Open Model for Restorative Justice: Is There Room for Punishment?" *Contemporary Justice Review* 12, 3 (2009), 289; Roach, "Changing Punishment at the Turn of the Century," 459; Dena M. Gromet and John M. Darley, "Punishment and Beyond: Achieving Justice Through the Satisfaction of Multiple Goals," *Law & Society Review* 43, 1 (2009), 1.

34   Daly, "Revisiting the Relationship between Retributive and Restorative Justice," 35 and 40.

35   Hadley Friedland, *Cree Legal Summary* (Victoria: Indigenous Legal Research Unit, 2013), 19–29.

36   "Dad Guilty in Freezing Deaths to Be Sentenced: Saskatchewan Man's Pun-
      ishment to Be Determined by Aboriginal Sentencing Circle," *Edmonton Sun*
      (January 8, 2009), 7.

37   Tim Cook, "Grieving Grandmother Calls for Change: Saskatchewan Reserve
      Where Young Sisters Froze to Death Needs Alcohol Ban, Counseling, She
      Says," *Globe and Mail*, February 4, 2008, A7.

38   Chris Purdy, "Healing Won't Happen in Jail: Life of Spiritual Guidance Needed,
      Say Elders, but a Judge Will Get the Final Say," *Globe and Mail*, February 14,
      2009, A8.

39   Mindelle Jacobs, "Don't Impair Justice," *Ottawa Sun*, December 9, 2008, 15. See
      also Rosie DiManno, "Jail Only Just Term in Freezing Deaths," *Toronto Star*,
      January 9, 2009, A2; Lysiane Gagnon, "A Telling Take on Yellow Quill," *Globe
      and Mail*, June 22, 2009, A15; Alex Kinsella, "Punishment Deserved," *Waterloo
      Region Record*, February 20, 2009, A8.

40   John Mohan, "Own Up and Bring Our Sanity Back," *Portage Daily Graphic*,
      April 15, 2009, 4.

41   "Letters to the Editor Column," *Winnipeg Sun*, January 20, 2009, 8.

42   Purdy, "Healing Won't Happen in Jail," A8.

43   "Father of Two Girls Who Froze to Death Needs Treatment, Not Jail, Judge
      Hears," *CBC News*, February 13, 2009.

44   Toby Goldbach, "Sentencing Circles, Clashing Worldviews, and the Case of
      Christopher Pauchay," Illumine: Journal of the Centre for Studies in Religion
      and Society 10, 1 (2011), 53, 57.

45   *Elder Protocol and Guidelines* (Edmonton: University of Alberta, Council of Ab-
      original Initiatives, 2012); "Guidelines for Participating in First Nations Sweats,"
      Steinbach Consulting <steinbachconsulting.org/uploads/7/0/0/1/7001863/
      sweat-protocol-sheet.pdf>.

46   Sections 732.2(2)(b) and 742.7(1) of the *Criminal Code* respectively.

47   Jennifer Graham, "Father of Frozen Girls Jailed, Judge Hands Man Prison
      Term Despite Sentencing Circle Decision," *Calgary Sun*, March 7, 2009, 7.

48   Judge Morgan noted that because the offence can merit a term of life imprison-
      ment, it in turn reflects the fact that the offence is a very serious one. See *R. v
      Pauchay* [2009] 2 C.N.L.R. 314 (Sask. P.C.).

49   George Pavlich, *Governing Paradoxes of Restorative Justice* (London: The Glass
      House, 2005).

50   Juan Tauri, "Explaining Recent Innovations in New Zealand's Criminal Justice
      System: Empowering Maori or Biculturalising the State?" *Journal of Criminol-
      ogy* 32, 2 (1999), 153; Paora Moyle and Juan Tauri, "Maori, Family Group Con-
      ferencing and the Mystifications of Restorative Justice," *Victims & Offenders* 11,
      1 (2016), 87.

51   Examples include Law Reform Commission of Canada, *Studies on Diversion*,
      working paper no. 7 (Ottawa: Law Reform Commission, 1975), 23–24; Cana-
      da, House of Commons, Standing Committee on Justice and Solicitor General,
      *Report of the Standing Committee on Justice and Solicitor General on its Review
      of Sentencing, Conditional Release and Related Aspects of Corrections. Taking
      Responsibility.* (Ottawa: Solicitor General, 1988), 75; Law Reform Commission

of Australia, Report no. 31, *The Recognition of Aboriginal Customary Laws*, vol. 2 (Canberra: Australian Government Publishing Service, 1986), vol. 1, 7.

52   Zellerer and Cunneen, "Restorative Justice, Indigenous Justice, and Human Rights," 253.

53   Julian V. Roberts and Loretta J. Stalans, "Restorative Sentencing: Exploring the Views of the Public," *Social Justice Research* 17, 3 (2004), 315.

54   For a similar argument with regard to Australia, see Russell Hogg, "Penality and Modes of Regulating Indigenous Peoples in Australia," *Punishment & Society* 3, 3 (2001), 355. A great deal of American literature makes similar arguments with respect to "tough on crime" and "war on drugs" policies as applied to Blacks and Latinos. See, for example, Paul Butler, "One Hundred Years of Race and Crime," *Journal of Criminal Law and Criminology* 100, 3 (2010), 1043; Deborah Small, "The War on Drugs Is a War on Racial Justice," Social Research 68, 3 (2001), 896; David Garland, *The Culture of Control: Crime and Social Order in Contemporary Society* (Oxford: Oxford University Press, 2001), 132.

55   "Systemic Racism," *Ottawa Citizen*, May 1, 1999, B5. In a subsequent editorial, the *Ottawa Citizen* demanded that "parliament should repeal differential sentencing"; "Badly Formed Sentences," *Ottawa Citizen*, April 5, 2001, A14; "Sorry's Not Enough," *National Post*, June 28, 1999, A19; "Crime, Time and Race," *Globe and Mail*, January 16, 1999, D6; "Aboriginals Deserve Equal, Not Special, Treatment: Overplaying the Race Card Is in No One's Interest," *Globe & Mail*, April 29, 1999, A12; Linda Williamson, "Different Strokes for Different Folks: This Is Social Engineering Disguised as Justice for All," *Toronto Star*, April 30, 1999, 17; "A Messy Prescription for Native Offenders" *Globe & Mail*, August 12, 2002, A12; Tanis Fiss, "Special Treatment Can't Right Wrongs to Aboriginals," *Guelph Mercury*, January 9, 2004, A9.

56   Rachel Dioso and Anthony Doob, "An Analysis of Public Support for Special Consideration of Aboriginal Offenders at Sentencing," *Canadian Journal of Criminology* 43, 3 (2001), 405.

57   Tamara Hage and Jamie Fellows, "Combatting Over-Represenation of Indigenous Youth in the Queensland Criminal Justice System Through Justice Reinvestment," *James Cook University Law Review* 24 (2018), 147.

58   Kirsten Anker, "Reconciliation in Translation: Indigenous Legal Traditions and Canada's Truth and Reconciliation Commission," *Windsor Yearbook of Access to Justice* 33, 2 (2016), 15.

59   Tonio Lappi-Seppala, "Penal Policy in Scandinavia," in Michael Tonry (ed.), *Crime, Punishment, and Politics in Comparative Perspective. Crime and Justice: A Review of Research*. v. 36 (Chicago: University of Chicago Press, 2007).

60   Michael Tonry, "Making Peace, Not a Desert: Penal Reform Should Be about Values Not Justice Reinvestment," *Criminology & Public Policy* 10, 3 (2011), 637.

61   Anthony Doob, "Transforming the Punishment Environment: Understanding Public Views of What Should be Accomplished at Sentencing," *Canadian Journal of Criminology* 42, 3 (2000), 323.

62   Anthony Doob, "Transforming the Punishment Environment," 329.

63   Anthony Doob, "Transforming the Punishment Environment," 331.

64 Anthony Doob, "Transforming the Punishment Environment," 331.

65 Anthony Doob, "Transforming the Punishment Environment," 334–35.

66 Crystal Garland, "Increasing Public Safety and Reducing Spending: Applying a Justice Reinvestment Strategy in Texas and Kansas," *Corrections Today* 69, 6 (2007), 65–66.

67 Nathaniel J. Pallone and James J. Hennessy, "To Punish or to Treat: Substance Abuse within the Context of Oscillating Attitudes Toward Correctional Rehabilitation," *Journal of Offender Rehabilitation* 37, 3/4 (2003), 13.

68 Nancy La Vigne et al., *Reforming Sentencing and Corrections Policy: The Experience of Justice Reinvestment States* (Washington, DC: Urban Institute, 2016), 42.

69 Nancy La Vigne et al., *Reforming Sentencing and Corrections Policy*, 37.

70 The Justice Center, *The Justice Reinvestment Initiative* (New York: Council of State Governments, 2018).

71 The Justice Center, *Justice Reinvestment in Ohio: How Ohio Is Reducing Corrections Costs and Recidivism* (New York: Council of State Governments, 2016).

72 James Le Blanc, "Rehabilitation Programs Will Help Offenders Change — And Enhance Public Safety," *Corrections Today* 70, 5 (2008), 8, 14.

73 Robin Walker Sterling, "Narrative and Justice Reinvestment," *Denver Law Review* 94, 3 (2017), 552.

74 Anne-Marie McAlinden, "'Transforming Justice': Challenges for Restorative Justice in an Era of Punishment-based Corrections," *Contemporary Justice Review* 14, 4 (2011), 383.

75 Ian Burns, "Ottawa Providing Nearly $10 Million in Funding to Support Indigenous Law Initiatives," *The Lawyer's Daily*, May 18, 2021.

11

INDIGENOUS CORRECTIONS AND PAROLE

There is certainly the potential for preventative programming and Indigenous justice processes to make significant strides toward ending Indigenous over-incarceration. The ultimate hope is to minimize the necessity to call upon incarceration, as is consistent with prison abolition, at least with respect to Indigenous Peoples. But that objective cannot be realized overnight. It may take years, even decades, to even approach accomplishing that goal. That means that significant numbers of Indigenous Peoples will remain in prison, and continue to find their way into prison, for the foreseeable future. That in turn means we must invest in effective initiatives for Indigenous Peoples within the walls of prisons, even as we engage in the long-term project of minimizing the need to incarcerate Indigenous Peoples.

It must also be conceded that prison cannot be completely dispensed with even should the long-term project be accomplished. We can hope to minimize the need for it to the maximum extent possible, particularly through preventative programming and justice processes with restorative emphases. But even those who most ardently oppose widespread incarceration acknowledge with a healthy dose of realism that it may in very narrow instances remain necessary. Even the most enthusiastic proponents of restorative justice do not propose a complete reliance on restorative justice. They often admit that some offences are so serious as to be inappropriate for applying restorative justice and that there are some offenders who are simply so dangerous or who simply will not respond to corrective efforts. Their point is that in Western justice systems, imprisonment is relied upon reflexively and uncritically for far too many offences.[1] Even some prison abolitionists hold that incarceration should be restricted only to those who are so dangerous to others that there is no workable alternative for them. But those abolitionists may still hold out the possibility of eventual rehabilitation even for those select few.[2]

It would be up to each Indigenous community where they want to draw the line. And it may be that some Indigenous communities may want to pursue objectives similar to those advocated by prison abolition. It could be, for example, that some Indigenous communities may want to limit the use of prison only to those who commit intentional murder[3] or those whose danger cannot be reasonably managed by any alternatives to prison.

This chapter explores possibilities for healing and rehabilitation grounded in Indigenous cultures within prison. It is based on a recognition that there will still be a need for Indigenous-based alternatives in a correctional setting for the time being, even as we pursue the long-term project of minimizing the need to incarcerate Indigenous people.

THE THEORY OF INDIGENOUS HEALING IN PRISON

James Waldram, medical anthropology professor with the University of Saskatchewan, connects colonialism with Indigenous crime and rehabilitation as follows:

> Emotionally, the scars are evident. Some men have talked of hate and bitterness. Others expressed profound sadness. They spoke of an inability as adults to love their own families and to trust people. And they demonstrated profound difficulty establishing positive identities for themselves.
>
> Trauma, it is argued here, also operates at community, societal, and cultural levels. Narratives presented in this chapter characterize some Aboriginal communities as pathological in a way that is clearly damaging to residents.... Current psychopathology, and other problems experienced by Aboriginal inmates, must therefore be seen as the product of events and circumstances operating at four levels: the individual, the community, the society, and the culture. Rehabilitative programs which ignore this fact, for instance by focusing only on the individual, will not likely be successful.[4]

Waldram presents as a solution Indigenous Elders adopting the role of both therapeutic healers and spiritual guides for Indigenous inmates. Because an Elder is also Indigenous, is possessed of considerable cultural and spiritual authority, and has often had similar life experiences to those of the inmate, the Elder can reach through to the inmate so that he or she is receptive to the Elder's teachings. Once an initial rapport is established, the Elder employs various methods of healing. The Elder can place the inmate's pain within the broader contexts of colonialism, racism, social conditions, and the events that have impacted the inmate's life. The Elder extends understanding and sympathy to the inmate and lets the inmate know that he or she remains valued as a person. The Elder can also instruct the inmate on his or her place in the world, his or her relationships to other people, to the Creator, to ancestral spirits, to the natural world, with the idea of gently discouraging future actions that harm others. The Elder can also instruct the inmate on cultural and spiritual values, thereby gently persuading the inmate to reform and become healthier. This also has the goal of building up an inmate's self-esteem in him- or herself as an Indigenous person. The Elder maintains a bond of compassion and empathy with the inmate, to assure the inmate that the Elder has the inmate's best interests in mind.[5] The Elder can also engage inmates with the healing process through cultural ceremonies such as talking circles, pipe ceremonies, and sweat lodges.[6] As we will see, the federal government of Canada has made some legislative allowances for this approach. An overview of the legislative regimes governing the corrections and parole of Indigenous inmates now follows.

CANADIAN CORRECTIONAL LAW

Section 80 of the *Corrections and Conditional Release Act* (CCRA) mandates that the Correctional Service of Canada (CSC) shall "provide programs designed particularly to address the needs of aboriginal offenders."[7] This provision aims to deliver services such as life skills training or substance abuse treatment, but designed to include the inculcation of Indigenous cultural values as part of the treatment or training. Another stipulation is to facilitate inmate participation in cultural activities, such as training in traditional spiritual practices or sweat lodge ceremonies. These services are often delivered by Elders or other members of Indigenous communities with similar cultural authority. The rationale behind these approaches is that the CSC has identified the loss of cultural identity as the underlying cause of Indigenous criminality.[8]

A primary objective of correctional programming is to prepare inmates for parole. Canadian correctional legislation contains directives to consider the circumstances of Indigenous offenders and alternatives that can lessen terms of incarceration. Section 102 of the CCRA sets out the criteria for granting parole as follows:

> The Board or a provincial parole board may grant parole to an offender if, in its opinion,
>   (a) the offender will not, by reoffending, present an undue risk to society before the expiration according to law of the sentence the offender is serving; and
>   (b) the release of the offender will contribute to the protection of society by facilitating the reintegration of the offender into society as a law-abiding citizen.[9]

The Parole Board of Canada's policy manual provides an additional gloss to this provision by mandating consideration of certain factors:

> Any systemic or background factors that may have contributed to the offender's involvement in the Criminal Justice System, such as, the effects of substance abuse in the community, racism, family or community breakdown, unemployment, income, and a lack of education and employment opportunities, dislocation from his/her community, community fragmentation, dysfunctional adoption and foster care, and residential school experience.[10]

Sections 84 and 84.1 allow Indigenous convicts to apply for parole and release, typically under supervised conditions, into an Indigenous community with a view toward reintegrating into that community. Notice to the community is required, which provides the Indigenous community an opportunity to propose a plan of supervision and reintegration. The manual also allows Indigenous Elders to be present in order to provide background information that will assist the Parole Board in reaching appropriate decisions.[11] A similar accommodation is allowing the parole hearings to be heard in Indigenous communities, also known as "releasing circles," which allows Indigenous communities to have input into the determinations.[12]

Even after the Parole Board grants parole, the delivery of correctional programming continues. The early stages of parole are often spent in a residential correctional facility, a halfway house. A halfway house, while not a prison, requires the offender to reside there and not be absent save under specific exceptions (e.g., supervised absences or employment). It is meant as a transitory phase in an offender's parole, neither full incarceration nor full freedom in the community, with the goal of gradual community reintegration. Many of the services previously mentioned as available in federal penitentiaries are often in halfway houses as well.[13]

There are indeed a number of halfway houses designed specifically to provide culturally sensitive services for the reintegration of Indigenous offenders. One type are the csc-operated Indigenous healing lodges within four federal minimum-security penitentiaries. They are the Okimaw Ohci Healing Lodge in Maple Creek, Saskatchewan, the Pê Sâkâstêw Centre in Mâskwâcîs, Alberta, the Kwìkwèxwelhp Healing Village in Harrison Mills, British Columbia, and the Willow Cree Healing Lodge near Duck Lake, Saskatchewan.[14] The other type is known as section 81 healing lodges and are operated by Indigenous communities themselves in partnership with the csc. They are the Stan Daniels Centre in Edmonton, the Buffalo Sage Wellness House in Edmonton, the Waseskun Healing House in Montreal, the Prince Albert Grand Council Spiritual Healing Lodge in Saskatchewan, and the O-Chi-Chak-Ko-Sipi Healing Lodge in Crane River, Manitoba.[15] It is easy of course to idealize Indigenous spiritual healing as an alternative route to rehabilitation and parole. Whether this works in practice is an issue we will now explore.

DOES IT WORK?

When culturally appropriate programming is effectively implemented and provided to Indigenous inmates, the evidence bears out that it produces positive results. Some of this evidence is anecdotal. A significant number of qualitative studies based on interviews with various Indigenous inmates have confirmed that practising Indigenous spirituality can contribute to inmates' healing, to increased self-esteem, and positive changes in lifestyle that make release and reintegration a real possibility.[16]

Sometimes success can also be found in improvements in the prison environment itself. For example, the Ma Mawi program, based in the Stony Mountain Institution in Manitoba, is a program designed for Indigenous inmates who have been convicted of domestic violence offences. It approaches the problem through a combination of healing and spiritual ceremonies, as well as educational components designed to help inmates understand and control their violence, establish healthier relationships, and develop parenting skills.[17] More specifically, the program is organized around twenty-nine sessions provided by the Elders to the inmates, with each session lasting 2.5 hours. The program was divided into four sections of sessions, with each session representing a geographical quarter of the medicine wheel. The first section, the south section, focuses on "to see," and it encourages inmates to seek initial insight into their problems and how those are tied to colonialism, cycles of violence, and substance abuse. The second section, the east, focuses on "to do." It encourages the inmates to learn how to express their feelings and engage in critical self-reflection. The third section, the west, focuses on "to think." The inmates learn to commit to positive relationships and personal improvement. The fourth section, the north section, focuses on "to know." The inmates engage in sharing circles and have personal goals to attain.[18] Many of the Indigenous inmates who were interviewed indicated that the program was a positive experience since it provided their first exposure to their traditional cultures and helped them understand and control their violence. Correctional staff also noted positive changes, including reduced aggression in the inmates and improved relationships between staff and inmates.[19]

Not all of the evidence is anecdotal, however — a consultation study of two available sources provides statistical proof that approaches to rehabilitation based on Indigenous cultures and spirituality are effective. One source focused on the case release files of 1,133 Indigenous inmates that had been stored in the csc's *Offender Management System*.[20] The other source was the information obtained through Joseph Johnston's study of 518 Indigenous inmates.[21] The recidivism rate for Indigenous offenders who had participated in cultural activities was 3.6 percent, compared to 32.5 percent for those who had not.[22] The recidivism rate was 14.4 percent for those who had participated in spiritual activities (e.g., sweat lodge ceremonies) versus 24.2 percent for those who had not.[23] The recidivism rate was 12.9 percent for inmates who had contacts or meetings with an Indigenous Elder, in comparison to 26.8 percent for those who didn't.[24] Additional confirmation came from a survey report based on interviews with fifty-six male and twelve female Indigenous ex-offenders who had not been charged with a Canadian criminal offence for at least two years following their release. While other factors such as family support and steady employment were important in keeping them out of trouble, a large percentage of the respondents indicated that participation in spiritual ceremonies (71%) and cultural activities (68%) were also significant.[25]

Success was also obtainable in a halfway house setting. The Stan Daniels Centre enjoyed a recidivism rate of 3.5 percent from the years 1988 to 2001. The recidivism study also suggested that the Indigenous healing lodge as implemented in Canada could provide a model worth implementing in dealing with American Indian over-incarceration.[26]

A 2011 evaluation of both CSC Lodges and section 81 healing lodges provides additional evidence. Sixty of every one hundred Indigenous men completed programming in CSC lodges, compared to thirty-three in minimum-security penitentiaries. The respective rates were sixty-four to thirty-two for Indigenous women.[27] Another measure of success is noted improvement in behaviour while within the institutions. Forty-two percent of correctional staff noted improved accountability and self-respect among the inmates, 28 percent noted increased cooperation and respect for others, 25 percent noted increased self-esteem, and 25 percent noted greater engagement with Indigenous culture. Favourable outcomes were also noted when it came to lowering several risk factors that the CSC had identified as tied to recidivism.[28]

Sometimes success also means a greater willingness to undergo and complete programs when they are culturally appropriate in comparison to standard programming. One consultation study found that Indigenous sexual offenders completed treatment programs less often than those of non-Indigenous offenders prior to the introduction of culturally sensitive programming. The differences in completion rates disappeared after culturally sensitive treatment was available.[29]

Despite these legislative and programming accommodations, there remain considerable problems with Indigenous inmates being denied access to meaningful programming and opportunities for parole. In 1996/1997, Indigenous offenders were granted parole at a rate of 34 percent compared to 41 percent for non-Indigenous offenders.[30] In 1998, it was found that Indigenous inmates waived their right to a parole hearing at a rate of 49 percent, versus 30 percent for non-Indigenous offenders.[31] Suggested reasons that have included many Indigenous inmates lacking knowledge of the parole process[32] and Indigenous inmates often mistrusting correctional staff so as to lack hope in the process.[33]

Howard Sapers, who completed an independent investigation of Canada's correctional system, concludes that part of the problem is ongoing systemic discrimination against Indigenous inmates when it comes to both parole and security classification decisions.[34] Sarah

Turnbull, sociology professor with the University of Waterloo, argues that the provision of Elder-assisted parole hearings is itself a continuation of the colonial status quo. She argues that the Parole Board has an implicit understanding that such hearings amount to little more than procedural tweaks that are only to be used in a small minority of cases. Elder-assisted hearings therefore do very little to fundamentally interrogate the role of colonialism in an Indigenous person's incarceration or to engage in an in-depth exploration of the Indigenous person's potential and possibilities for reintegration.[35]

It is apparent that despite some accommodations of Indigenous approaches to rehabilitation, and documented instances of success, not much headway has been made in addressing the problem of Indigenous over-incarceration. The discussion will now explore lingering obstacles as well as potential avenues to overcome them.

LACK OF RESOURCE COMMITMENT

While it is true that the federal government has implemented some culturally appropriate programs for Indigenous offenders, the resource allocations that are provided hardly reflect a serious effort to address the problem of Indigenous over-incarceration comprehensively and in earnest. Carol LaPrairie indicates that the availability of rehabilitative programs to Indigenous inmates varies greatly among institutions.[36] Participation in culturally sensitive programs was noted to be very low from January 1996 to June 2000, with the number of participants in certain types of programs ranging from 140 to 195 out of 4,819 Indigenous offenders.[37] The low level of participation was blamed on Indigenous inmates having very little access to culturally sensitive programming.[38] Sapers indicated before the Senate Standing Committee on Legal and Constitutional Affairs that the CSC had an annual budget of $1.8 billion, yet it allocated only $27 million of that for the delivery of core program services (i.e., all services available in federal penitentiaries, whether generic or Indigenous-specific).[39] He then went on to state that in light of this fact, it was hardly surprising that many Indigenous inmates had no access to culturally specific programs that could help them progress toward release.[40]

One study found that there were too few halfway houses that provided programming specifically for Indigenous offenders. For example, there is only one halfway house in Saskatoon, an urban centre with a significant Indigenous population.[41] Sapers released a 2012 report titled *Spirit Matters*, in which he concludes that Canada's support for only four section 81 lodges, offering a total of sixty-eight available beds, is simply inadequate. A key reason for this lack of funding was that in 2000, $11.9 million was allocated for the construction of new section 81 lodges. However, the Waseskun Healing House in Montreal was the only new section 81 lodge built under this fund. The remainder was instead used to create interventions for Indigenous inmates inside existing federal penitentiaries.[42]

Even for the existing section 81 lodges, the *Spirit Matters* report also noted the lack of support and resources available to them. This has meant a lack of staff retention and training, as well as a lack of structured programming that can address inmate needs.[43] csc-controlled healing lodges received $21,555,037 in funding, in comparison to $4,819,479 in funding for section 81 lodges.[44] The *Spirit Matters* report adds:

> Chronic under-funding of Section 81 Healing Lodges means that they are unable to provide comparable csc wages or unionized job security. As a result, many Healing Lodge staff seek employment with csc, where salaries can be 50% higher for similar work. It is estimated that it costs approximately $34,000 to train a Healing Lodge employee to csc requirements, but the Lodge operators receive no recognition or compensation for that expense.[45]

The report calls for more section 81 lodges and greater support for them. Indeed, the report suggests that financial support should not be any less than an increase of $11.6 million to reflect the fund that was allocated in 2001 for those lodges, adjusted for inflation.[46]

Even after release, there may be concerns about the lack of available services that can assist Indigenous people with effective reintegration. Another study found that Indigenous parolees often faced a lack of adequate housing or racist discrimination from prospective landlords. They were therefore vulnerable to residential instability, which increased their risk of reoffending. The study stressed the need for increased community supports so that Indigenous parolees could find adequate housing.[47] The *Spirit Matters* report also notes that there have been numerous issues with the implementation of s. 84 of the ccra, which is meant to facilitate parole and release for Indigenous inmates. The provision has been underutilized. For example, in 2010–2011, there were ninety-nine section 84 releases, even though 593 Indigenous offenders had expressed interested in a section 84 release.[48] The problems involved included:

1) There are only twelve Aboriginal Community Development Officers who are employed to develop bridges between Indigenous communities and Indigenous inmates. They face excessive caseloads that often cause them to lose focus on an Indigenous inmate's individual needs.

2) The process involved in applying for a section 84 release has become very cumbersome and lengthy, requiring at least twenty-five tasks for completion.

3) Indigenous communities are often not compensated by the CSC for the costs of programming, monitoring, or transporting an offender. This leads to resource deficiencies in the implementation of section 84 release plans.

4) The validity of programs and services under section 84 release plans, and whether plans adequately address an offender's needs, are decided by the CSC and not Indigenous communities themselves. This is "viewed as patronizing by many Indigenous people and communities."[49]

The report also calls upon the CSC to adjust its policies and resource allocations in order to fully implement Parliament's original legislative intent when the CCRA was first passed in 1992.[50]

Canadian governments should seriously consider investing greater allocations toward increasing culturally appropriate rehabilitative programming that is available to Indigenous inmates within federal institutions, within halfway houses, and for community resources post-release, if for no other reason than one of long-term expediency. As with preventative programming and Indigenous justice initiatives that have parallels to restorative justice, this may demand a greater investment in the short term. The 2011 evaluation of healing lodges noted that the annual cost per male inmate was higher for CSC-operated lodges than for minimum security institutions ($167,800 to $95,038), but it was roughly the same when comparing CSC-operated lodges for women ($218,545 to $211,093). The CSC attributes this increase in costs to the smaller bedding capacity of CSC-operated lodges, as well as the resources needed for Indigenous-specific programs and services.[51] To keep Indigenous inmates warehoused in the prison system, however, is far more expensive in the long term. The theme advanced here is that more resources should be poured into culturally appropriate programming with the idea of saving more in the long run by preparing Indigenous inmates sooner and faster for halfway house residency and ultimately offloading once full parole and reintegration is achieved. "Spend now, save later" is the idea. Resource allocations are not the only problem here, though — there are also issues with security classification.

SECURITY CLASSIFICATION AND PAROLE

Another barrier to accessing needed programming is that Indigenous offenders are placed in stricter security classifications in disproportionate numbers compared to non-Indigenous offenders. The 1990 Task Force on Federally Sentenced Women found that Indigenous women were much more likely to receive a higher security classification than non-Indigenous women.[52] The Native Women's Association of Canada estimated that as of 2003, Indigenous women comprised at least 50 percent of incarcerated federal women classified as maximum security.[53] A 2000 study found that Indigenous inmates were classified as maximum or medium security at rates of 27.7 percent and 34.7 percent, respectively, in comparison to rates of 20.3 percent and 24.1 percent for non-Indigenous offenders.[54] The security classification system can prejudice an inmate's ability to pursue reintegration through correctional programming and parole. The Canadian Human Rights Commission describes the effects of a maximum-security classification on female inmates as follows:

> Among the hardships imposed by this are the fact that maximum security inmates, unlike their minimum and medium security counterparts, are not eligible to participate in work-release programs, community release programs or other supportive programming designed to enhance their chances of reintegration. In fact, half of all maximum-security women are now being released directly from maximum security incarceration into the community after serving two-thirds of their sentence, without the benefit of preparatory programming.[55]

Tamara Walsh, law professor with the University of Queensland, also emphasizes the point that keeping long-term inmates in maximum security and then releasing them is detrimental. The inmates are released without having had adequate correctional programming or resources and supports to facilitate rehabilitation. Release under such circumstances is also potentially threatening to public safety.[56] And indeed, both the 2011 evaluation report on Indigenous healing lodges and the *Spirit Matters* report noted that a minimum-security classification is a prerequisite to being admitted to either a csc-operated lodge or a section 81 lodge.[57] The *Spirit Matters* report further noted that as of the 2010–2011 year, only 337 Indigenous inmates, a rate of 11 percent, were housed in minimum-security institutions. The prerequisite of a minimum-security designation had the effect of excluding nearly 90 percent of Indigenous inmates from a csc-operated or section 81 lodge. Thus, even with only sixty-eight section 81 bed spaces available, these have not been fully utilized due to the minimum-security prerequisite.[58]

Initial determination of security classification upon arrival in a federal penitentiary is made using the Custody Rating Scale. Under this scale, a score of 133.5 or higher on the security risk component qualifies an inmate for maximum security. It is here that prior history can operate as a static factor to the detriment of many Indigenous inmates. Penalties for an initial sentence amount to twenty points for five to nine years, forty-five points for ten to twenty-four years, and sixty-five points for twenty-five years or more. Being younger is also detrimental, with penalties for age at time of offence ranging from three points for thirty-four years of age to thirty points for being twenty-four years of age or younger. Twelve points are assigned for minor or moderate offences, while thirty-six points are assigned for serious or major offences. Penalties are also assessed for prior convictions, with three points for one prior conviction, six points for two to four prior convictions, nine points for five to nine prior convictions, twelve points for ten to fourteen prior convictions, and fifteen points for fifteen or more prior convictions.[59]

After the initial determination, an offender's security classification may be re-determined with the assistance of the Security Reclassification Scale.[60] Reclassification is to be considered at least once a year or when there is cause to believe that an offender should no longer be in minimum security, or every two years for offenders serving a life sentence for murder or terrorism.[61] The factors that are considered in whether to move an offender from one security classification to another are as follows:

a. The serious of the offence committed by the offender

b. Any outstanding charges against the offender

c. The offender's performance and behaviour while under sentence

d. The offender's social, criminal and, where available, young offender history

e. Any physical or mental illness or disorder suffered by the offender

f. The offender's potential for violent behaviour

g. The offender's continued involvement in criminal activities[62]

Note that the seriousness of the offence for which the offender has been imprisoned, and past criminal history, including youth offences, remains relevant to determining security reclassification. It is not hard to imagine that Indigenous inmates are placed at an obvious disadvantage during such redeterminations, as studies have shown that Indigenous inmates in the aggregate have worse criminal histories than non-Indigenous inmates.[63] One study, for example, shows that at least 80 percent of Indigenous federal inmates had previously served terms in provincial jails, compared to approximately 70 percent for non-Indigenous inmates.[64] Inuit and First Nations federal inmates were more likely to have served a previous adult community supervision sentence, at rates of 87 percent and 79 percent, respectively, in comparison to 72 percent for non-Indigenous inmates.[65] First Nations and Métis youth also have greater involvement with the justice system. First Nations offenders served terms in closed custody at a rate of 40 percent, terms in open custody at a rate of 39.5 percent, and underwent community youth supervision at a rate of 53 percent. For Métis offenders, the rates were 45.9 percent, 42.3 percent, and 57.3 percent. For non-Indigenous offenders, the rates were 27.5 percent, 24.9 percent, and 34 percent. First Nations inmates are more likely to be convicted for homicide offences, at a rate of 28 percent, in comparison to 24 percent for non-Indigenous inmates.[66] Inuit (39%), First Nations (39%), and Métis (33%) federal inmates were more likely to have committed a major assault crime than non-Indigenous inmates (26%).[67] Inuit offenders are far more likely to be convicted of sexual assault, at a rate of 62 percent, versus Métis inmates at 16 percent, First Nation inmates at 22 percent, and non-Indigenous inmates at 17 percent.[68]

These statistics have repercussions at least for initial security classification. Indigenous inmates were recommended for maximum-security placement at a rate of 21 percent, in comparison to non-Indigenous inmates at 15 percent.[69] The commissioner's directive on security classification does stress that CSC staff are to make a genuine effort to consider factors relevant to Indigenous offenders, such as history of family dislocation, lack of employment opportunities, lack of education, history of substance abuse, history of systemic or direct discrimination, and history of participation in Indigenous ceremonies and cultural activities.[70] It is a fair question to ask whether this part of the directive results or will result in any tangible benefits for Indigenous inmates while static factors involving prior history remain a substantial component of security determinations. Indigenous offenders continue to be placed more often in higher security classifications, and it is hard to ignore that the seriousness of the offence for which the inmate has been incarcerated as well as previous criminal history, youth history included, will represent enduring penalties for Indigenous offenders, even during reclassification. The security classification scheme, therefore, as applied to Indigenous inmates, may represent a form of systemic discrimination.

It is interesting to note, though, that a study by Cheryl Webster and Anthony Doob found that the use of criminal history had no predictive value whatsoever when it came to the involvement of Indigenous women with institutional incidences.[71] Indigenous women in maximum-security institutions were involved in institutional incidents at a percentage (28.6%) comparable to female inmates in medium- and minimum-security institutions (26.8%).[72] The study also found that correlation between their security risk score (based on previous criminal history) and involvements in institutional incidences were practically of zero strength. Indigenous women are thus more routinely placed into tighter security settings despite the fact that their criminal history has no predictive value for whether they are genuinely a risk to other inmates or staff.[73]

The security classification system has been criticized for not giving adequate attention to the social context that brings many Indigenous people into the prison system. Jena McGill, law professor with the University of Ottawa, notes that Indigenous women are far out of proportion subject to poverty, discrimination, and violent victimization.[74] She adds:

> The "one-size-fits-all" classification system employed by the CSC denies the complexity of Aboriginal women's lives by attempting to dissect them into discrete categories for the purposes of "needs classification," and problematically rejects any kind of contextual consideration of the impact that the systemic marginalization experienced by Aboriginal women in Canadian society is likely to have on their social histories.[75]

Patricia Monture-Angus, formerly a sociology professor with the University of Saskatchewan, adds with reference to both Indigenous men and women offenders:

> These risk scales are all individualized instruments. This must be seen as a significant and central problem for applying these instruments to Aboriginal people (male or female). This individualizing of risk absolutely fails to take into account the impact of colonial oppression on the lives of Aboriginal men and women. Equally, colonial oppression has not only had a devastating impact on individuals but concurrently on our communities and nations. This impact cannot be artificially pulled apart because the impact on the individual and the impact on the community are interconnected.[76]

A study by criminology professors from the University of Laval and the University of Montreal argues that contemporary Canadian policies of "Aboriginalizing" prisons amounts to reasserting Canadian hegemony over Indigenous Peoples via incarceration. Current risk assessment tools, while ostensibly race-neutral, result in more Indigenous inmates being assessed as high risk. This in turn equates to more Indigenous inmates being denied access to rehabilitative services.[77]

A particularly scathing critique comes from the Supreme Court of Canada in *R. v. Ewert*. The court concluded that the routine application of the security classification system did not violate *Charter* rights to equality and security of the person but it did contravene section 24(1) of the CCRA, which requires that the CSC ensure "that any information about an offender that it uses is as accurate, up to date and complete as possible." In so doing, the court recognized that the application of those factors to Indigenous offenders, who have lengthier criminal records and greater social instability in their lives, could lead to overestimation of their actual risk. And overestimation of risk in turn could result in higher security classifications, unnecessary denials of parole, and loss of access to rehabilitative programming.[78]

The *Spirit Matters* report admonishes the CSC to "seek ways of allowing those Healing Lodges to determine which offenders would benefit from the lodge's healing approach, regardless of their security classification, without jeopardizing the facility's physical and healing environment."[79] There are at least a couple of alternative strategies to addressing institutional security that also aspire to remedy the systemic discrimination latent in standard risk predictor instruments. One approach is to develop a classification scale specific to Indigenous offenders that addresses the concerns expressed by McGill, Monture-Angus, and others. The scale would have little or even no emphasis on static factors such as criminal history, and it would instead place primary emphasis on offenders' correctional needs and offender progress with behaviour while incarcerated.

There is reason to believe that such an alternative may indeed be workable. The Security Reclassification Scale for Women was developed as a gender-specific method of classification for female offenders. The nine items that are considered in this scale are as follows:

1. Correctional plan; program motivation

2. Maintains regular positive family contact

3. Number of convictions for serious disciplinary offences during the review period

4. Number of recorded incidents during the review period

5. History of escape or unlawfully at large from work release, temporary absence or community supervision

6. Pay level during the review period

7. Number of times the offender was placed in involuntary segregation for being a danger to others or the institution during the review period

8. Total number of escorted temporary absences (ETAS) during the review period

9. Custody Rating Scale incident history[80]

Note the de-emphasis on static factors involving the offence that was the basis of the original conviction, or previous criminal history, and a greater emphasis on progress with behaviour during the review period. Early field tests involving 580 files have found that the scale is reliably predictive of actual security risk.[81]

Given that there is evidence that Indigenous spiritual healing can improve offender behaviour and improve prison conditions generally, is there any legitimate reason why the Canadian correctional system should not develop an Indigenous-specific classification scale? The Supreme Court in *Ewert* admonished the csc to either research the extent to which existing actuarial tools sufficiently account for cross-cultural variance when applied to Indigenous inmates or to modify how those tools are applied to Indigenous inmates.[82] An Indigenous-specific scale could have little or no emphasis on static factors tied to previous criminal history. The scale instead would place emphasis on escape history, history of successful escorted temporary absences, and progress with culturally appropriate programming, with participation in cultural and spiritual activities, and with behaviour while in prison. If Indigenous spiritual healing continues to demonstrate its power to address the systemic factors behind Indigenous criminality, to lead Indigenous inmates towards positive reform, and to improve prison conditions overall, why should this not constitute the primary emphasis in an Indigenous-specific classification scale?

Another strategy is perhaps a search for alternatives to address institutional misconduct that do not necessarily have negative implications for security classification. The Stan Daniels Centre is noted for having strict rules enforcing curfew, cleanliness, conduct during supervised visits, and prohibiting drug use,[83] but, furthermore,

These more bureaucratic rules are counterbalanced by policies based in Aboriginal practices so that, for example, rule-breaking and inter-resident conflict are dealt with by a "sharing circle," a form of case conferencing, rather than a disciplinary hearing. Instead of receiving a fine, being put in segregation, or being sent back to the correctional institution, they may have to make an apology in front of a general meeting of the residents or make restitution by cutting wood for a sweat or by creating a piece of artwork dealing with forgiveness.[84]

Another avenue of reform involves risk assessment for the purposes of parole.

RISK ASSESSMENT AND PAROLE

When the Parole Board of Canada decides whether to grant an offender's application for parole, it must assess whether the application is meritorious such that public safety will not be endangered. There is no doubt that the board faces a difficult task. When a released offender goes on to reoffend, especially when it is a homicide offence, public fury naturally ensues. Examples include Eric Fish, who murdered two people in 2004, within six weeks after walking out of his halfway house,[85] and Daniel Jonathan Courchene, a known member of the Manitoba Warriors gang who was kept on parole despite several substance abuse-related parole violations and went on to attempt the murders of a police officer and a homeowner during a home invasion while on parole.[86] Be that as it may, as of 2002, these errors leading to homicide while on release amounted to only 0.3 percent of parolees.[87] In other words, the board rarely if ever gets it wrong such as to expose the public to mortal peril. The pertinent question for this study's purposes is how to facilitate the process such that the Parole Board can be convinced that releasing Indigenous inmates who apply for parole is good and safe.

An important consideration for the Parole Board in granting or denying parole is an actuarial risk assessment of whether the inmate is likely to reoffend. A federal corrections study concluded that risk assessment instruments aligned on eight central risk factors: 1) history of antisocial behaviour; 2) antisocial personality; 3) antisocial attitudes; 4) antisocial peers; 5) family/marital problems; 6) school/employment difficulties; 7) absence of positive leisure or recreational activities; and 8) substance abuse.[88] Factors such as antisocial peers and substance abuse are considered dynamic factors, which can change over time with sufficient treatment.[89] On the other hand, history of antisocial behaviour (e.g., criminal history) is a static factor that is not deemed to "change over time."[90] Percentages of inmates who were assessed as high risk to reoffend as of 2003 were 85 percent Inuit, 73 percent First Nations, 67 percent Métis, and 57 percent non-Indigenous inmates.[91]

Some research has indeed concluded that criminal history is a reliable risk predictor for both Indigenous and non-Indigenous inmates.[92] Indeed, one study found that from 2006 to 2009, Indigenous federal inmates had higher incidences of institutional misconduct than their non-Indigenous counterparts.[93] Consider, however, that colonial oppression and the enduring social conditions that it has left behind continue to play a critical role in Indigenous over-incarceration. To the extent that oppressive social conditions do much to bring Indigenous Peoples into contact with the justice system, the emphasis on static factors tied with criminal history may represent a form of systemic discrimination.

In fact, a 2017 research report by Public Safety Canada concluded that standard risk assessment tools have less predictive accuracy for Indigenous offenders than non-Indigenous offenders.[94] The authors admitted that they could not conclude with certainty the reason for the loss of predictive accuracy, although they speculated. One explanation was that systemic discrimination in justice system practices themselves, such as increased police attention and Indigenous offenders thus having more extensive criminal histories, had the result of artificially inflating Indigenous offenders' projected risk. Another reason was the failure of the risk assessment instruments to account for the unique historical and social factors (e.g., colonialism, intergenerational trauma) that Indigenous offenders face. A third explanation was a failure to account for the degree to which connection to Indigenous culture and spirituality can mitigate Indigenous offender risk and degree that the absence of those connections can exacerbate risk.[95]

The question then becomes how to address this. Consider that there is compelling statistical evidence that Indigenous spiritual healing can produce remarkably positive results with respect to recidivism post-release. This strongly indicates that Indigenous spiritual healing has the capacity to address risk factors and prevent recidivism — suggesting that perhaps where Indigenous inmates are concerned, static factors should be de-emphasized in favour of dynamic factors. The John Howard Society says of dynamic factors:

> Dynamic factors have been found to predict recidivism as well as, or better than, static factors and are also measured by several actuarial risk assessment tools. It is knowledge of dynamic factors that is necessary in order to assess changes in an offender's risk level. Through participation in rehabilitative programming, an offender may become less likely to recidivate, but corrections and parole workers would not be able to measure this change unless they assessed the offender's risk based on changeable factors.[96]

It may thus be useful for actuarial risk assessment of Indigenous offenders to de-emphasize static factors and instead focus on participation in culturally appropriate programming and spiritual healing, along with attendant offender progress in addressing dynamic risk factors. Culturally appropriate programming and spiritual healing can mould Indigenous inmates' behaviours such that they can prepare themselves for parole and reintegration. There remains a particularly thorny issue in this area though — the prevalence of Indigenous gangs in the prison system.

INDIGENOUS GANGS AND PAROLE

This is a phenomenon that is particularly worrisome among Indigenous Peoples. Indigenous gangs have their genesis in the Canadian penal system, as Criminal Intelligence Service Canada has reported,[97] and they now exist in significantly large numbers and with every expectation of expanding. There is no doubt that prison gangs present real security concerns. One study that found junior gang members were more likely to commit violent offences within the American prison system than inmates who were not affiliated with gangs to a statistically significant level. The study found, however, that inmates who had spent longer periods in prison were not significantly more likely to commit violent offences than unaffiliated inmates. The study was uncertain as to whether this indicated the accumulated stress of gang activity on an inmate's life or whether this reflected moving up in the gang hierarchy and therefore the inmate's capacity to give orders instead of having to carry them out.[98] Indigenous gangs can present real safety problems for both inmates and correctional staff. Guards at the Edmonton Institution, a maximum-security facility, reported that Indigenous gang members frequently assaulted other inmates as part of competition for the lucrative prison drug trade, as well as to keep the other inmates intimidated. They also are not afraid to take violent runs at the prison guards.[99]

It could be argued that by voluntarily joining a gang, an Indigenous inmate has engaged in self-labelling as one given to criminal activity and therefore greater scrutiny for the sake of both institutional and public safety.[100] Indigenous inmates have frequently complained that they face a double jeopardy phenomena — once for being an Indigenous offender and again for being identified as a member of an Indigenous prison gang.[101]

A approach frequently used by Canadian correctional officials has been to try to keep Indigenous gang inmates segregated from each other and sometimes even to keep Indigenous inmates segregated from members of rival Indigenous gangs. A report, however, describes the fallacies of such an approach:

> The next stage in the process is the segregation of known gang members. Gang members are isolated in units of their own and kept separate from other rival gangs. There are several problems with this approach. First and foremost, it is an attempt at "accommodation" of the gang phenomena and does not directly deal with the root causes of the problem. When we segregate gangs, we are essentially throwing our hands up in despair and saying that the only way that we can control the situation is by trying to "manage" them by monitoring their movement and activities and making sure they do not interact with other gangs. This approach puts an onerous strain on correctional officers who have to be vigilant in keeping track of which group members are where at what time. Secondly, this approach leads to increased tensions in institutions as gang members, encouraged in their agitation and animosity through segregation, search for opportunities to threaten and intimidate rival gang members (through glass windows, doors, open access areas).[102]

Approaches to gang activity may not, however, always require an iron-fisted approach. It is possible for more conciliatory or rehabilitative approaches to make progress. One Canadian study found that rehabilitative programs that emphasize cognitive-behavioural therapy reduced recidivism for major institutional offences among treated gang members by 20 percent in comparison to untreated gang members after a two year follow-up.[103] The study also concluded that the one-time $100,000 cost for treating a gang member made such an approach more cost-effective relative to the enormous year-to-year cost of housing criminals in the long term.[104]

Alternatives with an Indigenous cultural emphasis have also proven effective. An illustrative example, albeit not one that occurred in a prison setting, comes from Manitoba. The objective of the Ogijiita Pimatiswin Kinamatwin program is to facilitate a transition toward a better lifestyle for members of Indigenous street gangs. Participants learn carpentry skills and help develop or improve housing in inner-city areas. The program did not necessarily require the participants to cut ties with fellow gang members, only to desist from further criminal activity. From 2001 to 2006, thirty-four participants took part in the program, some of them with extensive criminal histories that include drug-related and violent offences. None of the participants were ever arrested during that period.[105]

One Canadian maximum-security prison tried a more conciliatory strategy to address the problem of Indigenous prison gangs: the Dynamic Intervention Approach. Measures that were employed in this approach included having correctional officers learn about the individual situations of the inmates, speaking with and listening to inmates, taking steps to address concerns expressed by individual inmates, ensuring access to educational and correctional programming for inmates, and ensuring access for Indigenous inmates to Elders so as to pursue spiritual healing. This approach produced a set of widely understood guidelines for proper inmate behaviour as well as a truce between correctional officers, Indigenous inmates, and the general prison population that led to a relatively safe and stable environment thereafter.[106]

Some Indigenous inmates who were interviewed in a consultation study expressed the view that gang affiliation is not a static matter and that Indigenous inmates are often willing to disassociate from prison gangs in order to reform behaviour or seek healing. The problem is that the gang member label stays with them despite any positive efforts, and this impairs their ability to improve their security classification and seek Elder healing and culturally appropriate programming.[107] The study recommended that correctional staff adopt a more flexible approach that gauges commitment and willingness to disassociate from the gang life-style and begin reformation, thereby increasing inmates' access to need-ed resources.[108] Perhaps these concerns could be incorporated into or addressed by this book's recommended Indigenous-specific classification scale, which would emphasize progress with spiritual healing, cultural programming, and behaviour.

Notes

1   Ross D. London, "The Restoration of Trust: Bringing Restorative Justice from the Margins to the Mainstream," *Criminal Justice Studies* 16, 3 (2003), 175; Sherman and Strang, *Restorative Justice: The Evidence*, 82–83.

2   Robert Ambrose, "Decarceration in a Mass Incarceration State: The Road to Prison Abolition," *Mitchell Hamline Law Review* 45 (2019), 732, 753; Allegra McLeod, "Prison Abolition and Grounded Justice," ucla *Law Review* 62 (2015), 1156, 1168.

3   Hadley Friedland, for example, notes that permanent banishment or even execution was possible in Cree legal orders, but only as a last resort. Hadley Friedland, *Cree Legal Summary* (Victoria: Indigenous Legal Research Unit, 2013), 21.

4   James Waldram, *The Way of the Pipe* (Peterborough: Broadview Press, 1997), 68.

5   Waldram, *The Way of the Pipe*, 71–75.

6   Waldram, *The Way of the Pipe*, 85–96; for other works with similar themes, see Emily R. Brault, "Sweating in the Joint: Personal and Cultural Renewal and Healing Through Sweat Lodge Practice by Native Americans in Prison," PhD thesis, Vanderbilt University, 2005; Lee Irwin, "Walking the Line: Pipe and Sweat Ceremonies in Prison," *Nova Religio: The Journal of Alternative and Emergent Religions* 9, 3 (2006), 39.

7   *Corrections and Conditional Release Act,* S.C. 1992, c. 20, s. 80.

8   Waldram, *The Way of the Pipe*, 83.

9   *Corrections and Conditional Release Act,* s. 102.

10 Parole Board of Canada, *Policy Manual,* vol. 1, no. 13 (Ottawa: Parole Board of Canada, 2008), 2.1–2.

11 National Parole Board, *Policy Manual,* 9.2.1–1.

12 Parole Board of Canada, *Parole Board of Canada: Contributing to Public Safety* (Ottawa: Parole Board of Canada, 2011), 7.

13 John Howard Society of Alberta, *Halfway House: Executive Summary* (Edmonton: John Howard Society of Alberta, 2001).

14 John McKay, *Indigenous Peoples in the Federal Correction System, Report of the Standing Committee on Public Safety and National Security* (Ottawa: House of Commons, 2018), 13.

15 McKay, *Indigenous Peoples in the Federal Correction System,* 14.

16 For a study that involved interviews with inmates in a minimum security institution designed specifically for Aboriginal inmates, see Connie Braun, "Colo-

nization, Destruction, and Renewal: Stories from Aboriginal Men at the Pe'
Sakastew Centre," MA thesis, University of Saskatchewan, 1998. See also Joseph C. Johnston, *Aboriginal Offender Survey: Case Files and Interview Sample*
(Ottawa: Correctional Service of Canada, 1997); Waldram, *The Way of the Pipe*,
129–50; Nicole Crutcher and Shelley Trevethan, "An Examination of Healing
Lodges for Aboriginal Offenders in Canada," *Forum on Corrections Research*
14, 3 (2002), 52; Theresa Howell, "Stories of Transformation: Aboriginal Offenders' Journey from Prison to Community," *American Indian Culture and
Research Journal* 40, 1 (2016), 101.

17   Evelyn Zellerer, "Culturally Competent Programs: The First Family Violence
Program for Aboriginal Men in Prison," *The Prison Journal* 83, 2 (2003), 171.

18   Zellerer, "Culturally Competent Programs," 180–81.

19   Zellerer, "Culturally Competent Programs," 183.

20   Raymond Sioui and Jacques Thibault, *The Relevance of a Cultural Adaptation
of the Reintegration Potential Reassessment Scale (rprs)* (Ottawa: Correctional
Service of Canada, Research Branch, 2001), 17.

21   Joseph C. Johnston, *Aboriginal Offender Survey: Case Files and Interview Sample*, Research Report R-61 (Ottawa: Correctional Service of Canada, 1997).

22   Sioui and Thibault, *The Relevance of a Cultural Adaptation*, 43.

23   Sioui and Thibault, *The Relevance of a Cultural Adaptation*, 42.

24   Sioui and Thibault, *The Relevance of a Cultural Adaptation*, 44.

25   Doug Heckbert and Douglas Turkington, "Turning Points: Factors Related to
the Successful Reintegration of Aboriginal Offenders," *Forum on Correctional
Research* 14, 3 (2002), 56.

26   Marianne O. Neilsen, "Canadian Aboriginal Healing Lodges: A Model for the
United States?" *The Prison Journal* 83, 1 (2003), 81.

27   Eugenia Didenko and Bernard Maquis, *Evaluation Report: Strategic Plan for
Aboriginal Corrections* (Ottawa: Correctional Service of Canada, Evaluation
Branch, Policy Sector, 2011), 57.

28   Indigenous men released from csc-operated lodges showed an aggregate 23%
improvement when it came to maintaining employment, 22% for familial and
interpersonal relationships, 24% for positive social interactions, 37% for con-
trolling substance abuse, 26% for personal/emotional needs, and 34% for attitude. The respective percentages for Indigenous men released from section
81 lodges were 16%, 22%, 22%, 31%, 25%, and 36%. The respective percentages
for Indigenous men released from minimum-security institutions were 14%,
18%, 15%, 25%, 20%, and 25%. The respective rates for Indigenous women
released from csc-operated lodges were 15%, 20%, 19%, 28%, 29%, and 35%.
The respective rates for Indigenous women released from multi-level security
institutions were 15%, 16%, 19%, 23%, 20%, and 25%. Didenko and Maquis,
Evaluation Report: Strategic Plan for Aboriginal Corrections, 70.

29   Lawrence Ellerby and Paula MacPherson, *Exploring the Profiles of Aboriginal
Sex Offenders: Contrasting Aboriginal and Non-Aboriginal Sexual Offenders to
Determine Unique Client Characteristics and Potential Implications for Sex Of-
fender Assessment and Treatment Strategies*, Research Report R-122 (Ottawa:
Correctional Service of Canada, 2002).

30   Andrew Welsh and James P. Ogloff, "Full Parole and the Aboriginal Experience: Accounting for the Racial Discrepancies in the Release Rates," *Canadian Journal of Criminology* 42, 4 (2000), 472.

31   Solicitor General of Canada, *Canadian Correctional Release Assessment, 5 Year Review: Aboriginal Offenders* (Ottawa: Minister of Supply and Services, 1998).

32   Joseph C. Johnston, *Northern Aboriginal Offenders in Custody: A Profile* (Ottawa: Correctional Service of Canada, 1994).

33   Johnston, *Aboriginal Offender Survey: Case Files and Interview Sample.*

34   Howard Sapers, *Annual Report of the Correctional Investigator, 2005/2006* (Ottawa: Office of the Correctional Investigator, 2005), 11.

35   Sarah Turnbull, "Aboriginalising the Parole Process: 'Culturally Appropriate' Adaptations and the Canadian Federal Parole System," *Punishment & Society* 16, 4 (2014), 385.

36   Carole LaPrairie, *Examining Aboriginal Corrections in Canada* (Ottawa: Aboriginal Corrections, Ministry of the Solicitor General, 1996), 84–85.

37   Sioui and Thibault, *The Relevance of a Cultural Adaptation,* 17.

38   Raymond Sioui and Jacques Thibault, "Examining Reintegration Potential for Aboriginal Offenders," *Forum on Corrections Research* 14, 3 (2002), 51.

39   Canada. *Debates of the Senate,* 2nd Session, 39th Parliament, volume 144, no. 36 (February 27, 2008), 857 <publications.gc.ca/collections/collection_2017/sen/Y3-392-36-eng.pdf>.

40   "ARCHIVED — Speaking Notes for Mr. Howard Sapers, Correctional Investigator of Canada, Appearance before the Standing Senate Committee on Legal and Constitutional Affairs, Thursday, February 14, 2008," Office of the Correctional Investigator <oci-bec.gc.ca/cnt/comm/sp-all/sp-all20080214-eng.aspx>.

41   Solicitor General of Canada, *Issues in Urban Aboriginal Corrections: Report on a Focus Group and an Overview of the Literature and Experience* (Ottawa: Solicitor General, 1998), 23.

42   Howard Sapers, *Spirit Matters: Aboriginal People and the Corrections and Conditional Release Act* (Ottawa: Office of the Correctional Investigator, 2012), 15–17.

43   Crutcher and Trevethan, "An Examination of Healing Lodges for Aboriginal Offenders in Canada," 56.

44   Sapers, *Spirit Matters,* 20.

45   Sapers, *Spirit Matters,* 4.

46   Sapers, *Spirit Matters,* 34.

47   Jason D. Brown et al., "Housing for Aboriginal Ex-Offenders in the Urban Core," *Qualitative Social Work* 7 (2008), 238.

48   Sapers, *Spirit Matters,* 24.

49   Sapers, *Spirit Matters,* 24–25.

50   Sapers, *Spirit Matters,* 33.

51   Didenko and Maquis, *Evaluation Report: Strategic Plan for Aboriginal Corrections,* 77.

52   Task Force on Federally Sentenced Women, *Creating Choices* (Ottawa: Correctional Service of Canada, 1990), 112.

53   Elizabeth Fry Society, *Discrimination Against Aboriginal Women Rampant in*

Federal Prisons Claims the Native Women's Association of Canada (Ottawa: Elizabeth Fry Society, 2003).

54 Andrew Welsh and James Ogloff, "Progressive Reforms or Maintaining the Status Quo? An Empirical Evaluation of the Judicial Consideration of Aboriginal Status in Sentencing Decisions," *Canadian Journal of Criminology* 50, 4 (2008), 479.

55 Canadian Human Rights Commission, *Protecting Their Rights: A Systemic Review of Human Rights in Correctional Services for Federally Sentenced Women* (Ottawa: Canadian Human Rights Commission, 2003).

56 Tamara Walsh, "Is Corrections Correcting? An Examination of Prisoner Rehabilitation Policy and Practice in Queensland," *Australian and New Zealand Journal of Criminology* 39, 1 (2006), 109.

57 *Evaluation Report: Strategic Plan for Aboriginal Corrections,* 40; Sapers, *Spirit Matters,* 3.

58 Sapers, *Spirit Matters,* 3–4.

59 "Security Classification and Penitentiary Placement, Annex B: Custody Rating Scale," Corrections Canada <csc-scc.gc.ca/acts-and-regulations/705-7-cd-eng.shtml#annexB>.

60 Correctional Service of Canada, *Commissioner's Directive 710-6 — Review of Offender Security Classification* (Ottawa: Correctional Service of Canada, 2009).

61 Correctional Service of Canada, *Commissioner's Directive 710-6,* 3.

62 Correctional Service of Canada, *Commissioner's Directive 710-6,* 6.

63 Alexander Holsinger, Christopher Lowenkamp, and Edward Latessa, "Ethnicity, Gender, and the Level of Service Inventory — Revised," *Journal of Criminal Justice* 31, 4 (2003), 309; c and Ogloff, "Progressive Reforms or Maintaining the Status Quo?" 479; Robert Hann and Willaim Harman, *Predicting Release Risk for Aboriginal Penitentiary Inmates* [(Ottawa: Solicitor General, 1993).

64 John-Patrick Moore, *First Nations, Métis, Inuit and Non-Aboriginal Offenders: A Comparative Profile* (Ottawa: Correctional Service of Canada, Research Branch, 2003), 44.

65 Moore, *First Nations, Métis, Inuit and Non-Aboriginal Offenders,* 16.

66 Moore, *First Nations, Métis, Inuit and Non-Aboriginal Offenders,* 17.

67 Moore, *First Nations, Métis, Inuit and Non-Aboriginal Offenders,* 17.

68 Moore, *First Nations, Métis, Inuit and Non-Aboriginal Offenders,* 17–18.

69 Moore, *First Nations, Métis, Inuit and Non-Aboriginal Offenders,* 19.

70 Correctional Service of Canada, *Commissioner's Directive 710-6,* 5.

71 Cheryl Webster and Anthony Doob, "Classification without Validity or Equity: An Empirical Examination of the Custody Rating Scale for Federally Sentenced Women Offenders in Canada," *Canadian Journal of Criminology* 46, 4 (2004), 395.

72 Webster and Doob, "Classification without Validity or Equity," 400.

73 Webster and Doob, "Classification without Validity or Equity," 401–2.

74 Jena McGill, "An Institutional Suicide Machine: Discrimination against Federally Sentenced Aboriginal Women in Canada," *Race/Ethnicity* 2, 1 (2008), 98.

75 Jena McGill, "An Institutional Suicide Machine," 99.

76   Patricia Monture-Angus, "Aboriginal Women and Correctional Practice: Re-
      flections on the Task Force on Federally Sentenced Women," in Kelly Hannah-
      Moffat and Margaret Shaw (eds.), *An Ideal Prison? Critical Essays on Women's
      Imprisonment in Canada* (Halifax: Fernwood Publishing, 2000), 52, 56.
77   Joane Martel, Renee Bressard, and Mylene Jaccoud, "When Two Worlds Col-
      lide: Aboriginal Risk Management in Canadian Corrections," *British Journal of
      Criminology* 51, 2 (2011), 235.
78   *R. v. Ewert*, [2018] 2 S.C.R. 165, para. 65.
79   Sapers, *Spirit Matters*, 30.
80   Kelley Blanchette and Kelly Taylor, "Development and Validation of a Security
      Reclassification Scale for Women," *Forum on Corrections Research* 16, 1 (2004),
      29.
81   Statistically significant correlations were found between srsw scores and in-
      volvements in major and minor institutional incidences, at r=0.33 and r=0.32
      respectively. The r= represents the use of a Simple Pearson's Co-efficient value,
      with -1 indicating a perfect negative linear relationship, while +1 represents a
      perfect positive linear relationship (i.e., strongest possible correlation). In an
      Area Under the Curve statistical calculation, a score of 1.0 means perfect pre-
      dictive power, while a score of 0.50 or less means no predictive power. The srsw
      had an auc score of 0.73. Blanchette and Taylor, "Development and Validation
      of a Security Reclassification Scale for Women," 29.
82   *R. v. Ewert*, para. 67.
83   Neilsen, "Canadian Aboriginal Healing Lodges," 75.
84   Neilsen, "Canadian Aboriginal Healing Lodges," 76.
85   "Man Who Fled Vernon Halfway House Charged in 2nd Slaying," cbc *News*,
      February 28, 2007.
86   "Shot Manitoba rcmp Officer Seeks to Sue Parole Board," ctv *News*, March
      12, 2002.
87   Lynne Cohen, "Law & Disorder: Are Parole Officers Dodging the Nasties?" *The
      Report*, July 8, 2002, 34.
88   Tanya Rugge, *Risk Assessment of Male Aboriginal Offenders: A 2006 Perspective*
      (Ottawa: Public Safety and Emergency Preparedness Canada, 2006), i, 6.
89   Rugge, *Risk Assessment of Male Aboriginal Offenders*, i–ii.
90   Rugge, *Risk Assessment of Male Aboriginal Offenders*, i.
91   Moore, *First Nations, Métis, Inuit and Non-Aboriginal Offenders*, 23.
92   James Bonta, "Native Inmates: Institutional Response, Risk, and Needs," *Ca-
      nadian Journal of Criminology* 31, 1 (1989), 49; James Bonta, Carol LaPrairie,
      and Suzanne Wallace-Capretta, "Risk Prediction and Re-offending: Aboriginal
      and non-Aboriginal Offenders," *Canadian Journal of Criminology* 39, 2 (1997),
      127; James Bonta, Stan Lipinski, and Michael Martin, "The Characteristics of
      Aboriginal Recidivists," *Canadian Journal of Criminology* 34, 3/4 (1992), 517.
93   Rick Ruddell and Shannon Gotschell, "The Prison Adjustment of Aboriginal
      Offenders," *Australian and New Zealand Journal of Criminology* 47, 3 (2014),
      336.
94   Leticia Guiterrez, Leslie Maaike Helmus, and R. Karl Hanson, *What We Know
      and Don't Know About Risk Assessment of Offenders With Indigenous Heritage*

(Ottawa: Public Safety, 2017).

95   Guiterrez, Helmus, and Hanson, *What We Know and Don't Know*, 9.

96   John Howard Society, *Offender Risk Assessment* (Edmonton: John Howard Society, 2000), 3. The studies being referred to are Paul Gendreau, Tracey Little, and Claire Goggin, *A Meta-Analysis of the Predictors of Adult Offender Recidivism: What Works!* (Ottawa: Public Works and Government Services Canada), 1996; R. Karl Hanson and Monique Bussière, *Predictors of Sexual Offender Recidivism: A Meta-Analysis* (Ottawa: Public Works and Government Services Canada, 1996).

97   *2003 Annual Report on Organized Crime in Canada* (Ottawa: Criminal Intelligence Service Canada, 2003), 5.

98   Gerald G. Gaies et al., "The Influence of Prison Gang Affiliation on Violence and Other Prison Misconduct," *The Prison Journal* 82, 3 (2002), 359. For a study that explains perceptions on the part of American correctional officials that gang-affiliated inmates were more likely to assault inmates than un-affiliated inmates, see Rick Ruddell, Scott H. Decker, and Arlen Egley Jr., "Gang Interventions in Jails: A National Analysis," *Criminal Justice Review* 31, 1 (2006), 33.

99   "Who's Running the Joint: Prison Guards Say Native Gangs are Booming Under the Soft Regime at the Edmonton Max," *Alberta Report*, August 16, 1999, 18–19.

100 Ovide Mercredi, *Aboriginal Gangs: A Report to the Correctional Service of Canada on Aboriginal Youth Gang Members in the Federal Corrections System* (Ottawa: Correctional Service of Canada, 2000, 7).

101 Mercredi, *Aboriginal Gangs*, 7.

102 Jana Grekul, *"When You Have Nothing to Live For, You Have Nothing to Die For": An Investigation into the Formation and Recruitment Processes of Aboriginal Gangs in Western Canada* (Ottawa: Public Safety Canada, Aboriginal Corrections Policy Unit, 2006), 75.

103 Chantal Di Placido et al., "Treatment of Gang Members Can Reduce Recidivism and Institutional Misconduct," *Law and Human Behavior* 31, 1 (2006), 108. This study was with reference to standardized programming that was accessible to both Indigenous and non-Indigenous gang members.

104 Di Placido et al., "Treatment of Gang Members," 109.

105 Lawrence Deane, Denis C. Bracken, and Larry Morrissette, "Desistance within an Urban Aboriginal Gang," *Journal of Community and Criminal Justice* 54, 2 (2007), 128.

106 Mercredi, *Aboriginal Gangs*, 14–17.

107 Mercredi, *Aboriginal Gangs*, 17.

108 Mercredi, *Aboriginal Gangs*, 17.

12

RECONCILIATION IN THE FUTURE

Many, if not most, people tend to see crime as a moral choice to be condemned and punished — and this informs tough-on-crime policies that rely on punishment through incarceration. It is a harsh approach that lacks a nuanced consideration of the adverse social conditions that drive many persons to commit criminal behaviour. Many empirical studies affirm that social conditions such as poverty, abusive and/or unstable home environments, and other factors play a strong role in increasing crime rates and recidivism. Other empirical studies have verified that these social conditions have an alarming prevalence in Indigenous communities. Countless reported legal decisions have also noted the presence of these conditions when it comes to Indigenous persons coming into contact with the criminal justice system. Many of these same decisions also trace the problems back to residential schools as an integral part of the colonization of Indigenous Peoples, either as the accused having suffered as a student in the schools or experiencing trauma that has spread across generations in Indigenous communities.

It is not overstating matters to say that residential schools have played the most important role in the grave problem of Indigenous over-incarceration. Is it the only causative factor? Certainly not. It could be suggested that Indigenous gangs hold out their own social allure to draw in more members, or racial profiling of Indigenous Peoples, or that land dispossession and subsequent poverty have also been contributing factors. Nonetheless, it is hard to contest that the problem of Indigenous over-incarceration would be nowhere near the magnitude that it has reached today, if at all, but for residential schools having spread severe trauma on a massive scale from generation to generation among Indigenous Peoples.

Reconciliation is envisioned here as a process that unfolds in two stages. The first stage requires that Canada act in genuine partnership with Indigenous Peoples. This requires far more than band-aid provisions; instead, a comprehensive set of initiatives are needed to tackle the problem at all of its temporal stages. It requires a fundamental overhaul of how Canada approaches criminal justice for Indigenous Peoples in order to minimize any need for their incarceration.

One proposal involves greater investment in social and preventative programming that both moulds healthier Indigenous communities but also minimizes, to the greatest extent possible, the need for any "after the fact" responses in the criminal justice system. Such programming must not be generic but must specifically include elements of Indigenous culture and spirituality so as to better serve the needs of Indigenous clients and communities.

Another strategy is to further support contemporary adaptations of Indigenous justice that resemble restorative justice. This requires a recognition that a bifurcation based on Canadian assumptions about less serious and more serious offences should not be a significant barrier to the implementation of Indigenous justice initiatives. This means applying Indigenous perspectives on justice to a greater range of harmful behaviour, beyond the minimal range of serious offences that conventional restorative justice is typically limited to.

A third proposal involves more investment in prison correctional programs that include elements of Indigenous cultures and spirituality to best meet the needs of Indigenous inmates who may still need to be incarcerated, while still contemplating their eventual reintegration. That also includes the development of Indigenous-specific risk scales that place greater emphasis on dynamic risk factors instead of static risk factors, so as to increase access to culturally sensitive services and further access to parole where it is merited.

The transitory phase involves working within a state framework, with the eventual hope that it can give way to revitalized Indigenous legal orders as Indigenous Peoples gain capacity and experience with administering justice in their own communities. And that can mean applying Indigenous approaches to justice to a still greater range of harmful behaviour than what could be expected in partnership with the state during the transitory phase.

It must be acknowledged that the hope expressed here is very speculative and idealized, and it may well lead to more of the politics of recognition that Coulthard critiques. Yet the limits of direct action that Coulthard and Alfred propose are significant as well. The Word Warrior approach articulated by Turner is, in the end, preferable here, for the reason that there is evidence that mainstream Canada can be willingly persuaded to change directions with respect to both Indigenous Peoples themselves and criminal justice policy generally. The proposals require, at least for the time being, Canada to invest resources in partnership with Indigenous societies to make the initiatives work. Certainly, these proposals place very significant demands for resources, but Canada is spending far too much as it is on tough-on-crime policies that are not only ineffective but even counterproductive. The proposals may make a greater initial demand for resources in the short term, but they will prove not just more effective but will also lead to considerable resource savings for everyone concerned in the long run. The Word Warrior approach, in this instance, tries to align Canadian self-interest with Indigenous aspirations.

On that note, much of what has been proposed here has amounted to drawing on prison abolition ideas but in ways that are distinctive to the circumstances and needs of Indigenous Peoples in Canada. It may be enough, at least in the context of Indigenous Peoples, if incarceration were almost completely minimized. It may be all for good, though, if mainstream Canada were to fundamentally rethink its uncritical reliance on incarceration and likewise embark on a course of prison abolition while reconciling with Indigenous Peoples. But of course, we are currently far from that point.

Canadian policies presently fall well short of what can be considered true reconciliation. The previous Tory government led by Stephen Harper pursued justice policies that were fundamentally inconsistent with reconciliation. Those policies sustained, even exacerbated, Indigenous over-incarceration and deprioritized more constructive policies. The Tory government pursued those policies despite substantial and growing empirical evidence that mass incarceration policies are counterproductive and that the alternatives are likely much more effective. Those policies were also followed without any meaningful consultation with Indigenous Peoples, which fell far short of the Canadian government acting in a genuine partnership or sharing mutual decision-making power with Indigenous communities. For Prime Minister Harper to provide a verbal apology but then pursue counterproductive policies that worsen problems for Indigenous Peoples amounts to mere "words" but without any "concrete action."[1]

It remains to be seen what directions the current Liberal government led by Justin Trudeau will take. Some but not all of the signs are encouraging. The current government has been willing to invest relatively more resources into Indigenous programming. They delayed for years to act on a campaign promise to repeal the mandatory minimums and only recently repealed a fraction of them. There is the allocation for revitalizing Indigenous legal orders — but the amount is small enough that some may dismiss it as a token gesture. The discovery of unmarked graves near the residential schools has apparently spurred additional allocations. Federal Indigenous Services minister Marc Miller announced in August 2021 an allocation of $107 million for healing services for residential school survivors and those affected by intergenerational trauma.[2] That allocation could be a promising sign.

There is also, of course, the spectre of governments changing hands — and that means that the priority given to Indigenous reconciliation can oscillate, and not always for the better. That in turn means that the years- or even decades-long commitment needed to see reconciliation through can end up frustrated through the vagaries of electoral change. That admittedly could end up justifying Coulthard's critiques of the politics of recognition.

It is perhaps easier for non-Indigenous Canadians to simply maintain the status quo and continue to dismiss Indigenous concerns as those of an inconsequential minority. I would discourage non-Indigenous Canadians from becoming comfortable with such an assumption, which is fallacious when considering future repercussions. The Indigenous population as of 2011 was estimated at 1,502,000, representing 4.4 percent of Canada's population. However, the Indigenous population is projected to grow at a rate of 2.2 percent, compared to a rate of 1 percent for non-Indigenous Canadians over the next twenty years. The Indigenous population is projected to amount to 1,965,000 to 2,633,000 by 2036, amounting to 4.6 to 6.1 percent of Canada's population.[3] The potential repercussions are staggering, and the costs associated with Indigenous over-incarceration alone should be proof of that.[4] Indigenous population growth combined with Indigenous over-incarceration cannot be considered anything less than a looming crisis, with the promise of incredible demands on resources. It is not difficult to anticipate similar repercussions when it comes to issues such as Indigenous over-representation in child welfare apprehensions and Indigenous underachievement in educational settings. Non-Indigenous Canadians and their leaders must become mindful of this reality.

There is, of course, no guarantee that Indigenous self-determination will necessarily solve these problems. What can be guaranteed is that the status quo will perpetuate or even worsen the problems, and that is simply unacceptable. Maintaining the status quo will not only entail grave repercussions for Indigenous Peoples, but for the rest of Canada as well. As John Borrows, Anishinaabe law professor at the University of Victoria, states: "Furthermore, it should also be apparent that Aboriginal issues are not an inferior field of study but a vital part of Canada's legal fabric. Aboriginal rights are not purely an Aboriginal issue, and they have a great impact on many people's lives."[5] It is time to move law and justice policy forward in a more progressive fashion that will liberate Indigenous Peoples from their colonial constraints.

Notes

1   Matthew Dorrell, "From Reconciliation to Reconciling: Reading What 'We Now Recognize' in the Government of Canada's 2008 Residential Schools Apology," *English Studies in Canada* 35, 1 (2009), 39.

2   "Ottawa commits $321 million for residential school searches and support services for survivors" *CBC News*, August 10, 2021 <https://www.cbc.ca/news/indigenous/ottawa-residential-schools-search-support-funding-1.6136139>.

3   Jean-Dominique Morency et al., *Projections of the Aboriginal Population and Households in Canada, 2011 to2036* (Ottawa: Statistics Canada, 2015).

4   Public Safety Canada, *Corrections and Conditional Release Statistical Overview: 2013 Annual Report*, 25.

5   John Borrows, "Tracking Trajectories: Aboriginal Governance as an Aboriginal Right," *University of British Columbia Law Review* 38 (2005), 287.

INDEX

foster care,
  conditions in, 32, 47
  Indigenous children in, 46, 53, 180
  see also child welfare system
Friedland, Hadley, 70, 162

gangs, 205
  Dynamic Intervention Approach and, 198
  membership in, 43–44, 82, 194, 198–99
  prison-based, 82–83, 125, 196–98
  youth, 51, 115
gender, 192
  inequality, 40, 42, 135
Gladue case, 89
  factors, 31, 86, 90
  limitations of, 90–96
  principles, 6–7
grandparents, 29, 162
  intergenerational violence and, 17, 23, 41, 43
  residential school attendance, 17, 23, 33, 41, 49, 54
Green, Ross Gordon, 152–53

Hage, Tamara, 168
halfway houses, 67, 180, 194
  Indigenous offenders in, 181, 183–87
Hannah-Suarez, J. Andres, 85
harm reduction programs, 116–17
Harper, Stephen,
  apology of, 1, 86
  policies of, 14, 16, 77–78, 111, 207
Hay, Carter, 50
healing lodges, 181, 183
  evaluation of, 185–86, 188, 192
  provision of, 67, 77–78
  section 81: 181, 183–85, 188, 200n28
health, Indigenous, 54, 83, 115, 179
  children's, *see* children, Indigenous
  poorer, 5, 12
  services for, 107–12, 114, 168, 206
  see also mental health, Indigenous
Hollow Water Holistic Circle Healing Program, 129, 143, 152–53
home environments, 53–54, 78, 205
  abusive, 1, 17, 24–25, 39–42, 51, 83–84
  instability in, 5, 32–33, 46–48, 88

safety in, 14, 22–23, 88
Howe, Brian, 107–9

Idle No More, 66
incarceration, 207
  abandonment of, 4–5, 7, 11–12, 70–71, 177–78; *see also* abolition, prison
  alternatives to, 79–80, 94–95, 122–27, 142, 161, 166
  Black people and, 5, 7, 11–12, 109
  contributing factors, 2, 22, 29–31, 47, 51, 89, 180, 205
  mass, 4, 11, 69, 73, 109, 112, 125–26
  over-, *see* over-incarceration, Indigenous
  preference for, 21, 78, 89–91, 107, 112, 166
  see also prisons
Indigenization, 154
  critiques of, 68–69, 115
Indigenous justice systems, 5, 152–60, 171, 186, 206
  federal government recognition of, 67, 72, 129–30
  restorative justice versus, 68–69, 97, 123–25, 135, 140–42, 162–67
  see also legal orders, Indigenous
Indigenous Peoples, 2–4
  Canadian state versus, 6–8, 9n10, 12, 63–72, 83–89, 127–30
  lack of respect for, 12, 63–64, 83–86, 110–11, 165, 207
  systems of justice, *see* Indigenous justice systems
  see also colonialism
Ingram, Marie, 77–78
institutions, Canadian, 105
  harm from, 22, 30; *see also* residential schools
  need for change in, 64, 68, 115, 183–86
  safety in, 188–90, 192–98
intergenerational trauma, 195
  conceptualization of, 5, 18, 38, 66
  criminal behaviour and, 47–49, 82–88, 125, 205
  family violence, 1–2, 23, 38–43, 53, 78
  healing, 66, 115–16, 208
  public opinion on, 3, 17–18